FAITH ON THE EDGE

FAITH
ON
THE
EDGE

RELIGION AND MARGINALIZED EXISTENCE

Leonardo Boff, O.F.M.

Translated by Robert R. Barr

1817

Harper & Row, Publishers, San Francisco

New York, Grand Rapids, Philadelphia, St. Louis
London, Singapore, Sydney, Tokyo, Toronto

The chapters comprising this book have been selected, edited, and translated from two volumes originally published in Portuguese as *Fé na Periferia do Mundo* in 1978 and *O Caminhar da Igreja com os Oprimidos* in 1980, 1981, and 1988 by Editoria Vozes Limitada, Petrópolis, Brazil.

The publisher gratefully acknowledges the advice and assistance of Dr. Michael Candelaria in the preparation of this edited translation.

Scripture selections taken from the New American Bible, Copyright © 1970 Confraternity of Christian Doctrine, Washington, D.C., are used with permission. All rights reserved.

FIRST EDITION

Library of Congress Cataloging-in-Publication Data

Boff, Leonardo.
   [Selections. English. 1989]
   Faith on the edge : religion and marginalized existence / Leonardo Boff : translated by Robert R. Barr.—1st ed.
     p. cm.
   Selected, edited, and translated from: Fé na periferia do mundo and O Caminhar da Igreja com os oprimidos.
   ISBN 0-06-060812-9
   1. Liberation theology.   2. Sociology, Christian (Catholic) 3. Church work with the poor—Catholic Church.   4. Catholic Church—Doctrines.   I. Title.
BT83.57.B5965213   1989
230'.2—dc20   89-45243
                                         CIP

89 90 91 92 93 HAD 10 9 8 7 6 5 4 3 2 1

Contents

FAITH ON THE EDGE

I. LIBERATING THE OPPRESSED

1. Pilgrimage of the Church with the Oppressed

TOWARD UNDERSTANDING THE DEBATE IN THE CHURCH

Throughout Latin America, with repercussions in every area of the Church, a debate is raging over the political, social, and liberating content to be ascribed to Christian faith. All the media, both capitalist and popular, are caught up in the controversy, which is being carried on at two levels: one ecclesial, the other social and analytical. Two groups in the Church are in a stand-off.

1. CONSERVATIVE CURRENT

The first group maintains that the mission of the Church is essentially religious. Therefore the Church should not interfere in politics, which is the secular purview of the state and political parties. The function of the Church is ordered to the realm of the spiritual and to the inspiration of temporal affairs as a derivative of religious practice. Jesus was clear: "My kingdom does not belong to this world" (John 18:36). Jesus refused to act as a political leader, and the deliverance he proclaimed and bestowed bore not on economics and politics but on the religious relationship between the human being and God, which is translated in terms of sin or grace, conversion or hardening of the heart. To extrapolate from this content is to ideologize faith and to manipulate it toward interests essentially foreign to the gospel.

2. INNOVATIVE CURRENT

The second group claims that the Church's mission is more than merely religious. The mission of the Church has the same scope as the salvation of which it is the vehicle. Salvation is integral; it concerns not only the spirit but the body and the world as well, since these too are called to the Reign of God. Faith, therefore, and the Church (the organized place where faith is experienced) possess, independently of the will of their religious agents, a structural political dimension. For Jesus also said, "The reign of God is already in your midst" (Luke 17:21). Jesus was sentenced to death under Pontius Pilate, who represented the imperial power. His crucifixion was not a matter of blind fate but the consequence of a message and practice in conflict with those of the prevailing powers. The memory of the founder of the Christian community is dangerous and subversive. Its content is one of liberation, and therefore its message inevitably prioritizes the poor and marginalized. The Christian community must always keep that memory alive.

Politically speaking, the first position favors the dominant classes in society, which are conservative by nature and tend to conceptualize life in society as made up of separate compartments. Let politicians stick to the political and not leave their podium. Let the priest stick to prayer and the pulpit.

The second position adopts the aspirations to liberation it finds among the classes kept in subjection, the classes whose interests require the social mobilization that will bring them more power and a greater voice in the decisions that affect their lives. This position sees society as a dynamic, conflicting totality, composed of a wide variety of overlapping arenas. Politics is not the exclusive purview of a few citizens among many. Politics belongs to everyone. The human being is essentially a political animal. Religion, likewise, is not the privilege of a few but the right of every human being, since every human being stands in relation to an ultimate meaning called God.

It is a function of thought—here, of theological thought—not only to distinguish positions, but also to try to determine the correctness of those positions. Theology, then, must determine, within the broader framework of faith as attested by the Scriptures and by the historical experience of the church community, the correctness of the two positions we have just outlined. It seems to us that the first position—that of a Church with an essentially religious mission—too readily identifies Christianity with religion. Obviously Christianity presents itself, in a first analysis, as a religion—as a series of rites, dogmas, prescriptions, and corresponding practices. But this determination falls short of its basic content. Christianity seeks to be the extension of the process of the incarnation of God, which has culminated in Jesus Christ but which continues to assume all other reality. Christian faith is concerned with everything, then, and not merely with the religious "compartment" of human existence.

Further, it is not enough to assert the essentially religious nature of the Church. The truth of religion is not only in religion but, principally, outside religion. Why? Because religion belongs to the world of signs and symbols, whose truth lies only in their expression of the reality they signify. In other words, religion is authentic only when it expresses the reality of justice, the reality of a love characterized by solidarity, and the reality of mercy, all lived and experienced and not merely proclaimed or symbolized in ritual. The entire biblical tradition represents the truth of religion in this way and regards it as the reason religion is pleasing to God. Biblical and theological tradition, therefore, is not concerned only with the right apprehension and expression of *certain* faith, or orthodoxy. It is also, and principally, concerned with *true* faith. True faith—the only actually salvific faith—is faith informed by love, faith that becomes the practice of solidarity and liberation: orthopraxy. It is thus not preaching but practice that decides the truth of Christian faith—practice that begets more equality and justice or, in religious language, practice that produces greater holiness.

3. SAVED BY PRACTICE NOT PREACHING

Once we understand this, we can see that only the second position is faithful to the integral mission of the Church. That mission includes politics within religion, for it has discovered the religious dimension of politics. Religious practice and ethical practice are not mutually exclusive. Once the correct priority is established, they can be articulated and interconnected. The challenge to Christian awareness today is to be a Christian in a world of the marginalized. Christian faith on our continent can maintain its truth and not degenerate into a totem whose principal function is to legitimate the status quo only if it strikes a solidarity with the poor of the continent. The liberation discourse intoned by the Church in recent years has no other mean-

ing than this. The *origin* of the Reign of God "does not belong
to this world." But the Reign itself, as Saint Augustine declared,
indeed becomes reality in this world.

We must take care to avoid two reductionisms. The one is
religious and goes by the name of theologism. The other is political and is called secularism. Pope Paul VI, in his celebrated
Apostolic Exhortation *On Evangelization in the Modern World*
(1975), forthrightly maintains that "the Church is certainly not
willing to restrict her mission only to the religious field and dissociate herself from man's temporal problems."[1] The Latin
American bishops assembled in Puebla, Mexico, in 1979, were
even more explicit:

Christianity is supposed to evangelize the whole of human life, including
the political dimension. So the Church criticizes those who would restrict
the scope of faith to personal or family life; who would exclude the
professional, economic, social, and political orders as if sin, love, prayer,
and pardon had no relevance in them.[2]

The intent here is to teach a correct understanding of Christianity: not as one region of reality (the religious arena), but
precisely as a process of God's liberating incarnation in all reality,
a process calculated to render that reality the material of his
Reign.

The second risk is that of a political reductionism—secularism.
With secularism the relevance of faith is restricted to the area
of the social and political. In the words of Paul VI:

Many, even generous Christians who are sensitive to the dramatic questions involved in the problem of liberation, in their wish to commit the
Church to the liberation effort are frequently tempted to reduce her
mission to the dimensions of a simply temporal project. They would
reduce her aims to a man-centered goal; the salvation of which she is
the messenger would be reduced to material well-being. Her activity,
forgetful of all spiritual and religious preoccupation, would become initiatives of the political or social order.[3]

Faith does have one facet turned toward society. But that facet
is not the whole of faith. The original or central facet of faith
is turned toward the eternal dimension of existence, and it is in
light of that orientation that faith contemplates politics, economics, and society as potential routes to the Reign of God or de-

partures from those routes. Salvation in Jesus Christ—the content of the gospel proclamation—must be articulated with the historical liberations that render concrete the meaning of salvation for history. "The Church strives always to insert the Christian struggle for liberation into the universal plan of salvation which she herself proclaims."[4]

The second version of the debate on the political content of Christian faith is conducted through analyzing our unequal society. In simple terms, how are we to appraise the peripheral and dependent capitalistic system of our countries, a system in which we find so much social injustice, so many poor, and so few beneficiaries of the development accomplished by the toil of all? There is a causal relationship between the capitalistic mode of production and the generation of increasing misery. Can a relative justice conceivably coexist with this capitalistic system? As we know, Paul VI's *Populorum Progressio* (1967) stigmatized the latter as a "woeful system."[5] Nor did the bishops in Puebla mince any words. They called it the "idolatrous worship of wealth," and spoke of the "idol of wealth," "materialism," a "closed humanism," and, finally, "practical atheism," or atheism in practice.[6] Yesterday's objections to communism and Marxism are today's objections to capitalism. Although this formal condemnation has traveled a long, difficult road, it has finally arrived. And yet an appreciable number of bishops continue to entertain the notion of integrating the marginalized into the existing system in such a way that all persons would receive all basic necessities without structural change. For these bishops, one of the proper functions of faith is to encourage development and progress by seconding the project of the state and the dominant classes. And so they practice a theology of development, taking their cue from the theologians of the capitalist metropolis in Europe and the United States. However, an increasing number of bishops see in underdevelopment the other side of the coin of a development cast in the mold of capitalistic accumulation. They see that the impoverishment of the many is produced by the enrichment of a few. For those who espouse this interpretation, faith acquires a social function of criticizing and encouraging the liberatory forces of the oppressed and marginalized. Thus these bishops side with practices of liberation and with a theology of liberation as developed by the peripheral theologians of Latin America, Asia, and Africa.

We enter the debate with eagerness and anxiety. To which side of the scales will the needle incline? The answer will be crucial for both the Christian community and the society of Latin America and Brazil.

LATIN AMERICAN PILGRIMAGE OF THE CHURCH

The population of Latin America consists by and large of people who are simultaneously believing Christians and socially and economically oppressed. Catholicism steeps the fabric of our peoples and has molded, in large part, the identity of our continent. Latin America currently claims more and more of the attention of the Church universal. Why? First, because it is here that the Church of the future is being molded. There are more Catholics in Latin America than on any other continent. Soon more than half of the members of the Church will live here. European countries, with their demographic decline and meager religious creativity—their theology, liturgy, and pastoral ministry consisting almost entirely of syntheses of material drawn from the past—are gradually losing their universal relevance. Second, it is in Latin America that the Church's principal new challenges are appearing. What is the relationship between the gospel and the liberation of the oppressed? How can Christian love be reconciled with participation in the wild class struggle taking place all around us? How can Christianity help overcome the relations of international injustice prevailing in the unequal relationships between rich countries and poor ones?

It is not irrelevant that Pope John Paul II made Latin America the destination of the first journey of his pontificate. The periphery is the vessel of hope, the bearer of the future. Europe is no longer the center of Christian history. Latin America is. Slowly, stubbornly, faith is taking flesh in our countries and acquiring a new face. A new way of being Christian is being tested.

In order to understand this evolution, let us take two different approaches. The first approach understands the Church against a broader background of the history of Latin America. The other discerns the levels of self-awareness achieved by the

Church itself and asks how, internally, with the resources of its own symbols, the Church has carried forward its evolution.

1. A CHURCH ALIGNED WITH THE DOMINANT CLASSES

Latin American church history divides into three periods according to the relationship between Church and civil state. The first period, from 1492 to 1808 (Latin American political emancipation), witnessed the reign of Latin American colonial Christendom. The second, from 1808 to 1960, was the time of the new Christendom. And the third, from 1960 to the 1980s, represents the new Christendom in crisis and the emergence of a Church of the people.

In the first two periods, the Church assimilated to the project of the dominant groups in a peripheral Latin American society dependent on expanding mercantile capitalism. Planting the Church in Latin America was one of the purposes of the colonial enterprise, which thought of its goal as propagating "the faith and the Empire." Throughout the colonial period—the time of the Empire and the first Republic—evangelization was in the hands of the dominant classes and thereby at their service. Of course, the Church has always been concerned for the people— the poor, slaves, and the proletariat. But its concern was steeped in a paternalistic helping mentality—the spirit of the groups composing society's dominant class. Its concern never *began* with the people, with their aspirations, with their capacity to transform things. The Church never expressed or organized its concern for the people from the social vantage point of the people. The Church had concern *for* the people, but it never produced activity *with* the people or *as* the people would desire. Hence any role played by the Church in defense of the Indians, in the movement for the emancipation of the slaves, or in support of the workers' struggles was insignificant. A few prophets like Bartolomé de las Casas in Mexico or Antônio Vieira in Brazil denounced the shameful collaboration of the Church with the systematic exploitation of Indians and blacks. Still the Church did not abandon this collaboration. Its ties were to the dominant bloc. No wonder, then, that the popes lamented Latin American political emancipation. *Etsi Longissimo*, a papal encyclical of January 30, 1816, condemning the independence of Latin American countries, urged obedience to "our most dear son in Jesus Christ, Ferdinand, your Catholic King." What the official Church was concerned about was the "terrible harm of rebellion." From the viewpoint of the people, of course, we must ask: Are not the poor, the people, ordinary folk, at least as "dear sons" and daughters "in Jesus Christ" as was Catholic King Ferdinand? For whom had rebellion meant such terrible harm? Would it not be the affluent, privileged classes? Why not denounce the "terrible harm" of the economic, social, and political oppression to which the people had been subjected for centuries? But no such denunciation was forthcoming.

2. A CHURCH INCARNATE IN THE SUBORDINATE CLASSES

In the 1960s, the pact between the Church and the dominant class entered into crisis. The problem is linked to the restructuring of the international market, with the globalization of production, capital, and finance. It is likewise the product of major new cogs in the machinery of imperialist domination (national security regimes, trilateralism, and so on). Social conditions have reached such a shocking level that no one possessed of any humanity can fail to be moved. The Church has significantly broadened its social base and is moving out to the middle and popular classes. A Church on the defensive against liberalism has gone on the offensive against underdevelopment. A Church centered on formal devotions and mass religious manifestations, a Church absorbed by problems of family and education has become a Church open to social and political problems. Suddenly it hears the cry of the oppressed.

In the early stages of this process, a sort of "ecclesiastical populism" emerged, and the Church was able to win over large sectors of the middle and popular classes without endangering its alliance with oligarchical groups. But the bedfellows grew uneasy with each other, and the Church faced an inevitable dilemma. Either it would side with the people and their liberatory aspirations, share their struggles and their marginalization, and accept the conflict occasioned by a breach with a tyrannical, elitist system, or it would maintain and extend its alliance with the capitalistic state and the classes that state represents, thereby assuring itself of peace for its pastoral activities but at the price of being unable to evangelize the poor or denounce the violation of human rights.

At the Second General Conference of the Latin American Episcopate, held at Medellín, Colombia, in 1968, the Church on our continent made a historic choice. It opted for the people—for the poor, for their integral liberation, and for the base church communities. Now we had the basic, official framework of a new Church, which proposed to take flesh in the classes kept in subjugation and subordination. This sort of language had not been heard since the time of the martyrs of the early Christian centuries.

The post-Medellín years (1968–1979) saw a gigantic effort on the part of the Church to translate this foundational choice into a new ecclesial practice. During those years the Church took on a new image: one of solidarity with the cause of the poor and the courage to face up to an authoritarian state; the image of a defender of the rights of the downtrodden; the image of a Church deeply enfleshed in popular milieus, with thousands of base church communities where the people gather to pray, reflect as community, and organize community practices selected with an eye to their meaning for liberation. Internal conflicts persist in the Church. It is not easy to abandon practices bound to the privileged persons and groups of society and adopt a new societal locus—that of the people—from which to speak, organize, and act. Gradually, however, the conviction is taking root that the Church's option for the people and their liberation is irreversible. We are witnessing the advent of a popular Church, a Church interlinked with the popular movement—with the people's struggle for justice, social participation, and voice in government.

This choice has cost the Church a price. Some nine hundred persons directly involved with the pastoral ministry have been persecuted, imprisoned, exiled, tortured, or killed over the past ten years—native Americans, laity, religious, priests, and even bishops.

3. THREE LEVELS OF CHURCH AWARENESS, THREE TYPES OF PRACTICE

Revolutions in Church and society are not introduced simply by way of new ideas. Ideas win an audience, and viability, only if new practices and attitudes have been tested beforehand in response to new social and historical challenges. In the Church, this has occurred particularly over the past ten years. It seems to me that we can distinguish three overall practices in the modern history of the Church, with their corresponding theories.

The first would be that of a *Church outside the world*, subsisting in the classic figure of the bishop. This view limits the activity of the Church to the strictly religious sphere. It understands society as divided into fully autonomous spheres immune from mutual interference. The Church is then the agent of the religious element in society. Business people and employers run the economic system. The Church is above the world, far from the conflicts of that world, beyond history. The Church is necessary for salvation, hence of universal importance. It speaks to a world outside itself, to which it has a divine mission. Such practices, with their legitimating theory, were acceptable in a social regime where there was no breach between the spheres of Church and society—where Church and society were identical. This is the model of medieval Christianity—theoretically a thing of the past, but still in control of the minds of many Christians. This view has not yet grasped the irreversibility of secularization or the legitimate autonomy of earthly realities. It lacks the courage to let the world be world. Left in the dust of history by the official documents of Vatican II itself (1962–1965), this position nevertheless endures. Practices are undone only by other practices. New theories only invalidate or curb them.

The second model—that of a *Church in the world*—presupposes Christian practices performed not only within ecclesiastical frameworks but also in the world. This was the Church of the great lay movements of the nineteenth and twentieth centuries and the Church of the Christian political parties. Vatican II assimilated and endorsed its implicit theory. Now the Church was in the world, not vice versa. But the world, in this thinking, was the world of modernity, of science and technology, with which the Church had earlier waged a historical conflict. The Church declared peace and became modernized. Now its discourse was articulated in terms of progress and development. The bourgeoisie heard and was pleased and lent its wholehearted support.

The third model—that of a *Church in the subworld*—has become

possible only because of the second. It begins with practices performed by Christians who have become one social body with
those who struggle against the twin consequences of development in capitalistic molds: poverty and exploitation. Development does not help the people. It transpires at the people's expense. A subworld emerges alongside the great world. Where
should the Church be present? Medellín defined the position of
the Church as being in the subworld of the poor. It abandoned
a developmentalist discourse and began to speak of integral liberation and justice for all. It chose to take flesh in the subordinate classes and supported the base church communities, the
natural locus of realization of the new face of the Church.

The significance of Medellín was precisely this turnabout in
the Church. Medellín defined the new social locus from which
the Church would henceforward organize its presence in the
world. Now the door was open for a new historical enterprise.
Now the gospel would be taken over by the poor and used by
them for the purpose for which it was written in the blood of
the apostles, evangelists, and martyrs: the integral liberation of
the oppressed.

A CHURCH UNDER THE SIGN OF LIBERATION: WHAT LIBERATION?

The Second General Assembly of the Latin American Bishops'
Council (CELAM), which was held at Medellín in 1968, confirmed the Church's three great "options" or choices: for the
poor, for their integral liberation, and for the base church communities. The decisive element in these options is the reading
of social and historical reality and the "politicopastoral" practice
they imply. The starting point for this reading and this practice
is the subordinate classes. The old perspective, from the top
down, generated a paternalistic helping mentality. For all its
mercy and generosity, this approach ultimately failed to respect
the poor. It refused to acknowledge that they were historical
agents capable of making their voices heard. It refused to acknowledge the justice of their claims and struggles. The new
reading is made from a locus in the base of society. It looks from
the bottom upward—from the grass roots to the rest of society.

It fully appreciates the potential of the people, especially for transforming society. Against the classic analysts of the function of religion in society (Marx, Weber, and Durkheim), who assigned to religion the role of legitimizing the dominant classes and pacifying conflicts instigated in the subjugated classes, the Church has shown that it need not be this way. The Church has the potential, out of evangelical motives together with a sheer grasp of the justice of its cause, to opt for and merge with the marginalized groups. Now it adopts a strategy of liberation, legitimating the longings of the people, withdrawing its authorization of their subjugation, and developing a religious view of the world (like that of the people, most of whom are profoundly religious) adjusted to the people's interest in a social transformation. At Medellín the Church found it possible to demonstrate its interest in various popular movements, in the maturation of a popular political consciousness, and in the liberatory effervescence that had come to characterize our continent since the 1950s.

The adoption of a strategy for liberation has deeply marked the pilgrimage of the Latin American Church from Medellín to the present. It has obliged the Church to take new steps. It has brought the Church to many impasses. And it has won the Church the good reputation it undeniably enjoys with the other regional churches of the world today. Let us briefly sketch the three great options adopted by the Church.

1. OPTION FOR THE POOR

The poor make up the vast majority of the population of our continent. According to the International Labor Organization, some 100 million Brazilians live in conditions of severe poverty. Of these, 70 million are destitute. These numbers reveal the presence of profoundly unequal structures, and in such a society an ongoing violation of human rights is inevitable. Long before being taken up by American President Jimmy Carter and the Trilateral Agreement, the cause of human rights constituted the core of the pastoral proclamation of the Church. But we must recover the true meaning of human rights. When we say "human rights," we ought to be speaking basically of the rights of the poor. We are denouncing the violence perpetrated on the helpless. In this area the Church has managed to make its social weight and credibility count in favor of those from whom society never hears because they are not allowed to speak. With all other criticism stifled, the Church has had the courage to rise up against the authoritarian state and cry out, "Not everything is permitted! You shall not oppress your brother and sister!" Of course, the Church has had to pay a price for this forthrightness—in slander, persecution, and repression. The blood of martyrs has flowed in rivers these last ten years. Often the oppressors have put their victims to death in the name of "God." What god would this be? The death-dealing god of the status quo is certainly not the Father of our Lord Jesus Christ, the giver of life.

2. OPTION FOR INTEGRAL LIBERATION

The Church's option for integral liberation has forced it to undertake a more lucid critique of the causes of the general impoverishment of Latin America. The principal cause of that poverty resides in the capitalist system that has been so savagely implanted in Latin America. The Church has moved beyond mere developmentalism and progressivism, which have benefited only the privileged classes. The deeper the Church has sunk its roots in the popular milieu, the more it has understood that it must speak of a liberation wrought by the people themselves. Here is a social process, to be reinforced at the grass roots, that generates a more equal, shared community life. The word *liberation* is pregnant with ethical and political protest. It denounces the prevailing oppression and promotes the breaking of chains.

When we speak of liberation, we must always be clear about what liberation we mean. On a first level, we mean the social liberation of the oppressed. This implies the historical surmounting of the capitalist system, the principal producer of oppression, and movement toward a society of greater sharing, a society with structures that generate more justice for all. In political terms, liberation involves moving toward a society of a socialist type, a participatory democracy. As we see, liberation is not a metaphor. It is a social and historical process.

On a second level, social liberation is never merely social. It constitutes a human phenomenon charged with existential meaning, dignity, and the grandeur of humanism. The struggle for more humanity, partnership, and greater social and political voice is a noble one; commitment to a society in which the greatest possible number of persons are the agents of their own destiny and share in creating the commonwealth is both meaningful and ennobling.

In the third place, in the light of faith this social and historical process contains elements of salvation (or perdition). It anticipates and makes concrete the dimensions of the utopia that Jesus Christ called the Reign of God. Therefore it possesses a transcendent meaning. It has repercussions on eternity. God's ultimate design is realized or frustrated in the process of social and historical liberation. Granted, this ultimate design has a spiritual dimension as well, and this is why we speak of integral liberation. Faith can discern this dimension of depth. Faith also helps to mobilize a commitment to the oppressed and to their liberation. Finally, faith celebrates the victorious presence of the liberation wrought by human beings in the power of their omnipresent and all-pervading God, while it also proclaims the consummate liberation already won in the life, death, and resurrection of another oppressed one, Jesus Christ. Jesus is the sign that our struggles and hopes for total liberation are not condemned to fade into the distance of some unrealized utopia. No, the Christian utopia becomes radiant, brimming *topos*. It acquires a local habitation and a Name.

3. OPTION FOR THE BASE CHURCH COMMUNITIES

The grassroots community is the place where the poor gather, meditate on the word of God, take a moral inventory of their lives, offer one another their help, and forge links with other popular movements. The appearance of base communities is the most important event to have occurred in the Church for centuries. So long throttled into silence by society and Church alike, the people now have the floor. This is a first liberation—the liberation of the captive word. The political importance of this event is unparalleled. A torn social fabric is being mended. A tiny, helpless flower is threatening the wild jungle of the prevailing antipopular, despotic order.

These three basic options have brought the Church to a number of impasses. The Church has come to realize that the ecclesial body is shot through with the same conflicts as rend society at large. The Church's colonial and neocolonial covenant with the dominant classes cannot be abandoned in a mere ten years' time. A shift in the social locus of the Church has meant a genuine conversion process for that Church.

Now the road is open to a new incarnation of the gospel in a still-unreached continent, the continent of the poor. And a new kind of organization can spring up in the Church, an organization that is more popular, more shared, more closely connected with the cause of justice and a life worth living.

PUEBLA: GAINS AND ADVANCES

From January 27 to February 13, 1979, bishops from every country in Latin America gathered at Puebla de los Angeles, in Mexico, to sketch out the framework of present and future evangelization on our continent. After a lengthy, stormy preparation lasting nearly two years, a hefty document was drawn up—over three hundred pages long in the Vozes Brazilian edition.

The document, a montage of literary genres, represented the bishops' vision for the evangelization of Latin America. Like all texts, this one was written from a particular social location. The bishops' location is that of sacred power, taking primary responsibility for the unity of the entire Church. Like all social locations, that of the bishops permits one kind of discourse while prohibiting another. It makes a certain kind of signifying intervention possible, while rejecting another and making it impossible. What we usually expect from the locus of power is a conciliatory discourse, reformist at most, rather than prophetic, denunciatory, or innovative.

Surprisingly, what actually occurred at Puebla was the conversion of the Latin American episcopate. The bishops became more serious about their option for the people and the poor. From the standpoint of the oppressed, they analyzed social, economic, and religious reality; detected the deep, and deepening, chasm between rich and poor; and pronounced their prophetic, evangelical demand for structural innovations in our society.

Their conversion took on even more significance in light of one prevalent concern. Many, especially those of privileged classes, wanted to present, through the media they control, the image of a conservative Pope and an assembly of bishops at Puebla determined to correct Medellín, especially in the matter of liberation. Instead, Puebla confirmed Medellín, plumbed the depths of its great options, and broadened the flanks of church consensus, thereby extending the bases of church support for liberation.

THE PUEBLA DOCUMENT: TEN CENTRAL STATEMENTS

As Pope John Paul II expressed it, Puebla is a "spirit," a response to the needs and challenges of the Latin American continent. The text of the Puebla document is not self-explanatory. It must be read in the context of the more comprehensive movement and process in which the Church is engaged. The moment of Puebla is the textual moment of a broader process that began with Vatican II and Medellín. Thus the starting point for analyzing the document must not be the various theologies of the debate that produced it but the predominant practices of a ten-year experiment that preceded it. From the standpoint of practice—of a Church striving more and more to act and think out of the viewpoint of the periphery—the text becomes most meaningful. Without this reference to church praxis, the text can seem theologically mediocre and pastorally irrelevant.

As we have said, the pilgrimage of the Church from Medellín to our own day has been characterized by a shift in the social location of the Church. The new locus demanded a redefining of the Church's mission and of its presence among the subjugated. Unless we understand the immediacy of practice in this period of the Latin American church, we shall not understand Puebla or the significance of that conference as the confirmation of a baptism received at Medellín.

In the light of this hermeneutical approach, we can distinguish ten major themes that, despite an occasional hiatus, make up the warp and woof of the Puebla document. These ten themes reinforce, confirm, and stabilize the course set at Medellín for the Church in Latin America.

1. ESTABLISHING A METHOD: THINKING AND LIVING OUR FAITH FROM THE STARTING POINT OF SOCIAL REALITY

The formal organization of the Puebla document is in itself significant. The material is laid out according to a methodology long consecrated by the practice of the base communities as well as by the theological reflection being constructed on our continent known as the theology of liberation. And what is that methodology? First, one *sees*, analytically. Next one *judges*, theologically. Both operations are performed with a view toward acting effectively upon reality. Finally, one *acts*, pastorally. First, then, the document undertakes a broad critical analysis of Latin American social reality, detecting the greatest anguish and highest hopes of our peoples. Then it engages in theological reflection: it rethinks, under the lens of faith, the challenges it has identified in the analytical moment. Finally, it indicates pathways of Christian practice, as imperatives flowing from the analysis of the first moment and the reflection of the second. Each chapter in the document is organized according to this same methodology: situation, theological criteria, pastoral options.

All genuine theology, as we shall see below in chapter 5, is performed *ante et retro oculata*, "with an eye before and an eye behind." It has one eye on the present, with which it discerns the signs of the times, and the other on the past, where salvation in Jesus Christ has burst upon our world. In the light of that salvation, theology interprets the signs of the present time in order to incarnate the faith and so accomplish the liberation of history. Thus any theological idealism—reflection on the faith simply in and for itself, in dissociation from its incarnation in time—is precluded. The Christian faith is not primarily a theory. It is primarily a praxis. The praxis has its theory, yes. But that theory must never, under penalty of desiccation, be developed without reference to praxis—or, in classic terms, without practicing faith, hope, and love.

Social and historical reality has the first word. Today this reality can no longer be approached naively, with the physical senses alone. This would be empiricism, and empiricism will never succeed in detecting the actual mechanisms of society. Nor will a functional analysis be adequate. Functionalism tends to limit its analysis to institutions and their function or dysfunction in society. Thus its action never exceeds reformism. It is incapable of questioning the structures of the system itself. Why? Because it attends only to the function of the parts and neglects the whole.

A more adequate approach pays close attention to the tensions and conflicts of productive forces, since they make up the foundation of institutions and their social and historical movement. The Puebla document moves immediately to the structural analysis of these forces and denounces the systems, structures, and mechanisms that "create a situation where the rich get richer at the expense of the poor, who get ever poorer."[7] Puebla's analysis considers the various parts composing the social whole: the historical, the economic, the political, the cultural, the ideological, and the religious.

The central problem in this method, which always begins with reality (interpreted socioanalytically), is how to articulate and link three qualitatively distinct discourses—those of social analysis, theology, and pastoral practice. The task is feasible, as the mere fact of liberation theology shows, but it is not without difficulties. One danger is theologism, valuing theology as the only valid discourse for reflecting on social reality. Another is sociologism, regarding the social sciences as the sole legitimate discourse. A third is bilingualism, which holds two discourses in parallel without articulating or interconnecting them. A fourth approach merely mixes all the languages uncritically; it results from a faulty articulation of all of them. Liberation theology on the whole has had to learn how to avoid all these extremes. Unhappily, Puebla frequently becomes mired down in a bilinguistic articulation. Its theology of Christ, the Church, and evangelization is not always adequately interlinked with a social analysis. But in those parts of the document where the overriding concern is not orthodoxy—in the passages where the bishops are speaking as pastors—we find a happy mutual articulation of situation, reflection, and action.

The Puebla document unflinchingly establishes and consecrates the three-stage methodology of seeing, reflecting, acting. Puebla asks explicitly that communities and persons "be taught how to *analyze* reality, how to *reflect* on this reality from the standpoint of the Gospel, how to *choose* the most suitable objectives and means, and how to use them in the most sensible way for the work of evangelization."[8] The bishops make a profession of supreme import: "Since the First General Conference of the Latin American Episcopate in Rio de Janeiro (1955), which gave rise to CELAM, and particularly since Vatican II and the Medellín Conference, the Church has been acquiring an increasingly clear and deep realization that evangelization is its fundamental mission; and that it cannot possibly carry out this mission without an ongoing effort to know the real situation and to adapt the gospel message to today's human beings in a dynamic, attractive, and convincing way."[9]

2. THREE PROPHETIC CONDEMNATIONS

Latin America's situation of extreme poverty and institutionalized injustice is "intimately connected with the expansion of liberal capitalism."[10] The latter is not the sole cause, but it is the main cause, and it manifests itself as an "international imperialism of money," a "neocolonialism" of "new forms of supranational domination."[11] Capitalism is condemned with invectives once reserved for Marxism: "system of sin,"[12] "materialism," "idolatry of individual wealth," "closed humanism," and "practical atheism," that is, atheism in practice.[13] This formal condemnation of the capitalistic system has a fundamental importance on our continent, where capitalism is the reigning system and where so many Christians defend that system as right and good.

In order to implement its project, the capitalist system needs powerful regimes. Puebla harshly condemns this abuse of power as producing increasing oppression and an ongoing violation of human dignity.[14]

Puebla lodges a second condemnation against capitalism's friend, the national security doctrine, which "suppresses any broad participation by the people in political decisions," "presents itself as absolute, ranking higher than persons . . . and institutionalizes the insecurity of individuals." Owing to its absolutist nature, the national security doctrine "could never harmonize with a Christian view of the human being," even though among its champions are those who "attempt to defend their attitudes with a profession of Christian faith."[15]

A third condemnation is reserved for Marxism, in the spirit of the social encyclicals. The criticism is joined to an acknowledgment of Marxism's well-taken "criticism of the fetishism of the market and of the refusal to recognize the value of human labor."[16]

3. SOCIAL AND POLITICAL DIMENSION OF FAITH

If this diseased condition, this "ongoing violation of human dignity," this "grave structural conflict," this "situation of social sin"—is societal in nature, then the therapy too must be societal. The bishops clearly state, "Our social conduct is part and parcel of our following of Christ."[17] Never in the history of Christian awareness has the political and social dimension of faith been so strongly asserted. "The Church criticizes those who would restrict the scope of faith to personal or family life; who would exclude the professional, economic, social, and political orders as if sin, love, prayer, and pardon had no relevance in them."[18]

But Puebla's highest endorsement of politics may well be its declaration that politics "flows from the very core of the Christian faith" and constitutes "a way of worshiping the one God." To proclaim "a Gospel bereft of economic, social, cultural, and political implications" is the same thing, "in practice, as to mutilate it, and is tantamount to a kind of connivance . . . with the established order."[19] By reason of this social and political dimension of faith, Christians may call for "structural changes" and the advent of a "new society."[20]

4. PREFERENTIAL OPTION FOR THE POOR AND AGAINST THEIR POVERTY

The social and political dimension of our faith acquires its historical application through the solemn, courageous preferential option for the poor made by the bishops at Puebla. On the strength of this option alone Puebla becomes a sacred event, destined to have a great influence on the history of our continent.

First, the option in question is a *choice*, which in its context must be identified with Christian conversion. "Service to [the poor] really calls for constant conversion and purification among all Christians. That must be done if we are to achieve fuller identification each day with the poor Christ and our own poor."[21]

The option for the poor is a *preferential* option. That is, while not excluding other persons, its solidarity is with the masses.[22] Paternalism is left behind. With this preference Puebla is defining the locus from which the Church must utter and proclaim the message of liberation. The gospel proclamation now begins among the poor, moving out from there to the rest of humankind. The poor become the central focus of the concrete universality of the Church and of its call to salvation. When the poor are the starting point for our discourse, all other social classes feel the repercussions. This does not occur when we speak from the standpoint of the mighty. In that case the poor are for all practical purposes excluded. This option has caused the Church misunderstanding and hostility. "Economically powerful groups feel excluded by the Church, which it seems to them has abandoned its spiritual mission."[23]

The Church's option is a preferential option *for the poor, against their poverty.* The "poor" here are those who suffer injustice. Their poverty is produced by mechanisms of impoverishment and exploitation. Their poverty is therefore an evil and an injustice. An option for the poor implies a choice for social justice. It means a commitment to the poor in the transformation of society and the elimination of unjust poverty. It means a struggle for a society of more justice and greater partnership.[24]

Puebla avoids speaking of "spiritual poverty." The bishops prefer to speak of "Christian poverty," or "evangelical poverty," by which they mean an actual sharing in the material living conditions of the poor through a simple, abstemious, austere life; the casting out of the internalized wealthy person's thinking through the conquest of covetousness and pride; and, finally, an attitude of spiritual childhood and total availability for service (a trusting openness to God). This kind of poverty is a mode of being without which the living experience of the gospel is impossible for rich or poor alike.[25]

Surely the poor have needs to be attended to. But they also have the ability to transform history. They have worth. They have the ability to evangelize. The Church wishes to join them in their struggles, their anguish, and their hopes, and thereby join them as well in building a more just and more free common life.[26]

5. DEFENSE AND PROMOTION OF THE DIGNITY OF THE HUMAN PERSON

The ongoing violation of human rights, especially the rights of the poor, is the open sore of the Latin American continent. Therefore a defense of the dignity of the human person "may be the prime imperative of this, God's hour on our continent," and a "serious obligation." It is an "integral part" of the task of evangelization, an "evangelical value."[27] Powerfully, Puebla declares, "God's love . . . for us must today become above all else a deed of justice in behalf of the oppressed, an enterprise of the deliverance of the very neediest."[28] Since Puebla's basic option is the viewpoint of the poor, that conference repeatedly speaks not only of "human rights"—the language of the bourgeois, individualistic tradition—but also of the "rights of the poor and the neediest," with special attention to emergent "social" rights.[29]

6. OPTION FOR INTEGRAL LIBERATION

Like fabric shot through with golden thread, the Puebla document is guided from start to finish by the theme of liberation: the creation of a genuine societal partnership and a popular voice in society through a process of integral liberation. "Our Churches have something original and important to offer all: their sense of salvation and liberation."[30] The urgency of liberation arises as a response to the terrible challenges of social contrasts and concrete oppression. The Puebla text adopts one of the formulas of *Evangelii Nuntiandi:** "The Church has the duty to proclaim the liberation of millions of human beings, among whom are many of the Church's own children."[31] This liberation "belongs to the very core of . . . evangelization."[32] It is an integral, indispensable, and essential part of the mission of the Church.[33] The Church "must offer people today 'an especially

---

*"Of the Gospel to be Proclaimed," an apostolic exhortation of Pope Paul VI, published in 1975, on the subject of evangelization in today's world, and widely regarded as one of the most beautiful documents in the entire history of the pontifical magisterium.

vigorous message concerning liberation,' framing it in terms of the 'overall plan of salvation.' "[34]

This liberation must be comprehensive, spanning two complementary, inseparable poles: "liberation *from* all the forms of bondage . . . [and] liberation *for* progressive growth in being." It must span all the relationships of reality.[35]

Being comprehensive, liberation refuses to tolerate reductionisms that are actually mutilations: at one extreme a neglect of "liberation from sin," and at the other, a neglect of liberation from "dependence and the forms of bondage that violate basic rights that come from God." Liberation begins in history and will culminate in eternity.[36]

All activities of the Church must acquire a dimension of liberation. Evangelization and liturgy must evidence a commitment to liberation, and education must explicitly proclaim Jesus Christ as the Liberator, presenting him to youth as the agent of an integral liberation. Even charismatic groups are invited to make a social commitment. In a comprehensive formula (adapted, in the Bogotá text) Puebla says, "The best service to our fellows is evangelization, which disposes them to fulfill themselves as children of God, liberates them from injustices, and fosters their integral advancement." This, then, is "integral liberation."[37]

It is faith that motivates Christians' concern for the liberation of their sisters and brothers. Their very discipleship of Jesus Christ requires they be persons committed to the liberation of both self and neighbor. In terms of the document, this means having the courage to "use every means available to comply with what may well be the original imperative of this divine hour on our continent: i.e., a bold Christian profession and an effective promotion of human dignity and its divine foundations."[38] "Latin America . . . needs persons aware of their dignity and their historical responsibility. And it needs Christians jealous of their identity."[39]

What Puebla asks is a vigorous synthesis "between the faith they claim to profess and practice on the one hand and the real-life involvement they assume in society on the other hand." These are the kinds of statements with which Puebla confirms the liberation practices of the Church as well as, by implication, responsible reflection on such practices.[40]

7. OPTION FOR THE BASE CHURCH COMMUNITIES

One of the most palpable phenomena of the Spirit in Latin America in recent years has been the emergence of the grass-roots Church among the poor and oppressed. Here the common people have succeeded in living their community faith, as they take the first steps in a liberation born and bred of that faith. The bishops have endorsed these experiments, declaring them to be "reason for joy and hope," "focuses of evangelization, and motives of liberation."[41] They constitute part of the wealth that our Church can offer to all. The base communities are testifying to their desire for a place and a voice in their social milieu equal to that of their neighbors. They are likewise testifying to their experience of Church as family. Such vitality gives rise to new ministries, and to "a new nearness to the Gospels and the quest for an ever new face of Christ, which is their response to the legitimate aspirations they feel for an integral liberation."[42] The significance of these communities transcends the area of religion. They become the locus of the appearance of a new kind of vital social community, a community of more partnership, solidarity, and participation. In these communities the Church has discovered the evangelizing potential of the poor.[43]

All levels and aspects of the Church are affected by the base communities—bishops and priests, deacons, vocations to the religious life, evangelization, religious education, ecumenism, popular piety, and prayer. The expression "Church of the people" is an expression charged with meaning.[44]

Finally, the bishops "are determined to promote, guide, and accompany" the base church communities, which head the list of the "many signs of hope and joy for those who are immersed in Christ's paschal mystery."[45] With them lies the future of the Church on our continent.

8. ADOPTION AND PURIFICATION OF POPULAR PIETY

To make an option for the poor implies making a choice for the religion of the people. Thus it likewise implies an option for the culture of the people, which subsists in the framework of a religious worldview. The Puebla document recognizes the legitimacy of the popular Catholicism by which the poor and simple live the message of the gospel. Catholicism is the "continent's cultural matrix."[46] This being the case, it is understandable that popular piety should be "an active way in which the people continually evangelize themselves," just as it is the conduit for their "cry for true liberation,"[47] which society denies them. Popular religion does have a negative side—its superstition, its fanaticism, its ritualism—and these aspects constitute a challenge to evangelization. But this is no impediment to the adoption by the Church of various aspects of popular piety in the liturgy and elsewhere. On the contrary, without it the Church would not be universal. "We must see to it that the faith develops a growing personalization and a liberative solidarity."[48]

9. PREFERENTIAL OPTION FOR YOUTH

Almost half of all Latin Americans are under eighteen years of age. Here, then, is great hope for the renewal, not only of society, but of the Church itself. But the majority of youth are condemned to a life in which there is no youth. As soon as they are physically able to work, they are swept into the productive process as if they were adults, to become full-fledged members of the impoverished masses. Many suffer hindrances in their capacity to help in the renewal of the social body by repression at the hands of governmental systems. But the young are the vessels of the future, and they constitute the object of a special option on the part of the Church. "The Church has confidence in the young"[49] and addresses them a very special appeal. It invites them to find in the Church "a place for communion with God and human beings, a place to begin to construct a civilization of love, to build peace and justice."[50] The pedagogy of the Church must try to steer youth in the direction of social and political action and structural changes by instilling in them a "preference for those who are poorer still." It is crucial that our youth become a factor in our society for the transformation of that society and of the Church.[51]

10. WOMAN'S ADVANCEMENT AND LIBERATION

The advancement of women was not one of Puebla's greatest explicit concerns. Here the conference was brief, to the point, and altogether aware that it could be setting the stage for future surprises. Puebla's viewpoint is the viewpoint of the poor. It sees women as constituting the most oppressed human group of all, since they are not only women but also poor. The Church itself has collaborated in the marginalization of women by refusing to open the way to their participation in its pastoral initiatives. But now the Church supports women's aspirations for liberation and advancement. Women must share in the transformation of society and share in it as women. The conference explicitly states that women should have a voice in pastoral planning and coordination, religious education, and the like. It regards women as candidates for new ministries. The chapter on Mary places great emphasis on Mary's commitment to the poor and to liberation, presenting her as the model of Christianity, especially the Christianity of Latin American women.[52]

On the whole, Puebla gets good marks. It confirms the direction taken by the Church at Medellín. The great choices of recent years have now been consecrated. The preparatory phase had been marked by uneasiness. Here was a Church basically guided by a concern for liberation, social justice, human rights, and an option for the impoverished and their way of gathering in Christian community (in the base communities). All of this had been new and frightening. But now the ghosts have been exorcised. The Church is now on a social course. For the moment, it is moving outward and plunging deeper rather than moving ahead. Its orientation to the liberation of the poor enjoys a far broader support base now and a great deal more official recognition. If Medellín was the baptism of the Latin American church, Puebla was its confirmation.

The Puebla document has many limitations, both theoretical and practical. These have been amply examined by various analysts, and we need not rehearse them here. Our concern has been to accentuate the points in the document that ought to encourage our great hope for the future of the Latin American continent. That hope receives a special stimulus where Puebla has contributed to Christian reflection and action upon the main contradiction of our social reality, the widening gap between rich and poor. And our hearts beat high when Puebla recognizes our swelling aspirations for liberation.

LOOKING TO THE FUTURE: A CHURCH MORE COMMITTED TO THE PEOPLE

What is the outlook for the near future?

Once more without going into great detail, let us sketch some prospects for the future and draw some conclusions for society and the Church.

1. NEW AGENTS OF THE FUTURE OF LATIN AMERICA

It is impossible to understand Latin America in a vacuum. One must take account of the correlation of world forces and the internal contradictions of the capitalist system. The imperialist industrial powers (European Common Market, United States, Japan) live in a sate of tension, to be sure. But these tensions are under control, thanks to the antagonism reigning between the capitalist and socialist camps. The conflict between rich nations and poor ones, however—between the dependent countries of the South and their exploitative centers of the North—is swiftly increasing.

Latin America seems fated to be swept even deeper into the capitalistic system now that that system has entered a new phase: the internationalization of capital. The state, the national bourgeoisies, and the transnational corporations form the new ruling classes, and there will be peace among them. The benefits of development are distributed among them alone, to the ever more radical exclusion of the popular classes. This imbalance in the economic order requires authoritarian political regimes with military muscle, however democratic these regimes may seem to have become under pressure from the North. World development is now the tool of a new international distribution of labor. The central nations retain the more dynamic, tidier elements of development, exporting the classic, polluting stages to the peripheral countries, under the guarantee of a trivial profit there. The end result is the marginalization, not only of the workers and the *camponeses*, but of the middle classes themselves, who must sit by helplessly as home control of development disappears.

The reason for the current deterioration of our interclass relationships is that, despite all repression and watchfulness on the part of the powers that be, the popular classes are in an ever better position to mount their protests and propose an alternative project—liberation. These classes make both economic and political demands. In the economic arena they call for an industrialization calculated to provide for the people's most basic needs. In the political arena they demand a more genuine share in political life, for the defense of the rights of the masses and the gradual development of a participatory democracy with roots in the various popular cultures of our nation, hence with a legitimation of these cultures. The underclasses are still subordinate, but they have more and more power to impose changes on the strategy of capitalist domination and thus prepare the historical conditions for a new, more socialized, more equal society.

2. A CHURCH INCARNATE IN THE SUBORDINATE CLASSES

We now see sure signs that the course taken by Medellín and consecrated by Puebla will only be further confirmed and deepened in the aftermath of Puebla. The spirit of Puebla has had a profound impact on John Paul II, who has so courageously denounced the social and historical oppressions of our world and carried the basic intuitions of liberation theology to the rest of the Church. Committed groups in Latin America are altogether aware that the ecclesiological experiments being conducted on our continent are of universal significance. What we have here is an incarnation of the faith and the gospel in a new world, the world of the subordinate classes, that newly emergent agent of history.

The foundation and core of Puebla, as we have just seen, will likely determine the shape of the Latin American Church of the future. The spirituality of a faith-inspired commitment and solidarity is flourishing, as Christians identify with the most unfortunate victims of capitalist exploitation. On a social and historical level, Christianity's positive involvement with the process of the liberation of the oppressed is too obvious to be denied. Soon it will no longer be necessary to establish the social and political dimension of faith by way of argumentation and rhetoric. That dimension may well become the flesh and spirit of Christian understanding.

In the *social* arena, the process of integral liberation will take on an altogether concrete form in history. Once economic, social, and pedagogical liberation is read by theology as one of the historical concretions of the Reign of God, that liberation will become the most important step in the Christian commitment. Integral, total liberation can come only by way of this specific mediation.

The preferential option for the poor will surely be interpreted in the line of thinking initiated by Puebla: as an option for the impoverished and a commitment to social justice. Medellín spoke of the Church and poverty. Puebla speaks of the Church and the poor. In the aftermath of Puebla we shall be speaking more and more of the Church and the impoverished. The urgency of this option will become greater as the deleterious effects of the system grow in number and kind and thereby render social contradictions still more acute.

The promotion of human rights will take on the concrete guise of the promotion of the social rights of the masses, the rights of the humiliated and the wronged. The Church will guide popular education toward a choice for an alternative society and a stronger, more forthright declaration of independence from the prevailing system. Middle and higher educational institutions of the Church will find a way to show their students the correctness of an option of faith for social justice, for an alliance of pure and applied science for the benefit of the popular sectors.

In the *ecclesial* arena, the principal theological axis of the body of the Church will be the People of God organized into a vast network of communities. The laity will surely have a much fuller share in the decisions of the Church, and woman will have an unprecedented importance in the base communities and other pastoral structures. All this presupposes a redefining of the shape and style of the priesthood and episcopate, with both offices being far more closely and organically bound to the People of God.

Everything points to a continued effort on the part of base church communities to achieve an organic, in-depth coupling of faith and commitment to liberation, the joining of religious practices and political and ethical practices. A more autonomous, regionalized local church will mean the assimilation of the values of regional popular cultures.

All meaningful historical events are fraught with tension. They all include the interplay of antagonistic powers and conflicting interests. Puebla was no exception. But we shall have to take seriously the admonition of Pope John Paul II, as he bade farewell to Poland to return to Rome: "We must have the courage to move in a direction no one has yet gone, just as Saint Peter once had need of a great deal of courage to leave Lake Gennesaret in Galilee and set out for Rome, where he would be a stranger."[53]

The surest, safest route for us today is not the pathway to the past—the road already traveled. The surest, safest route for us today is the still-unblazed trail leading straight ahead and to the future.

2. Christianity and the Liberation of the Oppressed

In Latin America the religion of the people can become a catalyst for developing theories and practices conducive to an alternative society, a society whose objectives are altogether different from those of the current leaders of history and especially from those of world capital. As we have just seen at Puebla, as earlier and less decisively at Medellín, the Church on our continent made a categorical option for the people, for the poor, for their liberation, and for their organization in base church communities. It showed itself ready to assist in constructing a more equal society with more partnership, where everyone will have a voice in decisions. The Church's commitment springs from an imperative of faith itself in its political and social dimension.

THE RELATIONSHIP OF RELIGION AND SOCIETY

What contribution can we expect from Christianity in the transformation of our society, with its manifest, ever-widening gap between rich and poor?

Two Reductionisms: Theologism and Sociologism

It is important to pose the problem correctly. As indicated earlier, we must avoid the two reductionisms of theologism and sociologism. *Theologism* is a theoretical aberration, typical of an ecclesiastical view of the world, in which Christianity is regarded as fallen full-panoplied from the skies, owing nothing whatever to history. A theologistic Christianity regards the relationship between the human being and God as the only genuine relationship in Christian reality as well as the only explanation of that reality. The only adequate discourse, therefore, is the theological discourse, which embraces the whole truth of Christianity. All other discourse bearing upon Christianity must necessarily be ideological.

The error of theologism lies in its failure to take account of the historical roots of reality—any and every reality. Christianity does not operate in a vacuum. It operates in history, in society. Like it or not, it is limited and guided by its social and cultural context—the context of a particular, limited population and particular, limited resources, structured within certain modes of production, distribution, and consumption. Of heaven though it be, Christianity never slips the bonds of earth. It contains an undeniable historical, human component of which it must take account.

The second reductionism, as we have seen, comes from the side of society and is called *sociologism*. Sociologism is typical of classical Marxism. In *The German Ideology*, Marx and Engels maintain that religion is simply and solely a variable function of the economic structure. Religion is "the opium of the people," says Marx in a celebrated passage, "the sigh of an oppressed creature, the soul of a soulless society, the spirit of a world without spirit. Overcome social contradictions and religion will 'disappear. For it will no longer have its underpinnings, and will lose its function."[1]

The error of this reductionism consists in its refusal to recognize an irreducible element in religion: the encounter of the human being with the Absolute—our experience of a limitless abyss, the "oceanic experience." It attends only to one side of religious truth—religion's relation to society. It is unable to see the other side—our relationship with the Absolute.

RELIGION AND SOCIETY: RELATIVE AUTONOMY

Today's scholars of religious phenomena, in the wake of Gramsci, Portelli, Godelier, and Bordieu, are gradually coming to realize the *relative autonomy* of religion. Regarding autonomy, religion is possessed of its own truth and articulates that truth in its own field—that of the sacred, the arena of the encounter with the Divine (theologism's point of truth). Regarding the relative, religion is rightly perceived as one of many elements in a given society, sharing all the opportunities and limitations of that society (sociologism's point of truth). In other words, a concrete religion (Christianity, for example) is not completely determined either by society or by a relation to the Absolute, nor is it completely independent of these two instances. It arises from the convergence of both.

The particular problem that interests us here is the extent to which religion has the power to transform society. As we know, Karl Marx and Max Weber, otherwise so opposed in their views, agreed on what they saw to be the twofold function of religion. Religion is a matchless force for legitimizing the power of the dominant classes. It is also a superlative means of achieving the domestication of the subjugated. To borrow an expression from the Gramsci school, religion functions as an "ideological apparatus of the state" in consolidating the hegemony of the dominant class over the prevailing worldview and politics. And yet, given certain contradictions, and with an increasing capacity for resistance and protest on the part of the subordinate classes, the status quo can begin to split, and ideology will lose its power to consolidate. Organic intellectuals (here, religious agents—pastoral ministers, priests, bishops, theologians, laity) can join the struggles of emerging elements for liberation from subjugation. Thus religion can have a place in a strategy of liberation, especially if the people possess a religious worldview, as they do in Latin America. Once these religious groups succeed in merging their interests with the causes of popular liberation, they can develop a religious view of the world adjusted to the liberation of the oppressed and thereby legitimate the longings of the oppressed for change. How? By drawing on their reservoir of the symbols of faith—here, the dangerous, subversive memory of the person and message of Jesus Christ, who was crucified under Pontius Pilate and who unquestionably preferred the poor and marginalized to those the world calls blessed.

Here the figure of the prophet assumes a unique importance. The prophet seizes upon the urgencies of the historical moment and carries them to the religious arena, thereby endowing religion with a potential for contributing to the transformation of society. Both Max Weber and Pierre Bourdieu have shown the decisive influence of the prophet in this context, against the Marxist refusal to recognize the importance of the individual working in a small group for the process of change. From the prophet emanate forces conducive to the structural innovation of society.

In light of these considerations, the great choices made by the Latin American Church at Medellín and Puebla acquire relevance. Here the Church has made a preferential option for the poor and for their liberation, seeking to legitimate their causes and deprive their oppressions of any authorization. Social change is not effected by the Church. It is effected by the people. But faith can be a factor for mobilization rather than restraint. It can offer a powerful spirituality of commitment to the causes of justice, freedom, and partnership. Why? Because faith is precisely the guarantee that the definitive good that constitutes its goal—God, the Reign of God, the Meaning of meanings—is already here in this very history, that God has begun to become reality in society itself, and that this occurs whenever just causes are fought for and realized. When all is said and done, justice, communion, and freedom are not merely supreme social benefits. For faith, they are part and parcel of the Reign of God.

FAITH AND POLITICS: EVERYTHING IS POLITICAL, BUT POLITICS IS NOT EVERYTHING

With increasing frequency, Christians are making political commitments, calling for a qualitive change in society, and doing so in virtue of their faith itself. Likewise with increasing frequency, Christians no longer look on politics as nothing more than a power struggle. Now they see it as "a way of paying worship to the one and only God," as the Puebla Final Document expresses it.[2] After all, *politics* means the common quest for the common good. The positions assumed by the Church in defense of human rights in recent years, especially the rights of the poor, the alliance with popular communities, and now the preferential option for the wronged and for their liberation, has sharpened the question of the relationship between faith and politics. The bishops themselves, meeting in Puebla, acknowledged the conflicting nature of this new position: "The enormously positive activity of the Church in defense of human rights and its dealings with the poor have led groups with economic power, who thought they were in the front ranks of Catholicism, to feel that they have been abandoned by the Church. As they see it, the Church has forsaken its 'spiritual' mission."[3]

Others, accustomed to a Christianity of social and devotional practices, now fail to understand the prophetic and social dimension that expressions of faith have assumed in recent years. The correct theoretical procedure will be that recommended by Aristotle on the first page of his *Politics:* first, to reduce this complex affair to its simple components, and then to establish a correct interrelationship among them without reducing them to one another. Let us begin with the category of faith.

WHAT IS FAITH?

Faith, in its original sense, is a mode of being through which a human being lives and interprets experience in the light of a supreme Meaning. Religions know this Meaning as God; Christianity recognizes it as God incarnate in the historical figure of Jesus of Nazareth. Faith, then, bears directly on God, not on politics. Faith defines our transcendent dimension—not our dimension as social agent, employer or worker, black or yellow, but precisely our dimension as human beings—with the power to overcome all taboos and move beyond all historical determinants by exercising our freedom and transcendence.

Faith is more than an attitude toward the ultimate meaning of life; faith also has a particular, defined content. For example, part of the content of Christian faith is the notion of God as a communion of Father, Son, and Holy Spirit. Love and communion are the fundamental realities of the Divine. All the more, then, should love and communion be fundamental for all realities created by that Trinity. The Son took flesh in our poverty. He was not a Caesar but a laborer. He preached an incredible hope: the Reign of justice, love, and peace, beginning on earth itself and culminating in heaven. His message stirred conflict. All of the mighty of his time rose up against him, as they felt their privileges endangered. His death was a sacrifice for the Reign of God. It resulted from the conflict he provoked and had to confront in fidelity to God and to his brothers and sisters. His resurrection demonstrates the truth of his cause and the triumph of the oppressed. The Spirit who had descended upon

Mary now completes the work of Jesus, dwelling in history as a yeast and ferment, especially in the community of Jesus' followers. In brief, God so loved human beings that he became one of us, preferring the weak and impoverished of this world and guaranteeing to all who would be converted a happy ending to their life story. For God promises a creation wholly transfigured into a new world, where there will be no more tears but only the Reign of justice. As we see, by virtue of the fact that it defines a Meaning of meanings—the supreme Meaning—faith embraces the whole order of existence, political practices included. In this sense faith concerns not only God but, indirectly, politics as well. Emmanuel Mounier was right: "Everything is political, but politics is not everything."

WHAT IS POLITICS?

Now let us turn to politics. A great deal of confusion reigns here, especially in the minds of Christians. It is important, therefore, to distinguish the various meanings of *political* and *politics*. We offer the following clarification, with a view to linking the arenas of politics and faith (and its organized Christian form, the Church).

1. The word *political* has three meanings. In the *comprehensive sense*, it means anything pertaining to society (to the ancient *polis*), such as the state (with its apparatus), civil institutions, guilds and unions, economic, cultural, and religious organizations. In this sense of the word the faith community (with its ecclesiastical apparatus, the hierarchy), is "political," as it is a subsystem of the comprehensive social system. Thus faith is a community organizational principle having an influence on the societal whole. In the *broad* sense, *political* refers to the various conceptions (ideologies) of social organization: capitalism, socialism, Marxism, social democracy, and so on. Each of these conceptions has its practices and its view of the human being and society, their happiness (in the Aristotelian sense of *politics*), and their future. Faith lived in community—in the Church—is part of the political inasmuch as it holds a particular vision of the world and of the human being, a vision it serves by criticizing, rejecting, or collaborating with other political ideologies. In the *ordinary* sense, *political* re-

fers to any undertaking in behalf of the common good, such as the promotion of justice, individual and social human rights, political honesty instead of corruption, and the like. In this ordinary sense, faith is highly political, since its ideals prioritize the values of cooperation, uprightness, and truth, so frequently exploited for the purposes of a capitalistic ethic of private accumulation.

2. *Politics* is that field of human activity ordered to administer or transform human society by acquiring and exercising the power of state. For two hundred years now, this power has been organized in parties, each having its ideology, program, strategy, and tactics. In this sense of the word, *politics* pertains to power, not to faith. Hence politics in this sense can be practiced without necessarily appealing to faith, although faith can be useful to politics by moderating the temptation of all power to absolutize itself. The Church, understood as an ecclesiastical apparatus (bishops, priests, and religious), may not participate as an institution in politics in this sense of the word. Faith does not oblige us to join or vote for a particular party, since there are always other means of performing political activity. Furthermore, a party imposes a particular discipline; it defines its tactics and the kind of obedience it requires. Faith cannot be framed and limited in this way, since it would then have to renounce its status as a supreme meaning. A lay Christian, in the light of faith, can and must make political choices, even when these options do not enjoy the institutional support of the hierarchy. The freedom to do so is guaranteed by the gospel, which is expressed not only officially (through the hierarchy), but personally as well.

3. *Politização*, "politicization," denotes any activity directed toward educating the people to have a popular voice in political and social reality, so that the poor exercise their share of social responsibility and acquire a critical spirit. Here the Christian community has a crucial pedagogical function. It teaches that the common quest of the common good is an ethical demand of faith itself and a way of anticipating the Reign of God, which begins right here on earth. We must rehabilitate the positive sense of this word, so abused by authoritarian, individualistic minds. Political participation is not a matter of mere spontaneity. It must be the object of education.

4. *Politicking*—politics in the pejorative sense—is the corruption of political activity that occurs when the state or social power is pressed into service for individual, group, or class interests. The Christian community may be involved in the mechanisms of politicking by virtue of the privileges it receives. The history of religion abounds with instances of the religious legitimation of authoritarian, unjust power. Today, however, religion is moving toward criticism and delegitimation of such power, with a view toward creating a more open society of genuine partnership.

As we see, faith has meaning for society and politics, but its meaning is not exhausted there. Faith also projects an eschatological meaning for human beings and their history. It is important to link the two dimensions, so that faith may reveal its humanizing dimension and politics may be practiced as a virtue (as a mediation of justice) and not merely as a technique of power. The bishops at Puebla formulated it powerfully and courageously: "For us today [the love of God] must become first and foremost a labor of justice on behalf of the oppressed (Luke 4:18), an effort of liberation for those who are most in need of it."[4] And politics is one of the most important instruments of social love.

FROM THE CENTER TO THE MARGIN: WITNESS OF A PROPHET

A point of view is the view from a point. Change the point and you change the view. There are various social loci (commitments and practices), and each affords (and blocks out) various views of reality. Viewed from their centers, from their skyscrapers and their fancy display windows, São Paulo and Rio de Janeiro do not look the same as they look from their outskirts, from the *barrios* with their miserable little shacks. In the center things are softer. On the periphery things scream at you. In the center, the mechanisms of exploitation are invisible. On the margin you can see them with the naked eye. These differences create different discourses and correspondingly different interests. The sociology of knowledge (and theology is knowledge) has shown the connection between social locus (class condition and social status) and the conceptions and interests of the knowing subject.

This understanding is important for the topic we now address: the movement of the Church from the center to the margin. For centuries the Church has occupied a social locus identical to or akin to that of economic, political, and cultural power—in a word, to that of the center. We shall make no critical, ethical judgment of this locus, which the Church has occupied from the time of Constantine (fourth century) and Theodosius (fifth century) to the present. Indeed, we believe that Christianity had no realistic alternative. Social conditions limited its "choice." With Roman culture in decay, it had to be the Church that assumed the direction of the social process. And so a Christianity sprang up that was tied to power, the power of the center.

But the locus of central power yields a reading of reality in layers, from top to bottom, with order, discipline, harmony, consent, and integration heading the list of values. Religious power may differ from other power in its divine origin, but its mechanisms obey the laws of all power. Church history confirms this assertion. All power is exercised upon persons. The center creates its margin. Participation in the exercise of political power has never been widespread in our culture, either in society or in the Church. Power has always been strongly centralized, leaving a broad, powerless margin.

Over the last thirty years, however, power in the Latin American Church has been shifting from the center to the margin. This across-the-board movement began with the Second Vatican Council (1962–1965), gained momentum at Medellín (1968), and culminated with the level of awareness attained at Puebla (1979). We cannot here analyze the historical and theological conditions that favored this conversion of the Church, which has meant shifting its traditional social locus from one social and economic milieu to an entirely different one. We may remark, however, that the church historian will regard this phenomenon as more traditional than traditionalism itself, since traditionalism longs only for a return to the relatively recent past, while with its current shift of social locus the Church is returning to its origins in the marginality and poverty of primitive Christianity.

This change of direction has taken place primarily in the countries of the third world. Its first spokesperson was Dom Helder Câmara, who on the eve of the Second Vatican Council met with a number of other Latin American bishops in Rome, as if in the catacombs, and launched an appeal for a Church that is poor and of the poor. This was the origin of the new social locus of the Church and the new viewpoint arising from that locus. "From the center to the margin" is the formula we use to describe this pilgrimage that the Church has undertaken but not yet completed. It is also the title of a book by one of the most prophetic and conscientious of our Brazilian bishops, Dom José Maria Pires, Archbishop of Paraíba, whom we fondly call Dom Pelé: *Do Centro para a Margem.*[5]

Dom José Maria's book outlines a practice and supports the practice with a theory of exceptional lucidity. The book shows what it means to think, live, and practice Christianity from a social location on the margin of society. Christianity will surely find its roots when it takes its position on the margin and creates its theory and practice from that margin. After all, Jesus, the apostles, and the first Christians lived on the margin of the powerful society of their time. The gospel as the good news is heard with all its impact only by those who are (actually or by option) on the margin of society. There that gospel rings forth as liberation for the oppressed, justice for the impoverished, and a political voice for the marginalized. For God prefers the poor and addresses first to them the coming of the Reign. We see all of this in Dom José Maria Pires's book. His bright vision gleams before our eyes as the tranquil, serene vision of someone who has made this understanding of the gospel and the Church bone of his bone and flesh of his flesh. Suddenly we see: with the margin as its starting place, the gospel reveals its native colors. Our gaze is purer now. We behold only the essential. Everything becomes convincingly clear, and we are moved by the impact.

A Christianity of the margin makes four significant discoveries. We shall examine these discoveries in terms of Dom Pelé's own fine presentation.

1. DISCOVERY OF THE PASSION OF THE PEOPLE

Life on the margin is harsh. Here the economic, social, and political system in which we live exhibits all its inequity and injustice, as it gnaws away at every aspect of life. From a position on the margin, it is easy to see, as Puebla saw, that capitalism is an antihumane "system of sin" and tantamount to atheism in practice.[6] In the words of Dom José Maria, capitalism is "irreconcilable with a Church that pleads for opportunity for all. A gradual socialization of goods and means of production corresponds much better with God's project for humanity."[7] This is not a lecture by a social scientist. It is the lesson of a pastor, a shepherd, who has transferred his social locus to that of the marginalized. It is the lesson of one who says, "I have heard my people's cry" (see Exod. 3:7), and then goes in quest of their liberation.

2. DISCOVERY OF INSTITUTIONALIZED VIOLENCE

The violation of the rights of the poor is not something that "just happens." It is a permanent, ongoing process. The poor are economic ciphers. No account is taken of them in official planning. Now we understand why the Church commits itself to upholding the dignity of the weak and oppressed.

3. DISCOVERY OF THE POWER OF THE POOR IN HISTORY

Despite the violence in which they are engulfed, the people have maintained an almost bottomless capacity for resistance and historical patience. Constantly they find new ways to join forces. Popular piety especially constitutes a cell of liberation, a breathing space, a place where hope springs anew and the meaning of life lives on.

4. DISCOVERY OF THE EVANGELIZING POTENTIAL OF THE LOWLY

Awash in social misery, still the people maintain the fundamental evangelical values of solidarity, hospitality, and sincerity. They evangelize the entire Church. Today they may be the only evangelizers of bishops and priests.

The margin is sending a message to the center. And that message is a challenge. Millions are beating on the door, asking one thing alone: the right to be people. By our response we shall all be judged.

echist knows, the priest nods yes, the bishop imparts his blessing on it all, and the Pope sacralizes it in the name of the Eternal. There is grandeur here and a strong sense of security. This security is necessary for the tranquil celebration of faith. This is the vision of the calm surface of the lake of faith. This is the believer's perspective.

But the moment comes when faith becomes theology. Theology is faith thinking and thought, critical and systematic. The theologian realizes that, beneath the calm—which is real, and not just apparent—serious problems are concealed, like the rough contours of the lake bottom. Theology must not fix its mind mainly on formulas. First and foremost, theology must think the mystery of God. And before the mystery of God all else pales by comparison. Our thoughts only graze this mystery, and formulas that once sounded so clear and cogent now seem mere stammering. Words do not do this mystery justice. Indeed, it is the quality of mystery always to make us "think again." And then it remains mystery in the new formulation as well. Once theology has realized the inadequacy of all its formulas, even the most consecrated, it puts its shoulder to the wheel once more and strives, not only to explain and enrich the definitions of the past, but also to restate its grasp of the mystery of God in a language comprehensible to each new generation. It seeks somehow to encapsulate Christian dogmas in more comprehensive formulations. This is the view of the lake of faith from the starting point of its mysterious depths. This is the perspective of the theologian.

After writing his *Summa Theologica*, the greatest cathedral to Christian faith ever built, Saint Thomas Aquinas sank into the mystery of God and fell silent. Returning once more to the surface, he could only say of his theology that is all seemed but one little straw to him now, for he had glimpsed the actual realities of faith.

BETWEEN THEOBUREAUCRACY AND DILETTANTISM

Both visions—that of the simple believer and that of the theologian—are valid and full of truth. The truth of each should be respected. Neither annuls the other. As believers we must give the reason for this great hope of ours (cf. 1 Pet. 3:15). That is, we must do theology. And theologians must be persons of faith. For without faith we shall not have an existential experience of our speculation. Like the brilliant moon, which would be dark without the sun, so theology needs faith in order to live.

This difficult tension can give rise to either of two theological pathologies, both frequently encountered in the Church. The first is that of the "theobureaucrats"—theologians who are merely technical experts in the formulas, dogmas, and teachings of church documents and theology manuals. Such theologians have precious little upon which to reflect. They are epistemologically naive. They pretend to be above the various schools of theology, that they may content themselves with parroting the theological vulgate.

Theologians who are merely technicians deny other theologians the right to innovation, the right to plumb the depths of the doctrine of the faith. Any liturgical innovation is promptly derided by them as a "sociological mass." Any step forward or in-depth progress in theology is immediately suspect. This spirit in the Church would have made it impossible for an Origen, a Saint Augustine, a Saint Thomas, a Duns Scotus, a Congar, and a Rahner—the very minds who nourish our faith and piety today—to exercise their creativity. Christian teachings and theologies were not cut from whole cloth. They were woven by theologians, who risked a great deal, who reflected a great deal, and who were sometimes misunderstood, even condemned. Saint Thomas acknowledges that theology "requires much toil, and they are few who bear this toil for love of the science of theology."[1]

The opposite pathological manifestation is that of a speculative dilettantism in theology. A theology that exempts itself from any commitment to the past or, worse, to the faith pilgrimage of God's people, will do its thinking, its reflection, "on its own," with such contrivance and "creativity" that agreements will become impossible. It will have no formula of consensus (a creed), nor any rite to express and celebrate the universality of one and the same faith.

The first pathology, rule of the theological technicians, inflates the institutional facet of the Church, with its rites and formulas, and falls into dogmatism, which has nothing in common with the receiving of dogmas. But dogmatism is by definition intolerant and repressive. It loses the sense of mystery, despite the goodwill and high sense of responsibility investing its practitioners, those living martyrs of duty. The second pathology, a speculative dilettantism, exaggerates the experiential facet of faith to the point where some of its practitioners are content to live an orgy of religious experiences, refusing to confront the word of revelation, tradition, and the magisterium. Generally these persons condemn themselves to isolationism.

THE CHALLENGE OF A RESPONSIBLE THEOLOGY

A correct theology will be a responsible theology—a theology loyal to the past but free to say a much-needed word to the present, a word that will be original, as the challenges of the present are original. We must move beyond what Pascal called the spirit of geometry. The spirit of geometry abuses divine realities. It forgets that there can be no mathematical, rigid measure for the mystery of God and human beings. The holy must be dealt with in a holy manner, in a spirit of refinement and unction. Unction is not the automatic perquisite of the devout and prayerful. It is the quality of those who have developed a sense of mystery, a feeling for the ineffable. The spirit of *finesse* (Pascal, once more) is embodied in an attitude of respect, in the ability to listen with an open mind, even when one has the duty of denouncing abuses in faith and discipline. It is not enough to be a watchdog of orthodoxy. (Some watchdogs bite!) One must do one's thinking and proclaiming in such a way that God's message may truly be good news, ever and again, anew to each generation. To this purpose, *multa praecognoscere oportet:* "one must know a great many things in advance," and not merely theology.[2]

As as have seen, theology deals with the pinnacle of human existence and the radical meaning of human life. Only intellectually decadent, anemic times refuse to come to grips with theology. All of the great minds of the past have grappled with the problems that constitute the very life of theology—God, or the ultimate meaning of the human being and the cosmos—precisely because these minds were great.

To theology has been confided the care of the sacred mystery residing in every existence, however humble and lowly. The atmosphere of this mystery must be cared for, hovered over, with the same unction with which we care for the sanctuary lamps in our temples, feeding and protecting them that their flame may never fail. Before mystery let every tongue fall still, let all discourse keep silence. Nothing of our uttering can be more than a sign, a nod. But as we strive to develop this sign, the life of the Spirit feeds the flame of the lamp. Then in humility can theology pronounce its word: "God is greater than our hearts" (1 John 3:20).

CURRENT THEOLOGICAL TENDENCIES

The Christian world has always interpreted the universally accepted data of faith and the gospel in the spirit of pluralism. Theological disputes have generally been confined within the Church's borders and have not spilled over into society or the mass media. In recent years, however, the variety of opinions in the Church has gradually become public. Why? Because this variety of thought can give rise to different practical positions on burning public issues: the position of the Church on problems of the land, the Indians, social justice, human rights, criticism of various social and political systems, and the like. Perplexed, many ask: What is the origin of these divergencies? Why are there progressive theologians, conservative theologians, and theologians committed to the liberation of the poor?

SOCIAL AND EPISTEMIC LOCUS

In order to understand this situation, which is a normal and not a pathological one, we must understand what is meant by the social or epistemic locus of a reflection—in this case, of theological reflection. Any idea, theory, or worldview, however universalistic and objective it claims to be, is bound up with the material conditions, theoretical and practical, of its location. These conditions enter in some fashion into the formulation of the very content of our ideas. To put it in the technical parlance of the sociology of knowledge and the language of epistemology (the philosophy of knowledge): all discourse refers to a social locus. By social locus we mean the positions, practices, and engagements of persons by virtue of their function and role in society.

If I am a worker, I shall see the world from the viewpoint of a worker and judge the social and economic system under which I suffer and survive by the criteria of a worker, the criteria of someone exploited and abused by the prevailing system. If I am the owner of a successful industrial enterprise or an executive in a multinational corporation, I shall paint a different landscape of reality—one of progress, wealth, and the smooth functioning of technology and capital. We each project our own worldview or ideology, and this ideology confers meaning on the world in which we live. This is our social locus.

Every social locus permits or prevents particular discourses. For example, the wealthy will naturally be in favor of capitalism and oppose any change in the system of ownership and distribution of goods. After all, any change will be to their disadvantage. Inevitably, they will be conservative in the areas of politics and religion but not, however, in lifestyle and fashion, consumership, or morals, since wealth will permit them all liberties. They will be dead set against any workers' revolution. The suffering workers, however, who have to subsist on the minimum wage, once made genuinely aware of their circumstances will necessarily become agents for change. They will call for a new set of rules for the social game, because change will improve their situation. They will be revolutionaries opposed to social immobility. In either case, the social locus permits certain ideas and prohibits others. It permits the wealthy to be conservative and to oppose the idea of revolution, while the opposite occurs with the conscientized worker. The social locus produces the epistemic locus. That is, the social locus guides the development of ideas and worldviews.

This state of affairs is simply an instance of the incarnation of the human spirit in the concrete material of history and social conflicts. Despite this limitation (and any incarnation is at once a limitation and a concretion), the human spirit can rise above contingent conditions, acquire a raised consciousness, an enhanced awareness of the scope and limit of a given intellectual proposition, and maintain a tendency to seek out the objective truth or falsehood of what is thus proposed for its acceptance. Concrete truth is never neutral. The mind has a tendency to try to see the world in a higher light than that of human interests alone. This is the transcendence of spirit. It explains why we can read the ancients and learn from them despite the lapse of so many centuries and despite the differences between their conditions and our own. Thus it is always useful to pay a visit to Plato, Aristotle, Isaiah, Saint Augustine, Saint Thomas, and especially the Gospels with their message of Jesus.

These considerations are important for understanding the "why" of various theological tendencies or the different positions taken by the bishops toward the most varied problems. Underlying the theoretical differences are different social loci. Divergent, indeed conflicting and antagonistic, interests are at stake. As the ancient Chinese sages said, "If you seek to comprehend someone, look not at his mouth but at his hands." Attend less to people's words than to their deeds. Deeds rarely deceive.

All critical thought, all science, struggles for the greatest possible distance from particular interests. In some ages people thought they had arrived at complete objectivity. But modern epistemology has shown this attempt to be impossible. A residue of ideology and particular interests will remain in any intellectual content. After all, thought is a vital activity, and life is never neutral and undifferentiated. We must never again be so epistemologically naive as to say that science attains to pure truth. But though we can mount to the heavens, we dare not scorn earth. The light of truth can pierce the darkness but cannot exorcise it altogether. Light will always leave a shadow at the side of the reality upon which it streams.

The question facing theology is this: To what cause is a particular theology committed? What interests, conscious or unconscious, underlie it? Critical thinking acknowledges its own hidden interests. Concealment, unconscious or conscious (alienation or perversion, respectively), belongs instead to ideology. Distinct interests help determine the choice of themes to be addressed. The theologian's engagement defines the degree of relevance to be conferred upon the various themes. For a conservative theologian, the themes of the liberation of the oppressed or the rights of the poor, will not have a great deal of relevance. By contrast, the sacraments, the divinity of Jesus, and the sacred power of the bishops will seem very relevant. Not that the conservative theologian denies the validity of the other themes. It is only that, for this particular person, they are not existentially meaningful. Why? Because of the theologian's social locus. By contrast, for a theologian engaged in the base communities, committed to the poor and their struggles, Jesus' liberation, the conflicts that led him to crucifixion, the Beatitude of the poor, and so on, will be very important themes. This theologian's social locus points up the relevance of these traditional subjects. The Bible and sacred tradition are like an immense archeological excavation. You can find everything there, from gold coins to clay shards. Each theological group takes what it wants from the past, because in the Bible and tradition we find various social loci, each producing its corresponding discourse. The proper, correct criterion for the thinking of theologians is always the practice of the historical Jesus. For Jesus not everything was true, not everything was right. For some things we must be willing to undergo conflict, even persecution, and, if need be, death.

It is not enough, however, to have a crisp definition of one's interest, purified in the light of Jesus Christ. It is not sufficient to define a great cause. One must develop that cause theologically. And to create theology, a believer must know theological grammar, biblical exegesis, and historical methods. A believer must be able to interpret the teaching of the magisterium and tradition and also to be conversant in the various fields of theological and scientific knowledge. Someone can take on the interests of the despoiled—make an evangelical option—and yet develop a catastrophic theology owing to errors of argumentation, whether because of historical mistakes, inadequacies of logic, or both; just as another theologian, committed to the interests of the (politically and economically) powerful, and therefore involved in a profoundly questionable cause from an evangelical viewpoint, can develop a theology that is logically correct and well constructed methodologically. The only proper and correct theology, then, will be one developed first in view of a good and relevant cause, and then through all methodological rigor, following the rules of theological discourse and in respect for reality, the Bible, sacred tradition, the magisterium, theological reason, the *sensus fidelium* (believers' sense of truth), and so on.

FOUR THEOLOGICAL CURRENTS

Let us now outline the various theological currents prevailing in our culture today. As we shall see, all are somehow socially committed in terms of their social locus. In order to show this, we shall borrow terminology from the political arena. Classifications matter little. What is important is the underlying motive which is always a cause to be espoused, a commitment.

1. Some theologians identify socially with those groups that, under the old regime, occupied a place of economic, political, ideological, and religious power. Small groups of elite controlled tradition, family, and property. Historically these have lost their hegemony. But the symbols of their opulent past and their hereditary wealth are alive and well. Their theologians are reactionary, engaging in activity that is anything but original: they oppose the activity of others. Thus they are antimodern and antidemocratic. They reserve their esteem for authoritarian systems and the feudal symbols of sacred and secular power. Change terrifies them. They have a sovereign contempt for whatever might originate with the people. They use the symbolic arsenal of the medieval history of Christianity to defend their threatened interests. Being elitist, they want the Tridentine Mass, in Latin, and a return to the great medieval syntheses. They live on lamentation. They maintain an apocalyptic outlook, and they sense communists and heretics lurking around every corner. Their ideology causes them to identify their private, exclusive interests with a defense of the values of orthodoxy and tradition. Actually they are too little traditional; if they were genuinely so, they would seek out the historical Jesus. But the real Jesus is supremely uncomfortable for them. They prefer a made-to-order Jesus, arrayed in all the magnificence of a Byzantine culture. Archbishop Lefebvre's movement, Dom Sigaud, and Dom Castro Maier, among others, fall into this category—that of a reactionary interpretation of Christian faith.

2. Another kind of theology starts from the locus of sacred power in the Church—the functions of the bishop, priest, and pastoral minister. This theology too, is generally traditional, as it originates in the social locus of power. Its worldview unfolds from the top down, from vertex to base. Power descends from

God to Christ, from Christ to the apostles, from the apostles to the bishops, and from the bishops to the priests. (There it stops.) Here is a theology of order. Everything is elucidated from the point of departure of divine revelation and is translated into dogmas, theological theses, propositions of the magisterium, and meticulously defined moral norms. Its main problem is how to apply such clarity to the dark confusion of life. There is a great deal of emphasis on the transhistorical nature of the Church and thus on the apparent (not real) neutrality of political and social questions. This theology mistrusts any new religious experience, for it is not in a position to control it. It is a theology of certainties rather than of truths. Thus any crisis or doubt is regarded as a pathological manifestation calling for an immediate remedy. The strength of this theology resides in its emphasis on authority and obedience, the basis of order.

This second kind of theology regards the world as a kind of appendage of the Church. The Church is *mater et magistra,** "mother and teacher," and has the answer to all the great questions of life. The danger of this theology is theologism and an excessive attachment to ecclesiastical practices. It seeks to solve political problems by moral means. Based on authority, it erects the kind of Church that dovetails nicely with authoritarian political regimes. One never lodges a basic criticism against this kind of Church. One criticizes it only tangentially on grounds that, while authoritarianism can fall into excesses, in which case it must be corrected, it is basically a good thing. A dictator can be good and also devout. But the inherent violence of the very fact of a dictatorship is left out of account. Theological reflection is linked to the mentality of an authoritarian state.

3. A third theological current is called progressive. It identifies the great theological problem of the modern world as the gap between modernity and Christian faith. It has discovered the autonomous value of science and technology. It accepts the democratic advances exorcised a century ago by the magisterium of the Church: freedoms of expression, conscience, and religion. It accepts secularization, not only as a consequence of the sci-

---

Mater et Magistra, the title of a 1961 encyclical letter by Pope John XXIII on the recent evolution of the social question.

entific spirit but also as an imperative of faith itself, which de-fetishizes the world, reducing all of its realities to their proper status as mere creatures.

This theology expresses the social locus of the upwardly mobile—university graduates who will be joining a progressive, dynamic bourgeois society. This theology encourages the modernization of the Christian institution, the Christian liturgy, the Christian ethos. It created the Second Vatican Council, supplanting the official neoscholastic theology of the Roman Curia. It is open to a dialogue with all the modern sciences. It is willing to face any problem. It is the frame of reference of the majority of bishops and clergy today.

But this critical theology is not critical enough. It rarely recognizes that the scientific and technological enterprise is more than just an instrument for subjecting nature to human will. Today that enterprise represents a mighty weapon of capitalist domination (in our Western system) in the hands of a small group of countries that hold all the others at arm's length—on the periphery—and in a state of dependence. Progressivism evades the basic question, the question of the profoundly unequal relationships that prevail among nations and between classes, and the price others have to pay for the benefits of accelerated development in the central countries. It is possible to prostitute this theology as a religious ideology for the justification of the modern status quo—at the service of a little group of enlightened elite who become the sole beneficiaries of progress won by the labors of all.

4. A fourth current has sprung from the third. Its point of departure is not modernity and the social locus of a progressive bourgeoisie but rather the people, the social locus of the popular, oppressed classes. It strives for the liberation of these classes and seeks to help them win a voice in the historical process. It never ceases asking how far Christian faith can go in helping to build a more humane and just world for all without losing its identity and transcendent reference. It speaks not of the world but of the subworld, not of critical persons in a culture at last come of age but of nonpersons[3] subjected to processes of exploitation and dehumanization.

Obviously this form of theology can come into being only on

the periphery, in the third world, in Latin America, Africa, and Asia. At present it constitutes the most promising of all the theological currents. It has been officially adopted, in its basic framework, by the Latin American episcopate at Medellín and Puebla. This is the current of thought that frames our own reflection.

ALL THEOLOGY IS COMMITTED: LATIN AMERICAN THEOLOGY

It is scarcely out of epistemological considerations that Latin American theology has been denied legitimacy in the name of a universal theology—as if there could be such a thing as a universal theology. Here we must recall Aristotle and Saint Thomas, who examined the nature of the sciences long before the advent of modern epistemology. For Aristotle, a universal science is a contradiction. Every science has a limited object appropriated by way of a specific outlook. Following Aristotle, Aquinas held that in order to constitute a grammatical reflection on faith, even theology must be a regional science.[4] Theology contemplates all realities, yes, but only in the light of God—only from the outlook of faith. The mere fact of having the Absolute as its object does not render theology itself absolute or universal. Theology may not ascribe to itself qualities attaching to God alone—divinity, universality, absoluteness. This would suppose an identification of the human idea of God with the reality of God, which is the error of idolatry. Faith is universal in its quality as complete openness to God as the Meaning of meanings and the only Absolute Being.

On the concrete, existential level, faith is always historically situated in a language peculiar to the particular circumstances in which it is lived and experienced. The universality of faith exists only in the particular. This being the case, there is no reason why there should not be a variety of theologies. Indeed, we readily distinguish patristic theology, of a wisdom tenor; scholastic theology, of a scientific, systematical character; modern theology, which is historical and existential; and so on. We also speak of the theology of Saint Augustine as being different from that of Saint Thomas, which in turn differs from the theologies of Barth or Rahner. Each particular theologian has systematized the universal datum of faith in a peculiar, particular manner, using the theoretical tools of his or her particular day and age. The result is always a particular theology, not a universal one.

LEGITIMACY OF LATIN AMERICAN THEOLOGY

Theology is the fruit of the encounter of faith and reason. But reason is always historical. Its object is never the void. Reason always operates under limited conditions, and these conditions are always specific to a particular era. Thus reason always avails itself of the tools of a given age. Classical theology (which has mistakenly been called universal) was constructed with the help of contributions from biblical, Greek, Roman, Germanic, and in modern times scientific thought. It is only one kind of theology, it is not all of theology. It is a specific mode of rationally assimilating the content of faith.

Furthermore, theological production depends a great deal on the theologian's social locus, as we have already observed. Like everyone else, a theologian is a social agent, operating from a particular place in society. Nor is it a cozy place, this matrix of relationships between the theologian and other agents; these relationships can be competitive, cooperative, or conflicting. All theology is engaged and committed. After all, it is addressed to someone, it is constructed in a given language and no other, and it has repercussions on a situation and is shot through with multiple conflicts. This reality is not subject to our will. It will do me no good to stamp my foot and say, "My theology is neutral, official, apolitical!" Such language only betrays the epistemological naivete of the one using it. Speaking in this way will inevitably mean catering to the interest of one group and excluding another, and thus a division will already be present and operative.

Our ongoing question must be, not to what extent my theology is free of particular interests and ideology, but to what interests and ideology my way of doing theology is committed. Whom does this particular theology serve? And the criterion of theological authenticity is confrontation with the interests of the gospel—criticizing the interests of theology in light of the interests and commitments of the historical Jesus. There is no doubting the historical fact that, as Pope John II recalled to the bishops at Puebla, Jesus "identified with the deserted." His "commitment was to the neediest." He was "never indifferent to the imperatives of social reality." Only in the critical crucible of the gospel does theology find its authority, as its attunes its interests to the interests of God in Jesus Christ.

There is a Latin American theology that has already produced good fruit, at the theoretical, spiritual, and especially the practical level. It springs from reflection on Latin American problems in the light of Christian faith.

A REFLECTION WHOSE STARTING POINT IS THE PASSION OF THE POOR

The basic problem facing theology as a practice originating in a particular social locus is not how to proclaim the gospel to the critical, enlightened, secularized unbeliever of today, but how to proclaim the good news of Jesus Christ to the believing nonperson—to the exploited, miserable largely Christian masses of our continent. Proclaiming the gospel to the sophisticated, secularized unbeliever is the particular concern of European theological reflection. There the principal interlocutor is the nonbeliever, and religion itself is at stake. By contrast, the question concerning Latin American theologians is how to proclaim the good news to the nonperson whose dignity has been violated. Here the matter at issue is no longer religion but society. For Europeans, the great question is how to reconcile faith and modern science, the Church and the industrialized world, piety and secularization. For us Latin Americans, the burning question is the relationship between faith and social justice, between evangelization and liberation, between spirituality and politics, between the raw fact of class struggle and Christian love. What can we do to help the people's collective heritage of faith become a factor for integral liberation, starting with liberation from hunger, economic exploitation, and cultural marginality, and extending to the most exalted forms of spiritual liberation?

Unless we mean to be the cynical enemies of our own humanity, these questions must not be thrust aside in the name of a false pacifism. Circumstances in Latin America are conflictive in the extreme, and they have been courageously denounced as such by the bishops assembled at Puebla. The present Holy

Father invites us all to call injustice by its proper name. Then we must say, in every way we can, as Bishop Darcy Ribeiro of Rio de Janeiro has said: "In Latin America, the poor are nothing but fodder for the productive process." A few lions are devouring vast flocks of sheep. What partnership, what coexistence can prevail between a wolf and a sheep? A cat's discourse to a mouse on the value of cooperation and dialogue must not hoodwink us if we hope to survive. Theology must know which side it is on, as Jesus knew: on the side of the Samaritan (who was the heretic of the day), against the Levite who simply continued on his way oblivious to victim who lay in the ditch.

A faith willing to confront these altogether concrete questions can be articulated only in terms of liberation. Neither the Pope nor the bishops gathered at Puebla have preached resignation to the poor and almsgiving to the rich. They have proclaimed the urgency of liberation, of social justice, and of the conversion of an entire society to more equal relationships of partnership.

How is one to reflect upon and have a living experience of the Holy Trinity, Jesus Christ, grace, the sacraments, eschatology, and the Church, in a framework of these Latin American exigencies? To answer this question is to create Latin American theology today.

4. Spirituality and Politics

THEOLOGY OF LIBERATION: THE ARTICULATE CRY OF THE OPPRESSED

Liberation theology represents the first great theological current born on the periphery of the metropolitan centers of culture and theological production that has had a repercussion on the entire Church. Initially formulated in Latin America, liberation theology today constitutes a frame of reference and reflection for all groups who regard themselves as oppressed: the Christian poor of Africa and Asia, the oppressed minorities of the United States (blacks and Hispanics), and the various feminist movements.

Liberation, in the understanding of such theology, is not simply one topic among many that theologians address in the course of their theoretical practice. Liberation is the comprehensive backdrop against which theologians reflect on the entire content of their faith. It could not be otherwise, since these theologians do all their thinking with a view to promoting and adopting practices that promise to transform society. The next question, then, is: How is such a theology constructed? What mediations, what tools does it use to build its discourse?

What Liberation Is Meant?

The best characterization of the liberation that interests Latin American theologians is *integral liberation*. It means the liberation of the whole human being and all human beings—the liberation of all oppressed dimensions, personal and social, of human life in all of the subjects of that life, without the exclusion of anyone or anything. The process is a comprehensive one, spanning economics (liberation from material poverty), politics (liberation from social oppression, and the appearance of a new human being), and religion (liberation from sin, the re-creation of men and women in their total realization and actualization in God).

These phases are not successive but simultaneous. Thus a struggle for economic liberation is also a struggle for political and religious liberation. In other words, justice and grace are affairs of economics too. And the same dialectic governs a political or a religious liberation: the other two instances are simultaneously present, with each of the three areas opening out upon the other two. The liberation we mean, then, is never a metaphorical one but always a real, historical one.

In Latin America the oppressed are the poor, whose faces are so touchingly depicted in the Puebla Final Document, and the signs of whose poverty are listed in *Evangelii Nuntiandi*: "Famine, chronic disease, illiteracy, poverty, injustices in international relations and especially in commercial exchanges, situations of economic and cultural neo-colonialism sometimes as cruel as the old political colonialism."[1] Liberation from all of these oppressions is more than an academic problem. It is a political, human, religious, even messianic problem as well. The theology of liberation reflects on the theological dimension of this historical process.

ANTECEDENT OPTION: FOR THE POOR, AGAINST THEIR POVERTY

Unless it is to vanish in a cloud of euphemisms, a theology of liberation must demand of theologians a clear definition and awareness of their social locus. Liberation theologians have elected to see (social) reality from the perspective of the poor, to analyze the processes of this reality in the interests of the poor, and to act for liberation together with the poor. This option is a *political* one, since the theologian by definition is a social agent occupying a particular place in the correlation of social forces—in the case of the liberation theologian, a place at the side of the poor and oppressed. At the same time, this option is an *ethical* one: the theologian refuses to accept the situation as it is, experiences ethical indignation in the presence of the scandal of poverty, and takes an interest in the advancement of the poor; but the advancement of the poor will be possible only if there is a structural change in social and historical reality. Finally, this option for the poor and against their poverty is *evangelical*, since, according to the Gospels, the poor are the primary addressees of Jesus' message. They constitute the eschatological criterion of the salvation or condemnation of the human race and every one of its members (Matt. 25:31–46).

The all-consuming interest of the theology of liberation is the creation of an activity by Christians that will actually tend to the liberation of the poor. Everything must converge on practice (love). But how is Christian love to become effective? It must acquire a better knowledge of reality—of the mechanisms that produce poverty and the paths that lead to a society of justice for all. This is where liberation theology's three mediations enter the picture. A mediation is a means adopted by theology to achieve its goal of historical, integral liberation. The three principal mediations of the liberation theology are the socioanalytic, the hermeneutic, and the pastoral. They correspond to the three methodological moments of seeing, judging, and acting.

THE SOCIOANALYTIC MEDIATION: SEEING

Having defined our basic option—for the poor and against their poverty—we must now execute a correct analysis of the system that generates this mass poverty. An option for the poor does not of itself guarantee the quality of this analysis. The latter must be carried out by means of a series of adequate tools borrowed from the social sciences. What kind of analysis are we to adopt? What social theory will govern it? Here we see the importance of determining the social locus of the analyst and thereby the extrinsic purpose of the analysis (here, the liberation of the poor). This interest, this extrinsic purpose, should be openly declared, inasmuch as a social analysis is never completely disinterested.

Today's social analysis has two basic tendencies: the *functionalistic* tendency, which sees society principally as an organic whole (generally the view of the powers that be), and the *dialectical* tendency, which contemplates society as a set of forces in tension and conflict owing to their diverse interests (generally the view of the powerless). The former tendency works toward reform, concerned as it is with the functioning and perfecting of a system regarded unquestioningly as a good system and therefore one to be maintained and preserved. The latter, the dialectical tendency, concentrates on the conflicts and imbalances affecting the impoverished and calls for a reformulation of the social system to a point where it will offer more social and economic equality and thereby more justice for all.

Liberation theology prioritizes the dialectical analysis of social reality. This is the socioanalytic tool that best corresponds to the objectives of faith and of the Christian practice of the liberation of the marginalized and powerless. Many currents of liberation thought use the set of analytical tools developed by Marx and the Marxist tradition—by the various socialisms, by Gramsci, by French academic Marxism, and by other theoretical Marxisms. However, they typically distance themselves from Marxism's philosophical presupposition of dialectical materialism. In other words, some of us use the scientific side of Marxism only, avoiding the philosophical side. But all of us analyze social conflict from the data of social anthropology, social psychology, and history. Everything in our mediations must converge upon a structural and causal understanding of the unjust, inhumane, and dehumanizing poverty of so many millions.

THE HERMENEUTIC MEDIATION: JUDGING

Hermeneutics is the science and technique of interpreting texts (or realities) whose meaning is no longer immediately available to people today, so that the original meaning of these texts or realities may nevertheless be understood. The Christian Scriptures, like so many of the other great documents of our faith, are too far removed from us temporally and conceptually for us to understand them directly. We have to interpret them. Through the hermeneutic mediation we develop the theological criteria by which to measure and assess—or "read"—our socioanalytic text (the reality previously analyzed). Only then can the page of social reality, with its contradictions, be appropriated theologically—be transformed into a page of theology. What does God have to say to us concerning the problem of the poor, which we have now grasped through scientific rationality? Reason is not enough here. Faith must come into the picture.

By means of faith, Scripture, and sacred tradition as embodied in the teaching of the Church, the *sensus fidelium*,* and the teach-

---

*"Sense of the faithful." The people have a "sense" of God's truth, however, little they may express it in theoretical form as theologians would.

3. Theology and Political Commitment

Our pluralistic society is the scene of a conflict of interpretations of reality. The religious interpretation is one of the oldest, but it is far from being the only one. Today it is no longer even the dominant one. The interpretation of reality enjoying the greatest authority in our culture is the scientific, technological interpretation. And yet, despite the accumulation of knowledge, despite the process of disenchantment with the world, despite the process of rational analysis and radical criticism of all forms of religion, in spite of indifferentism, agnosticism, and militant atheism, millions upon millions of religious men and women are guided by the religious interpretation of reality in the basic questions of life. Religion, especially religious reason (theology), constructs reality after its own fashion. How solid is this construct? By what laws is it governed?

BELIEVER'S VIEW, THEOLOGIAN'S VIEW

You can look at a lake in two ways. You can simply contemplate its serene, tranquil surface, the smooth, diaphanous mirror of its waters. Or, while continuing to be aware of the surface, you can "think deeper"—realize that a lake has a bottom, sometimes a very deep bottom, one with mountains and valleys, chasms and crags (some projecting from the water), perhaps even monsters dwelling in its depths. Both the surface and the depths make up one and the same lake. The views alone are different, not the lake. Only the levels of awareness are different, not the reality.

The lake is like the Christian structure. In the Church we find canon law, liturgical regulations, dogmas, the creed, and the catechism. Here everything is clear. The faithful believe, the cat-ing of theologians, we identify the presence or absence of God in the reality around us. What our social analysis calls structural poverty, faith calls structural sin. What our analysis calls the private, "excluding" accumulation of wealth, faith calls the social sin of selfishness.

In other words, theology's task vis-à-vis social reality is carried out on three levels. First, we appraise the situation in terms of salvation history, in the light of theological categories like Reign of God, salvation, grace, sin, justice, charity, a faith that becomes genuine only when it leads to practice, and so on. We judge whether this kind of society is or is not in basic conformity with the divine design. This is theology's prophetic moment.

Second, we critically read the faith tradition itself from the viewpoint of liberation. We ask how far a certain understanding of the Reign, of grace, of sin, of human activity in the world, unintentionally reinforces precisely what it ought to try to overcome: the enormous gap between the rich and the poor. We must avoid bilingualism here—constructing a theological discourse divorced from any socioanalytic discourse—as well as the opposite pitfall, a simple juxtaposition of the two discourses disregarding the epistemological differences between them. We must articulate our two discourses, interconnect them, in such a way that what will emerge is a theology that can actually interpret, in the light of faith and tradition, the challenges of social reality, especially that of the poor.

Third, we engage in a theological reading of all human praxis, regardless of its ideological definition. The theological resides not in discourse but in practice. It belongs to theology to identify the presence or absence of the Reign of God in any kind of historical practice or form of social coexistence. Christian faith develops its own image of the human being, of society, and of history's present and future. No concept in the reservoir of Christian meanings can be completely exhausted in a particular political practice or social system. But these concepts nevertheless can be identified in social formations and are thereby helpful to Christians in making their choices. Christian faith, then, helps in selecting the socioanalytic tools best calculated to expose the injustices perpetrated on the poor.

THE PASTORAL MEDIATION: ACTING

A socioanalytic reading of reality, articulated with a hermeneutic reading, leads to pastoral practices of liberation. This is the third mediation invoked in constructing liberation theology.

Action has its own laws, which differ from those of analysis and theological reflection. First, we must attend to the whole interplay of social forces (economic, political, ideological, repressive, religious), lest we fall victim to a naive voluntarism. Human beings do not do whatever they wish. Human beings do what they are permitted by the particular conditions of reality. We must exercise pastoral prudence, which is not fear, but the wisdom to distinguish between what is viable and what is not.

Subsequently, we must organize our activity in such a way that the Church itself, as a vehicle of Christian faith, may be the agent of that activity. Now we can recover the liberating dimension of the liturgy, of religious education, and of theology and apply them to direct pastoral action. The Church acts directly on consciences and values. This can be the point of departure for its sacred pedagogical mission of raising people's awareness in a way that will lead them to commit themselves to struggle for liberation from the oppressions that affect all human beings, especially the very neediest. Church groups must seek connections with other social groups whose aim, like ours, is structural change and the liberation of the oppressed. What the Church contributes to the process of liberation is an awareness of the religious, transcendent dimension of that process. The Church looks on liberation from a comprehensive, integral viewpoint, seeing it as one step in a possible anticipation of the salvation of Jesus Christ.

Finally, Christians and organizations of Christians can and should, without compromising their status as members of the Church, engage in activities beyond the purview of the Church's structure. We must always keep our strategic goal before us: a liberation that will mean a different kind of society, one in which love and sharing will be less difficult. Historical circumstances may sometimes force us to rest content, provisionally, with reformist means. These are merely tactical steps, not strategic goals. But they too must point in the direction on integral liberation.

COMMITMENT: ESSENTIAL COMPONENT OF LIBERATION SPIRITUALITY

The Christian commitment to the humiliated and the wronged of this world is not supported only by a critical analysis of reality and a rigorous theological discourse on that analysis. It is also supported by a practice and a spirituality of solidarity and identification with the oppressed. It is this powerful spirituality that sees a service performed for our sisters and brothers as a service to Christ himself. We join our passion for God with a passion for the people. The Christian identity is based on the stimulus of prayer, meditation on the Scriptures, and the experience of a community of faith. Only in this way can the believer come to a visceral, existential grasp of the fact that the processes of genuine liberation make historically concrete God's own deed on behalf of his people.

TENDENCIES IN LIBERATION THEOLOGY

Liberation theology's starting point is ethical indignation in the face of the "humiliating scourge" of poverty,[2] together with an encounter with the Lord in the effort to search out, in the company of the poor, the pathways of liberation. This experience operates at the grass roots of our society in a number of different ways. Accordingly, we observe a number of different tendencies within the theology of liberation itself—different components of one and the same theological effort.

1. SPIRITUALITY OF LIBERATION

Just as there can be no social revolution without a political mystique, so there can be no act of integral liberation without the provocation, inspiration, and encouragement of an ardent spirituality. This requires something more specific than simply connecting faith to some kind of action. Here the challenge is to connect *spirituality and politics*, faith and historical liberation. The great themes that foster this outlook are: the justice of the

Reign of God; poverty as solidarity; the Exodus; the following of Christ; the cross as the price of all authentic liberation; resurrection as the triumph of those who suffer injustice; and the Church of Easter.

2. A LIBERATING REREADING OF THE SCRIPTURES

From a starting point in the longings of the poor, we reread the foundational texts of our faith. There it clearly appears that the message of Jesus is good news indeed, that the whole of Scripture is steeped in the theme of liberation. Without excluding other biblical texts, we nevertheless place special emphasis on those texts and situations concerned with oppression and liberation: the circumstances of the people of Israel, who produced the sacred texts, as an oppressed people familiar with slavery, exile, and the ongoing threat of the great powers of those times; the prophetic tradition, sensitive to the social themes of justice and poverty; the figure of Jesus, a poor, fragile person of this world, as both historical and transhistorical Liberator; Jesus' preferential option for the poor; his message of the Reign of God as total liberation of all creation; the primitive communities' practice of sharing their goods and living an evangelical communion.

A reading of the Scriptures from the locus of the mighty of this world can easily mask or "spiritualize" the theme of liberation present in the sacred texts.

3. A LIBERATING REREADING OF THE CONTENT OF THEOLOGY

Another component of liberation theology is the effort to extract from the principal theological categories and treatises, as developed by tradition, the dimension of liberation present in them. In Christology, in ecclesiology, in the teaching on the sacraments, in the treatise on grace and sin, in eschatology, and so forth, Latin American theologians have already made important theoretical contributions to a spirituality calculated to enable believers to live their faith in an engaged, liberation-oriented manner.

4. THEOLOGICAL REFLECTION ON THE SOCIAL ANALYSIS: LONGINGS FOR LIBERATION

The next component of liberation theology is a more rigorous approach to the steps just outlined. This approach begins with the reality of poverty, interpreted socioanalytically, and identifies especially the longings for liberation expressed by the oppressed. It interprets this reality in the light of faith and points to practices of actual, concrete liberation. A great deal of skill is required to articulate the various discourses with one another in such a way that liberation theology will be genuinely theological and effective as well.

5. THEOLOGICAL REFLECTION ON THE SOCIAL ANALYSIS: THE STRENGTH TO RESIST

The next component proceeds by the same steps as the one just sketched. But now the accent shifts to the people's strength to resist the mechanisms of oppression and captivity that engulf them. Liberation theology will not recognize a theology whose starting point is simply captivity as a viable alternative. A theological reflection on the people's capacity for resistance, a theological appreciation for and evaluation of the areas of freedom the people have preserved (popular piety, with its sense of festival, solidarity, and the like) will be part and parcel of any theology of liberation. Oppression is never complete. There are always little islands of freedom, and always liberation processes are under way.

6. THE PEOPLE AS AGENTS OF THEIR OWN LIBERATION

The true subjects of liberation are the oppressed people themselves. The various elements of popular culture, especially the people's radical piety, their popular forms of organization, and the base Christian communities, are native forces for liberation and consciousness-raising. The nurturing, purifying, and enriching of these elements constitute the pathways of a popular liberation.

7. POPULAR PEDAGOGY OF LIBERATION

Another approach extensively uses the contributions of Brazilian educator Paulo Freire. The people are helped to discover the pathways of their own liberation—techniques that begin with their values, culture, and practices. This approach is particularly useful in religious education and the grassroots ministry. Without exercising concrete practices of political participation, democracy, and liberation, no society of free and liberated men and women can come into being.

8. REREADING HISTORY FROM THE VIEWPOINT OF THE DEFEATED

Latin America is the scene of a serious effort to reread history from the standpoint of the memory of the marginalized—the Indians, slaves, *mestiços*, all of the poor. Past and present, previously read through the ideology of the dominant classes, are reinterpreted. The purpose of this rereading is to raise the people's consciousness and thereby furnish the struggle for liberation with its necessary roots and props. *Nova História da Igreja na América Latina* (*New History of the Church in Latin America*), in a projected thirteen volumes, is the ripest fruit of this new undertaking.

9. PHILOSOPHY OF LIBERATION

A philosophy developed in the framework of liberation adopts two tasks. The first is dismantling the prevailing philosophy, which has concealed the oppression of our peoples. To this end, the philosophy of liberation selects as its point of departure the situation of exclusion and exteriority that victimizes the "other"—the one outside the oppressive system. The second task of a philosophy of liberation is constructive. With its starting point in a praxis of liberation, it explains and clarifies the real categories that will permit the people to generate a more human and humanizing society, a society of broader social participation. Politics as an ontology of relations with authority holds the place of a *philosophia prima** here.

10. THEORY OF THE THEOLOGY OF LIBERATION

Liberation is not a blind practice. It has a theory and a grammar. It has a rigorous theological discourse, in epistemologically

---

*"First philosophy." Aristotle used this expression to designate metaphysics, the search for the ultimate foundations of all reality.

legitimate articulation with the other fields that contribute to this kind of reflection on faith. It is a sign of the autonomy of theological thinking when theology succeeds in developing its own methodological steps and takes account of its scope and limits. This final phase of liberation theology is characterized by a concern to acquire full status as a way of carrying out the task of the "intelligence of the faith." The epistemological contribution of Clodovis Boff, *Teologia e prática: teologia do político e suas mediações*[3] is a landmark event in this area.

All these components serve the goal of liberation. To liberation theologians, the goal is not theology but the concrete liberation of the oppressed. Whenever that concrete liberation occurs, the Reign of God is at hand.

MARXISM IN THEOLOGY: FAITH MUST BE OPERATIVE

The question of Marxism in theology is an emotional issue. We must discuss this question without the kind of emotion that will distort it. Otherwise we shall strive in vain for a reasonable degree of theoretical lucidity. A negative reaction on the part of both the Church and the capitalistic order to the question of Marxism in theology is understandable. Their respective dislike springs from different reasons, however. The Church, like any entity concerned with its own survival, opposes it because, were philosophical Marxism to triumph, public religion would disappear and atheism would be preached systematically as part and parcel of the process of educating the people. Capitalism opposes it because Marxism rejects private ownership—the basis of the capitalists's property and power—as the dominant system of a social formation.

As we see, opposition to Marxism in theology obeys the imperatives of the instinct for survival. And the reasoning behind the opposition is altogether legitimate. But it can close us to Marxism's potential for elucidating social and historical problems. We tend to forget that the greater part of the human race lives under regimes of Marxist inspiration. This fact alone represents a serious challenge to all who have not yet lost a minimal sense of solidarity with the destiny of humankind. In principle, as the bishops declared at Puebla, the Church "accepts the challenge and contribution of ideologies in their positive aspects."[4] Furthermore, as the Second Vatican Council has declared, "The Church admits that she has greatly profited and still profits from the antagonism of those who oppose or persecute her."[5] Besides, systematic opposition does not silence the dignity of Marxism's persistent questions: *What sort of solidarity, if any, do you capitalists and Christians maintain with the world's oppressed? What are you doing to promote the creation of social structures and formations likely to generate more social initiative, more freedom, and more justice for the greatest possible number of persons?* The infamous answer given by a North American capitalist is consummately inhumane and insensitive: the best way to help the poor is not to be one of them.

WHERE IS THE REAL PROBLEM?

Historically, Marx and his followers originated and developed Marxist thought as a way of responding to these questions with practical policies. Marxism is not primarily a theory; Marxism is rooted in concern for practice. Specifically, it is concerned with social conflict and the emancipation of the oppressed. Marxism inaugurates the second Enlightenment by asking how current reality can be transformed into a more humane, and thereby truer, reality. Questions of reality no longer belong to the academic philosopher; they are posed by the activist. If we hope to grasp anything useful about Marxism, we must begin by realizing that Marxism is not just another academic school of thought, like Aristotelianism or Kantianism or Hegelianism. Nor are we to imagine, initially, a closed body of doctrine. Instead we are dealing with a type of liberatory practice that calls for a theoretical moment in order to be effective. Marx insisted that his theory could always be changed in light of new demands of practice. The activist asks, What is the adequate theoretical framework for a more pertinent grasp of social reality, with all of its mechanisms and contradictions, its blockages and their viable resolutions, that I may act upon it in a way likely to transform it? Here lies the core, the great persuasive force of Marxism, and it must be honestly confronted. Fear of Marxism is fear that Marxism may be true. And when we fear truth, we begin to control and repress. If there is any truth in Marxism, we ought to adopt it and incorporate it into our own broader, Christian vision of reality.

Certain epistemological obstacles block an adequate view of Marxism. The dominant interpretation has created an ideological current linking it with atheism, violence, barbaric repression, depersonalizing collectivization, concentration camps, and so on. There is no denying that these sorts of things have all occurred in movements claiming to be Marxist. But the dominant interpretation is born of prejudice, and it may be fallacious. These abuses are no Marxist monopoly. The social inequity and injustice required to implant capitalism in a society defy description. And Christianity itself was subject to unspeakable abuses of heretic burning and witch hunts during the days of the Holy Inquisition. Of course, Marxism must explain its totalitarianism (and an adequate apologia has not been forthcoming). But let us be reasonable. Marxism is not simply identical with totalitarianism, as the prevailing Western ideology would have us believe, any more than capitalism is simply what its most caustic critics of the Leninist camp represent it to be, or any more than Christianity is identical with the machinations of the Holy Inquisition. We must move around these epistemological blind spots and look at what is really at stake in Marxism.

Various Meanings of Marxism

Pope John XXIII, in *Pacem in Terris* (1963), and Paul VI, in *Octogesima Adveniens* (1971), help us make the needed distinctions. First John cautions us: "It must be borne in mind . . . that false philosophical teachings regarding the nature, origin and destiny of the universe and of man [cannot] be identified with historical movements that have economic, social, cultural or political ends, not even when these movements have originated from those teachings and have drawn and still draw inspiration therefrom. . . . Who can deny that those movements . . . contain elements that are positive and deserving of approval?[6] Marxism's atheistic philosophical worldview is one thing, then, and its historical practice—in the movements that claim Marxism as their inspiration and in the new kind of society they have created, especially in the framework of socialist principles—quite another.

Paul VI, for his part, proposes we make "distinctions between Marxism's various levels of expression." Marxism, the Holy Father explains, is at one and the same time (1) a historical practice of class struggle, (2) an economic and political practice, (3) a theoretical (philosophical) practice—dialectical materialism— of an atheistic and materialistic stamp, and (4) a scientific practice, "a rigorous method of examining social and political reality" that furnishes certain thinkers with "the claim to decipher in a scientific manner the mainsprings of the evolution of society"— historical materialism.[7]

We note that each of these "various levels of expression" situates Marxism on a different epistemological level and therefore calls for a different evaluation. It is one thing to appraise Marxism as a metaphysics (a doctrine of being as such), and quite another to appraise it as science (a methodology of knowing). The Holy Father does observe that "it would be illusory and dangerous to reach a point of forgetting the intimate link which radically binds [these various levels in the expression of Marxism] together, to accept the elements of Marxist analysis without recognizing their relationships with ideology."[8] Nevertheless, the very distinctions Paul introduces show that he does not regard Marxism as some great, unshatterable monolith. Some discontinuity must operate among the levels or they would not be qualitatively different epistemologically. Let us note, then, that the Holy Father does not condemn Marxism as a whole; he rather cautions us to be on the lookout for certain illusions and dangers. The connection between one level and another—for example, between dialectical materialism (atheism) and historical materialism (science)—is not necessary and intrinsic but historical and contingent. It is therefore legitimate to divorce them in practice. The adoption of a *methodological* atheism by modern science (the refusal to hypothesize divine activity to explain natural phenomena) does not make the results of science atheistic, any more than Freud's atheism invalidates his representation of the human psyche or Jung's theism confirms his analytical psychology. The discourse upon things (science) and the discourse upon the ultimate meaning of life (religion) are qualitatively distinct discourses epistemologically. The fact that one is dealing with an ideology different from one's own is no justification for ignoring this distinction.

WHICH KIND OF MARXISM MAY BE USEFUL TO THEOLOGY?

Let us now address two specific questions. First, among the kinds or levels of Marxism the Pope lists, which kind will be useful to theology? Second, which kind of theology will be useful to Marxism?

Before addressing these questions, let us evaluate each of the four types of Marxism in light of our Christian faith. As to the first meaning, Marxism as a historical practice of class struggle, suffice it to recall that the class struggle, before all else, is an analytical datum. Social groups are marked by divergent, antagonistic interests. Conflicts and tensions therefore prevail among the groups embodying these interests. Marxists have their way of solving this problem. They try to overcome relations of exploitation and exclusion and create a society of cooperation and equality. Marxism is less interested in the moral condemnation of a class society than of its political rout through the defeat of the dominant capitalist class and the victory of the working class, with the intent of creating, not a reproduction of the system it has defeated, but a new kind of social relationship based on social ownership of the means of production (in the area of economics) and socialization of the means of power (in the area of politics). According to Marxism, the confrontation is between oppressed and oppressor, and it is a struggle to the death. But the outcome will be a quantum leap to a new form of coexistence marked by partnership and social participation.

Christians too wage this struggle. They too dream of a society where there will be neither rich nor poor, but where relationships of justice, partnership, and political participation will prevail among all. They find this dream in their gospel. They too are committed to a liberation that will generate a genuine social partnership and a political voice for all. This is the great mandate of the Final Document issued by the bishops at Puebla in 1979: to fight the causes that produce the class struggle, principally the privilege of socially meaningless ownership. Rather than seeking a confrontation with the oppressor (in the analytic not the moral sense), a Christian will seek to reach that oppressor's conscience by every means, nonviolent if possible, otherwise with that degree of violence justified by ethical criteria and for one reason or another inevitable. Christians will bring their activity to bear upon both poles of the relationship between oppressed and oppressor—since, on the principles of Christian anthropology, the spirit of oppression pervades the heart of both and both are therefore in need of conversion into new human beings—without the spirit of vengeance and retaliation: first the oppressor, since this is the primary pole, then the oppressed. Finally, the struggle assumes a different tone because of the Christian conviction that oppressors too are sons and daughters of God, created in the image and likeness of the Father and hence always the object of love and forgiveness, always the addressees of God's summons to conversion and solidarity. A commitment to the impoverished is worthy of the Christian calling because the poor are violated in their dignity as daughters and sons of God and sisters and brothers of one another. Finally, a commitment to the poor is eminently Christian because Jesus made this commitment.

Marxism as an economic and political practice, second, must be judged politically by the kind of society it produces and by the conditions it establishes for the realization of social happiness (in the Aristotelian sense). Theology can say this: were the socialist or communist ideal to become historical reality, it would offer Christian faith a better opportunity than does capitalism for a limited, categorical realization of the transcendent Christian utopia. The fact that the first socialists were Christians is significant here. It does not, however, imply a legitimation of the socialisms prevailing today. With their bureaucratic tyranny and suppression of individual liberties, they scarcely represent a viable moral alternative to capitalism. The socialist ideal can and should be realized in other ways.

The third degree of Marxism—Marxism as a theoretical (philosophical) practice—is altogether to be rejected by faith as directly opposed to Christianity. Philosophical Marxism comes forward as a radical philosophical materialism (as opposed to a vulgar mechanistic one) and an alternative to any and all philosophy of spirit. Granted, only from 1877–1878, with Engels's criticism of Eugen Dühring (in the *Anti-Dühring*), can we define the Marxist worldview as dialectical materialism. The latter was explicitly held, not by the historical Marx, but by his friend and colleague Friedrich Engels. Marx was a radical atheist personally, however, and this fact provides Soviet Marxism, which espouses dialectical materialism, with a reasonable basis for claiming to constitute the orthodox Marxist current. Engels and his successors erased the distinction between nature and history, explaining absolutely everything in terms of a dialectic of matter.

The three basic theses of Engels' *Anti-Dühring* are as follows: (1) The unity of the world consists in its materiality; (2) the fundamental "forms" of all being are space and time; (3) movement is the form of the existence of matter. A differentiation of movement (mechanical, chemical, biological, conscious) is responsible for any apparent qualitative diversity in the fabric of the single, monistic principle, matter. All transcendent reference to history or meaning beyond space and time is to be denied. God is an empty syllable, a projection of the oneiric (from the Greek for "dream") depths of the alienated human mind. Thus, the metaphysics of the *Anti-Dühring* is opposed to all spiritual or religious conceptualizations, including those of Christianity, with which there can never be any reconciliation.

The fourth meaning of Marxism refers to a method of social and historical analysis known as historical materialism. Here the Christian judgment can be more favorable. In science, the only valid explanation is the one that best explains the problems addressed by a given science. The medievals themselves laid down rules for a correct relationship between science and faith. To the extent that it reveals the truth of things, science is regarded as an instrument of God himself, who is the supreme Truth. Whether or not the practitioner of the science happens to be a believer is beside the point. Theology has no difficulty in accepting this. Indeed, it must accept it, under pain of falling into error concerning the deity itself by stubbornly closing itself off to light shed by the sciences. So states Saint Thomas in various places in his writings, as he responds to the criticism lodged by the traditionalists of his day (Platonists of Augustine's school) against his use of the theoretical tools of Aristotle, a pagan, in the task of constructing a Christian theology.

What, then, are the terms of the scientific theory of historical materialism? First, we are dealing with a theory, not a dogma. The historical Marx was keenly aware that his theory was an open construct that would have to develop in order to live. Historical materialism lays no claim to concrete knowledge, any more than does any other legitimate theory. A theory seeks to furnish us with an arsenal of abstract tools (concepts, models, paradigms) by means of which knowledge of the concrete can be produced. The object of the knowledge in question here is composed of social and historical moments and their conjunctures. Our theoretical tool is called materialism because it is an alternative to an idealistic interpretation of these same moments. Idealism, typical of the Western tradition that culminated in Hegel, prioritizes the idea (the consciousness that any age has of itself) as the ultimately determining factor in the formation, structuring, and evolution of human societies. Marxism maintains that it is the material conditions of the production and reproduction of life that constitute the ultimate foundation of the entire social and historical structure, including its ideological, juridical, and political components. It is not that these components are a simple mirror image of the economic component. (Marx always denied this, whatever the dogmatic Marxist party line may say to the contrary.) No, they are relatively autonomous and function under their own laws while always maintaining (only) an ultimate reference to the economic infrastructure.

Scientific Marxism is also historical. That is, it holds that, far from being defined once and for all, the material conditions within a social whole vary historically in dialectical relation to all of the other components of that whole. Like any other scientific theory, Marxist historical materialism should be acknowledged as valid, if indeed it is valid. And it is worth (only) whatever light it sheds on problems under discussion. But Marxist historical materialism is eminently valid in its criticism of capitalism and its proposition of socialism. Thus the exploited classes are well advised to use it as a theoretical weapon in seeking their liberation. Indeed this is its original purpose. It is a valid scientific theory and can help Christians acquire a better knowledge (only an approximate knowledge, of course, as with any scientific theory) of social reality, especially the conflicts of that reality, together with its mechanisms of popular marginalization.

Pastoral ministers and other agents of the Church generally encounter Marxism when they enter the cultural world of the poor. There they encounter it not as philosophical, atheistic materialism but as the only tool at the disposal of the poor either for understanding their exploited condition or as a route to organization, the formation of a critical awareness, and the mobilization of the popular sectors.

To What Kind of Theology Can Marxism Be Useful?

We have asked what kind of Marxism may be useful to theology. And we have answered, Marxist historical materialism—Marxism as a scientific theory of social and historical reality. It can help us to understand not God, grace, or the Reign of God, but the formation, conflicts, and development of human societies. Now let us ask a further question. To what kind of theology can Marxism (as historical materialism) be useful? In broad terms, to the kind of theology that in the light of faith reflects on the concrete captivity and/or liberation of oppressed human groups. In some theological schools a theological meditation on the sorrowful passion of humanity is missing, as participants simply abide by the classic themes of God, the Holy Trinity, Christ, the Church, the sacraments, and eschatology. They show little concern for the people to whom their reflections are addressed. Liberation theology, however, would regard itself as having betrayed both God and neighbor were it not to reflect, in the light of the message of Jesus—so poor and helpless in this world and yet the Son of the almighty Father—on the sin of economic, political, cultural, and spiritual oppression and on the grace of liberation that is touching millions of the humiliated and wronged of our world.

Where does the Marxist theory of history enter into the construction of this theology? Marxist historical materialism impinges upon the theology of liberation in the broader stage of theological elaboration. Liberation theology means to be, and is, authentic theology—discourse upon God. Thereupon it takes account of the fact that the God of Jesus Christ is a God who is sensitive to the cry of the oppressed, a God who wills to liberate his people from their oppression under all the Pharaohs of history. The God of Jesus Christ is not indifferent to the cry that rises from the earth begging for justice and humanity. This God takes sides with the oppressed against their oppressors.

Furthermore, liberation theology is theology because it rereads and interprets, in the light of the God of Jesus Christ, conflicting social reality. But here a problem arises. How may we come to as scientific an understanding of this reality as we possibly can? A merely empirical or functional conceptualization of society will be inadequate, however satisfactory it might be in the eyes of the idealists and the mighty. Here a political, ethical, and evangelical option for the poor against their poverty helps theologians select the series of scientific instruments that will afford them as adequate a knowledge of social reality as possible. Theologians thus committed to the poor will select the tools that hold the most promise for doing justice to the cry of the oppressed. In the methodological moment of seeing, of rationality and objectivity, the theologian can validly and usefully appropriate the Marxist theory of history. To emphasize: the theologian can use this Marxist contribution *only in the moment of the knowledge of conflicting social reality*. Once this operation is complete, the theologian enters upon the specific activity of theology itself—a reading (of this Marxist social analysis) in the light of faith, that is, under the lens of the Scriptures, the magisterium, the social teaching of the Church, and so on.

To accuse liberation theology of infiltration by Marxism, then, is to fly in the face of the facts. The problem is not theology; the problem is science. Marxism does not enter into the whole of the theological operation. It enters into the moment of the theologian's apprehension of social reality. Theologians use this method rather than another because this is the one that seems to them to constitute the most adequate tool for denouncing the ideological falsifications perpetrated by capitalism when it conceals the real causes of impoverishment, especially the accumulation of wealth in the hands of a few to the exclusion of the great majority of the population. This analysis is more in harmony with the intent of faith to liberate oppressed and oppressor alike. But faith as such is not bound to this method. It uses it only when it needs to see clearly its relationship with society and with the conflict of interests prevailing therein. Faith's ties are to God and to God's revelatory word. It does not lose its identity when it seeks a clearer view of what it believes (theology) concerning one of the terms of its relation (society).

GRANDEUR AND SUPERIORITY OF FAITH

For a person of faith, the use of historical materialism cannot represent a lethal danger. Only for anemic mentalities, imbued with a "faith" that does not really believe in its own stature and superiority, does Marxism represent the avenging angel. Only then is Marxism's historical materialism an evil. Faith, of its very nature, moves along a far vaster horizon—that of the Absolute, before which we can fall to our knees without demeaning ourselves, a horizon with room even for the contribution of Marxist theory of society, to the extent that that theory sheds light on social and historical problems. We Christians must overcome a superstitious attitude toward the Marxist method of analysis as a kind of antisacrament distilling curses whenever it is performed upon all who come in contact with it. It need be none of this once we know how to articulate correctly the discourse of faith with the Marxist scientific discourse. In our Western system, it is capitalism, not Marxism, that must be denounced as the most immediate and real curse of the great masses of poor.

What liberation theology espouses is not theology within Marxism, but the use of Marxism (in the form of historical materialism) by theology. Theology, not Marxism, is the major term, and theology has a grammar of its own. But in its quest for a liberating effectiveness in society, theology appropriates, under its own terms and after its own fashion, the contribution of Marxist rationality and builds its own synthesis in the light of its own theological criteria.

Marx developed his scientific socialism over the course of his ongoing polemic with a religious, utopian socialism. This was a step he had to take if he hoped to prevent the secular and the scientific from perversion by elevation to the status of a mystique. Today we are gradually coming to understand that Marxism and theology not only do not contradict each other, they require each other. They correspond to two distinct human dimensions, rationality and hope, respectively. Perhaps the time has come to construct a synthesis of a socialism that will carry scientific credentials and yet open out on a limitless, transcendent future. Perhaps Christians will find it within themselves to overcome their historical prejudices and make a courageous contribution to such a synthesis. New avenues to truth must not be encumbered with roadblocks of fear or exaggerated prudence. No one has the right to place obstacles in the way of an approach to a fuller truth.

SPIRITUALITY AND POLITICS: TO BE A CONTEMPLATIVE IN LIBERATION

The outstanding characteristic of Latin American church life in recent years has been an increasing awareness of the Christian responsibility in faith to help create social changes, to help society move in the direction of more justice and societal participation for the masses of the poor in our countries.

SPIRITUAL SHOCK: ENCOUNTER WITH GOD IN THE CLASS OF THE POOR

In the light of faith, in evangelical solidarity with the very neediest, increasing numbers of groups within the Church, including entire national episcopates, now seek to live and teach the Christian faith in such a way that it will be a motivating force for the integral liberation of the human being. Thus a vast, systematic liberation process, sprung from the unity of faith and life, is under way at the heart of our Christian communities.

Simultaneously, the corresponding critical discourse has developed. The theology of liberation is practiced in the interests of integral liberation, especially that of the most oppressed members of society. But what sustains both the practice and the theory (the theology) of liberation is a spiritual experience of encounter with the Lord of the poor. Underlying any innovative practice in the Church—including, and especially, any genuine and genuinely new theology—is a latent religious experience. This total existential experience, this "word," is the source from which all else springs. The rest is an effort to translate this word into the framework of a historically limited reality. Only from such a starting point can the great syntheses of the theologians of the past be explained.

Any spiritual experience means an encounter with a new, challenging face of God, emerging from the great challenges of historical reality. Great social and historical changes are charged with an ultimate meaning, a supreme demand, which religious minds recognize has having proceeded from the mystery of God. God has meaning only when appearing as the only radically important piece of a given reality, blazing away amid the lights and shadows of the rest of that reality. Here God is seen not as a closely defined, limited category in a religious framework but as an event of meaning, of hope, of absolute future for men and women and their history. This experience breeds a peculiar, typical experience of the mystery of God.

This, then, is the subjective moment of the experience of which we speak. But we can enunciate the same phenomenon in strictly theological language. Let us put it this way: God, in a will to self-communication, inserts a concrete self-revelation into history. Human beings grasp a new face of God because God's self-revelation actually contains this new face. It is God who posits the sacramental signs, chooses the emissaries, inspires the creation of an adequate discourse, and stimulates the practices consistent with the revelation in question. There will always be attentive spirits, who will identify this new divine voice and be faithful to its challenges.

In recent years, it seems to us, God has burst upon our continent like an erupting volcano. The divine will has prioritized the poor as the sacrament of this self-communication. The ruler of the universe assures us that our poor hear the divine call for solidarity, identification, justice, and dignity. And the particular churches have obeyed that call (Latin *ob-edire*, from *audire*, "to hear"). In the face of the scandal of poverty, God urges us all to act in behalf of the poor against poverty, to the end that we may all enjoy the fruits of justice. The required activity holds a clear liberation dimension sprung from the incarnation of a Christian faith that now seeks to cling to the Lord present in the poor. To struggle at the side of the poor, to be enfleshed in their longings, to commune with Christ present in the poor is to live in Christ's discipleship.

Holding to the Christ of the poor means being a "contemplative in liberation": *contemplativus in liberatione*. It implies a new way of seeking holiness and mystical union with God. A spiritual collision with God's new manifestation has produced specific new traits in the spirituality lived and practiced by so many Christians committed to the integral liberation of their sisters and brothers. This spiritual collision is the basis of the theology of liberation.

Before describing this new spirituality, however, let us briefly examine the great spiritual tradition of the Church, underscoring the original contribution of each major stage in its development. The problem in the contemporary stage is how to be a contemplative in liberation, how—in our pastoral practices, in our contact with the people—we may live a vital, concrete encounter with God. Perhaps by reflecting on this topic against a background of the Christian spiritual tradition we may more easily locate the specific difference of this new Latin American spirituality.

THE SPIRITUAL DIFFERENCE: SYNTHESIS OF PRAYER AND LIBERATION

Surely the most classic formulation of the quest for a unity of faith and life developed in the monastic tradition, whose maxim was *Ora et Labora*: "Pray and Work." Historically its dominant tendency consisted in the sovereignty of *Ora* over *Labora*. The core of the organization of the spiritual life is the moment of prayer and contemplation. True, this component alternates with work. But prayer monopolizes all real value and expresses it through the signs of the religious field: liturgy, the divine office chanted in choir, exercises of devotion, and the whole gamut of religious expression. Work is not regarded as a direct route to God. Work can carry us to God only when bathed in the influences of prayer and contemplation. Work is secularity, profanity, and "pure nature." It constitutes the area of ethical expression but is the locus of a testimony whose meaning is developed and expressed only in the area of prayer. Prayer prolongs work inwardly and alone renders it sacred.

Theologically this understanding of the sacred and secular approximates the erroneous doctrine of monophysitism, which understood Jesus as having a preponderance of divine over human nature. Only the nature of prayer redeems the profane nature of toil. Never the twain shall genuinely meet: on one side prayer, on the other, work. The conjunction *et*, "and," represents this theological bilingualism. On the positive side, this spirituality has elevated and rendered prayerful the toil of countless Christians over the centuries, sprinkling every corner of the so-called secular and profane with religious signs.

But the social and historical development of the Western world moved toward a relative autonomy of the profane, toward a culture of work. Operationality and efficiency are the twin pivots of modern culture, a culture whose finished expression is embodied today in the scientific and technological enterprise. The maxim has been turned around. We have discovered the divine and Christic character of creation. We have discovered human toil as a form of human cooperation with the divine action. God has not left us a finished world but has willed to associate us to the task of transforming it. Work possesses its own dignity, its own sacred nature, and it needs no baptism of prayer or supernaturalizing "good intention." Work is sacred by its own creational nature, for it is part and parcel of the Christic project. The supreme value of work is not that it be executed with a right intention, but that it be executed *rector ordine*—that it be ordered to building up the earthly city intended by God in anticipation of the heavenly one. The deed of justice, especially, performed in a commitment to the poor, is the be-all and end-all of contact with God in prayer. Tradition is explicit here (see Isa. 1:10–20; Jer. 22:16), and Jesus refers to this tradition directly (Mark 7:6–8). It is not what we preach but what we practice that wins us salvation (see Matt. 25:31–46). Prayer has its place and value. But the authenticity of prayer is measured by its expression in true, ethically correct practice.

In its most radical form, this spirituality has led to a contempt for prayer, both liturgical and devotional. This is a spirituality of the divine character of matter and of work brought to bear upon matter. Not surprisingly, then, its unwarranted radicalization places exclusive emphasis on the all-pervasiveness of an implicit "prayer" not restricted to the area of explicit awareness. The component of truth in this erroneous extreme is its recognition that the presence of God is not automatically, and surely not exclusively, realized simply by speaking of God or even speaking to God. By contrast, the presence of God is indeed always realized, objectively, in a correct practice of truth and justice in history—with or without an explicit consciousness of God. Here again, the preeminence of work over prayer only leads to a spiritual monophysitism—a new one this time, with the "nature" of physical work predominating over that of the spirit. And prayer becomes just another kind of work and practice. It has no specificity as prayer. It is as if we were trying to solve the difficulties of the *Ora et Labora* simply by saying "*Labora et Ora*" instead, with no more unity between faith and life, prayer and action, than before.

The synthesis that must be developed, and the one that is being developed in Latin America, is a synthesis of prayer *in* action, prayer *within* activity, prayer *with* the deed. What must be eliminated is a divorce between prayer on one side and action on the other—prayer severed from a lived commitment to the liberation of the oppressed. The correct relationship of prayer and action consists of prayer offered in the very process of liberation, when we experience an encounter with God *in* our sisters and brothers. Every great saint in history has managed this vital, concrete synthesis, and it has always constituted the secret of an authentically Christian life.

In Latin America, however, we are in something of a new situation, or at least one with particular accents. The problem is not simply that of the relationship between prayer and activity. The problem is the relationship between prayer and liberation precisely—between prayer and political, social, historical, transforming action. In its correct formulation, the question must be posed in terms of *spirituality and politics*. How is one to make a radical commitment to the liberation of the oppressed and at the same time a commitment to the source of all liberation, God? How can passion for God, the characteristic of any genuinely religious human being, be steeped in a passion for the people and for justice to the people, which is the distinctive note of the political activist? In order to be solid and complete, this synthesis must draw on all of the wealth of the *Ora et Labora*—prayer as a special encounter with the Lord—and draw on, as well, all of the truth present in a *Labora et Ora*—the entire religious value of work, the salvific worth of action toward realizing a society of justice and partnership.

The synthesis constituting the object of our quest is not a verbal one. The problem is not how to manage a correct correlation of terms. The problem is how to *live* a Christian practice imbued with prayer and commitment. How can commitment spring from prayer and prayer well up from the heart of commitment?

PASSION FOR GOD IN A PASSION FOR THE IMPOVERISHED

The experience of a vital, authentic faith effects a unity of prayer and liberation. But the experience of faith must be correctly understood. As we have said many times, faith is first of all a vital experience of all things in the light of God. Faith defines the *whence* and the *whither* of our very existence, which is God and God's design of love communicated and realized in all things. For the person of faith, reality is not primarily profane or sacred. It is simply sacramental. Creaturely reality reveals God, evokes God, comes steeped in the divine reality. Thus the experience of faith unifies life, for it contemplates reality as unified by the fact that God is the origin and destiny of its every part and parcel. A living faith is a way of life. It therefore carries a contemplative attitude toward the world. It sees tokens, traces of God on all sides. But it is not enough that faith be alive. It must also be true. And faith is only true when it becomes love and justice. To be pleasing to God, it is not enough to accept God. One must build the Reign of God, which is a Reign of truth, love, and justice. Only a committed faith is salvific faith and therefore true. "The faith that does nothing in practice . . . is thoroughly lifeless. . . . Without works faith is idle. . . . Faith without works is as dead as a body without breath" (James 2:17, 20, 26). Sheer belief is of no avail. "Do you believe that God is one? You are quite right. The demons believe that, and shudder" (James 2:19).

Christian faith knows that Christ is in the poor in an especially concentrated sacramental way. Not only do the poor have needs that must be alleviated; they possess a singular wealth of their own. They are the chosen vessels of the Lord, the prime addressees of the Reign of God, the potential evangelizers of the Church and of the whole human race.[9] The believer has a view of the poor that is more than socioanalytic. Over and above identifying the passion of the poor and the causes of the mechanisms of their impoverishment, the believer gazes upon the class of the impoverished with the eyes of faith and sees the suffering face of the Servant of Yahweh. Nor is this gaze satiated with the moment of contemplation, as if the believer were merely using the poor as a means to union with the Lord. Christ identifies with the poor in order to be served and welcomed *precisely in them*. Their miserable condition provokes a movement of the heart: "I was hungry . . ." (Matt. 25:35). We are truly with the Lord in the poor, then, when we commit ourselves to struggle against the poverty that demeans persons and contravenes the will of God, to struggle against the fruit of a relationship of sin and exploitation. The true faith itself, precisely by virtue of its truth, implies and demands a commitment to liberation: ". . . and you gave me food . . ." (Matt. 25:35). If we undertake no liberating action, then not only do we not love our neighbor, we do not love God (1 John 3:17). "Let us love in deed and in truth and not merely talk about it" (1 John 3:18).

This spiritual experience bestows unity on the relationship between faith and life, between spirituality and politics. But just how do we maintain this unity? How are we to foster it in the face of so many forces of decay and dissolution? The vision at once contemplative and liberating does not emerge spontaneously. It is the most significant expression of a living, true faith. But how are we to establish this consistency between contemplation and liberation?

Here two poles emerge: prayer and practice. The question cannot, however, be answered by way of either a polarization or a juxtaposition. We should surely fall anew into one of the "monophysitisms" just criticized. We must create a dialectical articulation of the poles. We must regard them as two reciprocally open, mutually involved spaces. However, one pole will have priority: prayer.

Through prayer, human beings express what is noblest and most profound in their existence. Through prayer they rise above themselves, transcend all the grandeurs of creation and history, assume an "ecstatic" position by which they "stand out" from themselves, strike up a dialogue with the supreme mystery, and cry, "Father!" Not that they leave the universe behind. On the contrary, they sweep it up and transform it into an offering to God. But they do deliver themselves from all bonds of earth: they denounce all historical absolutes, relativize them, and stand naked and alone with the Absolute, with whom they then proceed to create history. Here God is discovered as the Holy. With God we are before the supremely momentous, the Definitive. And yet this God, so holy, so absolutely momentous, is revealed as an engaged God, a God who wants to "get involved," a God sensitive to the sobs of the oppressed, a God who can say, "I have witnessed the affliction of my people . . . and have heard their cry of complaint against their slave drivers, so I know well what they are suffering. Therefore I have come down to rescue them . . ." (Exod. 3:7–8). Thus the God who says to us in our prayer, "Come," also says in the same prayer, "Go." The God who calls us to the divine union also calls us to make a commitment to liberation. God commands that our passion for God in Jesus Christ be lived in a passion for our suffering, needy brothers and sisters.

The activity of service to our sisters and brothers, in solidarity with their struggles for liberation, springs from the depths of the prayer that reaches the heart of God. Prayer fosters the outlook by which the believer sees in the poor, in an entire class of exploited persons, the sacramental presence of the Lord. Without a prayer born of faith, our eyesight would grow dim, seeing only the surface of things, failing to descend to the mystical depths in which we enter into communion with a Lord present in the condemned, awaiting us all in the humiliated and wronged of history.

Conversely, the pole of liberating practice refers us to the pole of prayer, that nourishing, supportive wellspring of strength for the struggle. Prayer guarantees the maintenance of Christian identity throughout the liberating process. For a Christian, liberation, in order to be genuine, must anticipate the Reign of God. It must render Jesus' redemption a matter of concrete history. Faith and prayer permit us to see our own human effort, which so often seems to have so little lasting value, as an integral part of the historical construction of the Reign.

Social practice has its concrete, this-worldly solidity, and this in itself would have sufficed to justify it. But in fact, the meaning of social practice is not exhausted here. Our human efforts have a transcendent value, a salvific meaning as well, and faith reveals this dimension of transcendence. For a person of faith, then, a service of liberation in behalf of one's sister or brother constitutes a genuine *diakonia* to the Lord, an association to his work of redemption and liberation, and therefore a genuine *leitourgia* in the Spirit. This is what it means to be a *contemplativa in liberatione*. Contemplation is not reserved to the sacred space of prayer or to the sacrosanct enclosure of church or monastery; it finds its place also in a social and political practice watered, cultivated, and fertilized by a faith living and true.

It is the noble heritage of the Latin American Church that the bishops, priests, religious, and laity most committed to the cause of the poor (the cause of their justice, their rights, their dignity) are also the most prayerful. They join together God and their neediest neighbor in one and the same movement of love and dedication.

A NEW SPIRITUALITY: PRINCIPAL CHARACTERISTICS AND CHALLENGES

What are some of the more significant traits of this new spirituality, this contemplation lived in a context of liberation?

1. PRAYER MATERIALIZED IN ACTION

The prayer of liberation gathers up all the material of the committed life—the struggles, the collective efforts, the mistakes, the defeats, and the victories of that life—returns thanks for the steps already taken, and makes its petitions not individualistically but with a view to the whole spiritual pilgrimage of a *contemplativus in liberatione*. The prayer of liberation is a prayer for those who suffer and for those who inflict the suffering. The conflict of the liberation process finds a special echo in prayer. To confess one's sins becomes a spontaneous, joint concern of the entire community, where no one hides behind ethereal words but all open their hearts, revealing matters of the utmost intimacy. Here is a prayer that reflects the liberation of the heart. We especially notice and confess any inconsistencies between what we profess and how we live—any lack of solidarity and commitment by which our Christian lives may be impaired.

2. PRAYER AS A SELF-EXPRESSION OF THE LIBERATION COMMUNITY

Private prayer has its permanent, unquestionable value. But in our committed groups, prayer is essentially a sharing of experiences and practices, enlightened by the light of faith and the gospel and criticized in that light. The experience of prayer is not limited to the splendid intimacy of the soul alone with the Alone. Here is a prayer that opens the praying subject out to others. Here is a prayer heard not only by God but by our neighbor, for it communicates to that neighbor. We word our prayer in such a way as to comfort and encourage one another. We talk aloud to God about someone's problems—just before rushing to that person's assistance. No "holy shame," no false modesty conceals our divine visitations and illuminations. For most of us, our soul is an open book. This in itself is a manifestation of the process of personal liberation transpiring at the very heart of the community.

3. LITURGY AS CELEBRATION OF LIFE

The canonical liturgy has the power to unite. It expresses the catholicity of our faith. But the more closely our communities wed faith to life, spirituality to politics, the more they express this shared celebration of life in liturgy. And a rich creativity appears whose worth and sacred nature are assured by the people's refined sense of the sacred and exalted. The people avail themselves of symbols of special meaning for their group. For example, they choreograph their own dances and use them in plays to be presented to others of their group. The resulting spiritual dramas, performed to the accompaniment of bodily expressions having a special meaning and importance for the people, are frequently rich and moving.

4. CRITICAL PRAYER

Liberation prayer frequently becomes a vehicle for critically examining the practices and attitudes of community members. Our people are able to listen to criticism from one another without undue sensitivity or personal offense. The important thing here is to be sure we use objective criteria: the Reign of God, liberation, and respect for the pilgrimage of the people. We simply confront the practices of our lay ministers with these criteria. True conversions emerge from this sort of sincerity and loyalty, affording us a great deal of help in our evangelization.

5. POLITICAL HOLINESS

Christian tradition is peopled with saints who were ascetics—who overcame their passions and faithfully observed the laws of God and the Church. It knows almost no saints who were politicians or activists. But the liberation process has created the matrix of another type of holiness. Christians must continue to battle their own passions. This is clear. But now they battle the mechanisms of exploitation and destruction of the community as well. New virtues emerge, difficult but genuine: solidarity with one's sisters and brothers, the members of the impoverished class; participation in community decisions, and fidelity to these decisions once they are made; victory over one's hatred of the agents of the mechanisms of impoverishment; an ability to see beyond the obvious and work for a future society not yet in sight and perhaps never to be enjoyed at all. This new type of asceticism makes its own demands and calls for particular sacrifices if one is to remain pure of heart and celebrate the spirit of the Beatitudes.

6. PROPHETIC COURAGE AND "HISTORICAL PATIENCE"

From their faith and their prayer many committed Christians have drawn the courage to confront the powers of this world in a struggle for the cause of the people and their trampled dignity. In this they show their apostolic *parrhesia*—the courage to "speak up" to someone of higher rank—oblivious to the risk of persecution, imprisonment, loss of employment, torture, even physical annihilation. And paradoxically, along with this evangelical courage, they have the "historical patience" to bear up under the hardships of a long, slow journey in the company of the people they love. They have acquired a sensitivity to the measured pace of a people accustomed to repression. They have confidence in these people, in their courage, their capacity to struggle despite their limitations, mistakes, and intellectual backwardness. They have a keen belief in the power of the Spirit, who acts in the lowly and the suffering. They believe in the victory of their cause and the rightness of their struggle. This attitude springs from a contemplative vision of history, whose only sovereign is God.

7. An Attitude of Easter

Liberation always comes at a price. Death and resurrection are to be accepted with evangelical joviality and serenity. Sacrifices, threats, even martyrdoms inspire no fear. Hardship of any sort is accepted as part of following Jesus. Our communities have a powerful sense of the cross. They look on it as a necessary step along the road to victory. When justice triumphs, when the people win their struggle and life is worth living, they experience resurrection. Historical liberation is a share in Jesus' resurrection. It is experienced as the temporal anticipation of the fullness of eschatological triumph. And it is celebrated as it is experienced, for it is the power of the presence of the Spirit at the heart of history.

We could list other characteristics of this kind of prayer, which is coming to be more and more frequently practiced in communities committed to the liberation of the very neediest. Our communities maintain a union of prayer and action, faith and liberation, a passion for God expressed in a passion for the people. New possibilities are constantly being created for the emergence of this new kind of Christian, the Christian deeply committed to the cities of earth and heaven alike, convinced that the latter depends on how we shall have busied ourselves in the creation of the former. Heaven is not the enemy of earth. It actually begins on earth. Both realms of existence are under the rainbow of grace, of God's deed of liberation in Jesus Christ.

This is not mere theology. This is the life and spirituality of a great many Christians.

LIBERATION MESSAGE OF THE BIBLE FOR THE OPPRESSED OF OUR TIME

We can say much about the Bible, since much is found in it. Biblical exegesis and theology have become so sophisticated that scholars do not have time to keep abreast of even the most important publications, which now come to them from all over the world. Despite all this wealth, however, we must try to identify in a few words the principal element of the Holy Scriptures.

STARTING POINT FOR A READING OF HOLY SCRIPTURE

The starting point of Scripture will not be the same for all generations. Every age has its problems, reading and rereading the ancient foundational texts of our faith, the Old and New Testaments, in its own way. What is the principal message of the Bible for us today? Before answering this question, we must try to grasp who we are today.

It is important to be clear about the standpoint from which we regard the sacred texts. Certain Christians today use the biblical texts to justify choices that divide human beings and destroy their unity. Some today actually persecute, repress, torture, and kill their fellow Christians in the name of God. And their victims are many. Here the agonizing question arises: Of what god are they speaking? Those who murder in God's name have their reading of the Bible, and those who denounce injustices in God's name and are murdered for it have theirs. Who is right? Is just any reading of the Bible correct? Or will some readings always be given the lie by Scripture itself because they contradict its principal, basic intent? What is the correct viewpoint from which to read and interpret the inspired texts?

Let us examine the point of departure from which liberation theology reads the sacred texts. After all, we read them with our own eyes and no one else's. What eyes do we have—here and now, today? Which passages arrest our gaze? Which phrases attract our attention? What messages do we underscore in red? We ascribe more importance to certain biblical viewpoints because they answer the problems that affect us today. What are our principal concerns today?

We are not referring to a list of personal problems. Certainly life's burdens are different for each of us. Every human being has existential questions that are individual and personal, and it is legitimate to read the word of God in light of these questions, that that word may give its answers and question its reader in turn. But what we wish to do here is identify certain basic concerns of the *entire* faith community. What are the great problems facing the Church today in Brazil, in Latin America, and throughout the world? With these concerns in mind, we can discern the principal element for us today in the message of the Holy Scriptures.

The universal Church has become aware of the agonizing disparities that prevail among the various parts of the world. A few wealthy countries are surrounded by their many poor neighbors. These latter writhe in hunger, destitution, and marginality. We cannot help thinking of the rich man and Lazarus, Jesus' parable on the destinies of each (Luke 16:19–31). The world in which we live is not a world of peace and concord but of confrontation, where the bonds of justice are dissolved at the international level. The consequences are disastrous: social injustice, wars, terrorism, and the global threat of a nuclear conflict in which there would be no winners, only losers. Peace, justice, concord, and communion are the great longings of today's world. What do the Christian Scriptures have to say about all of this?

Latin America is awash in these calamitous circumstances. A continent of Christian and Catholic tradition is the scene of the cruelest injustices. A whole people is reduced to a faceless mass, deprived of a voice in the decisions that will determine the fate of their nations. Teeming populations are overwhelmed by poverty and long for liberation. Endemic diseases wipe out whole families. Illiteracy prevails everywhere. Millions eke out a living on a subsistence income—if that—and are helpless to do anything about it because they are politically impotent. There is no escaping the fact: this society is riddled with sin. But a biblical faith can help people recover the dignity of which they have been robbed. How? What picture of God does the Bible paint? Is God a God of resignation or of liberation? Is the God of the Bible insensitive to the suffering Jobs of today, or is this a God who takes sides with those who suffer? Is this a God whose heart is sensitive to the affliction of the little ones?

These are the questions that arise from the wounds of our social and political lives, and they incline us to look in particular directions when we read the sacred text. When we begin to read, so many things seem important. Then suddenly some things in Scripture seem more important than others. Why? Because they have more to say to our particular circumstances. Scripture tells us that true faith is completely bound up with the practice of love. It tells us of a God who is communion and liberation; of human beings reduced to the condition of nonpersons by sin, but called to be free sovereigns of the world, sisters and brothers of one another and sons and daughters of God; of Jesus Christ, the eternal Son of God, who took flesh in our circumstances of nonpersonhood to mold us into liberated, divinized persons; of the Holy Spirit, who prolongs, down through the centuries, the work inaugurated by Jesus Christ; of the Church, the community that seeks to live Jesus' project in the power of His Spirit; and, finally, of a world destined not for destruction but for glory. Let us say something briefly about each of these elements of the scriptural message.

1. TRUE FAITH LEADS TO A PRACTICE OF LIBERATION

Faith is first of all a mode of existence, a fundamental attitude of life. In the Bible, to live the dimension of faith means living in the light of the all-encompassing reality of God. It means regarding the world, history, and human life from the viewpoint of God. Faith therefore implies an encounter with God as supreme Meaning of existence, as the Reality that counts absolutely, as the omnipresent Being whom nothing can escape. To believe means primarily to entrust and surrender ourselves to God as the supreme realization of our lives. The opposite of faith in this sense is not the pure and simple denial of God. The opposite of faith in this existential sense is fear. Those who believe in God have no fear. They know that they are in the hands of the one who has full knowledge of each and every person's life pilgrimage, who holds in loving hands the meaning of all quests. This attitude of unrestricted abandon to God embraces all dimensions of human life. It creates a particular manner of behaving in the world and underlies a typical interpretation of reality. For persons of faith, absolutely everything is a vessel and vehicle of God's design. Everything is a sacrament of his presence. Everything is bound, doubly bound ("re-ligion"), to God. Everything, then, is relative, in two senses: relative because it is related to God, and relative because it is derived, because it is not absolute. Only God can be the Absolute.

Besides constituting a basic attitude of surrender and abandonment to God, faith implies accepting God's design. God has a project for human beings and the world. To accept this project and to prepare ourselves to implement it are the tasks of faith. It is not enough, then, to "have faith," in the sense of simply having just any faith. It is not enough to cast ourselves into the arms of God. We must have true faith. What faith is true faith? What faith truly reaches God and not some idol or some projection of our insecure, unconscious minds? True faith is faith that manifests itself in practices that actualize effective love. True faith is faith the moves out from an attitude of unconditional surrender and dedication to God to an attitude of dedication to our brothers and sisters, in the form of service, solidarity with them in their need, and the molding of relations of partnership and justice among human beings. True faith is faith that liberates me *from* selfishness and false assurances and *for* the discovery of others in their need. Only a faith like this is faith in the biblical God, in the Father of our Lord Jesus Christ. Only a faith like this serves and implements the plan of God, which is to create a world of reconciliation and justice and thereby to inaugurate God's Reign, beginning right here in this world and culminating in heaven. And the Reign of God beings to form where love flourishes, where justice appears on the earth, where partnership and communion are inaugurated, and where liberty gains strength and substance. God is encountered only when these values are experienced and lived. Those with God on their lips but injustice in their hearts—those who believe in God but create no communion—neither profess nor believe in the true God. Their god is an idol. What kind of God is the real God—the true God attested to in Scripture, from the first page to the last?

2. A God Who Is Communion and Liberation

For the biblical experience, God is first and foremost the Holy. The Holy is the Utterly Other, the one who dwells in light inaccessible, the one beyond all we can think or imagine. One does not trifle with this God. In the sight of this God, human creatures must remove their shoes, like Moses at the burning bush. That is, they must behave with supreme respect, for they are in the presence of the Absolute. Several biblical passages teach us this. No one can approach God and live; no one has ever seen God; and so on. God is the Sublime, the Sacrosanct, the Mysterious, the Ground of being and life.

And yet this God of all transcendence is not an impassive God, a God indifferent to the human drama. This is a God who can say, "I have witnessed the affliction of my people in Egypt and have heard their cry of complaint against their slave drivers, so I know well what they are suffering. Therefore I have come down to rescue them . . ." (Exod. 3:7–8). This God is Yahweh the Holy, and Yahweh takes sides. This God defends the rights of the oppressed, is the mainstay of the abandoned orphan, protects the poor against the depredations of the mighty, and strides forth as the strength of the weak against the arrogant sway of the proud. The biblical God is an ethical God. The worship that pleases Yahweh does not consist in sacrifices, long prayers, and a plethora of rites, but in mercy, justice, and uprightness of heart. Yahweh hates the lie and the exploitation of one human being by another. Yahweh's servants are not those who cry, "Lord, Lord!" but those who obey the divine commands and implement the divine will, which is ever to seek the right, the just, the sociable. God alone is light. Only they are with God who walk in the light, that is, those who are sincere. Those who live by love know that they are with God, because God is Love and is not found apart from love.

Therefore God adopts a commitment to all who suffer injustice and are violated in their dignity. Anyone who injures the image of God—anyone who wrongs a human being—violates God himself. Yahweh is not indifferent to the crimes of this world. This God demands conversion and the reestablishment of just relationships. Otherwise human beings will not enter into the Reign of God or taste the divine blessing.

God has a project and implements that project throughout the course of history. Human wickedness cannot destroy it. Nothing can separate the Planner from the plan. God brings it to fulfillment, using even human weakness to do so. God's project in history is the inauguration of the Reign. The Reign of God is the sovereignty of Yahweh over all things, through the triumph of truth, justice, love, and concord. The Reign of God stands against the reign of fallen Adam, hard-hearted in the will to dominate, in acquisitiveness and selfishness. Plainly, Yahweh's project is built amid conflict. It must advance by way of conversion, which is the stripping away of all that can interfere with human beings' communion with God and with one another.

All human beings are sons and daughters of God. And this God, so opposed to any kind of injustice, nevertheless loves them all, especially the ungrateful and the evil! The Gospel of Luke clearly tells us this in chapter 6, verse 35: God goes out in search of human beings. God does not wait for the lost sheep to return but goes out looking for it (Luke 15:4–7; Matt. 18:12–14). Here is the God of the prodigal. Here is the God of the sinful tax collector who repents (Luke 15:11–32; 18:9–14). Here is the God of the destitute, of the fallen, of those who feel that God has abandoned them. Here is the God of the lost coin, who is so glad when that coin is found. The smoldering wick will not be quenched, nor the bruised reed broken off forever. Yahweh is a compassionate God, a God who offers forgiveness and salvation to every creature.

Through Jesus Christ, the biblical God is revealed as a Parent of infinite goodness. The right to call Yahweh our Parent is not won through human effort. The name of parent expresses the very reality of God as creative source of all things. God sustains and preserves all things with power and love, like a mother or a father. In calling Yahweh our "Father," our Parent, we accept our status as daughters and sons of our creator. We express the fact that Yahweh is a superabundance that never closes in upon itself but that always gives itself, in love and communion overflowing. Our creator is our parent because we are that creator's children. We come to know Jesus as the "only begotten of God," only to discover that, in Jesus, we too are the daughters and sons of God. When we say, with Jesus, "Abba"—"Daddy"—we express a conviction that is the fruit of Jesus' own experience: that this all-pervading, all-sustaining Mystery is not a terrifying reality but rather the One who waits and watches for us at home, where our journey will end. Far from threatening us with terrible deeds, this Father and Mother of ours is the only being in the universe who accepts us with absolute, and absolutely personal, love.

The God of Jesus Christ, recognized by the faith of the apostles and accepted by the Christian community, is a Trinity: Father, Son, and Holy Spirit. The ultimate principle of the world and of history is not a solitary being, then, but God the Family— God-Communion. From all eternity, Yahweh is a bond of loving relations, an unfathomable Mystery—the unoriginated Origin of all—called "Father." This Mother and Father emerges from the depths of the divine mystery in an act of self-communication and self-revelation within the Godhead itself, and this emergence is the second person of God: "God the Son." Now Parent and Child—"Father and Son"—join in an embrace of love and in doing so express and give origin to the Holy Spirit, who is the Oneness of the first and second persons. This Trinity has not remained enclosed but has communicated itself, making human life its temple. The Trinity dwells in us and our history, divinizing each of us.

Who are we to be thus the object of Yahweh's love? How do the biblical authors regard the human being in the light of God?

3. THE HUMAN BEING, IMAGE AND CHILD OF GOD

All other beings have been created by divine command. Only human beings appear by invitation. Humans alone have a vocation. Adam and Eve are persons in dialogue, able to respond to God's call. They are not creatures like the others; they are the image and likeness of God. They are children of God, members of God's household. Created to be intermediaries between God and the world, Adam and Eve function as God's representatives to the world. They have won from God the world as their inheritance, the inheritance the child receives from the Parent.

As God is Creator, then, so we human beings also are to be creators of good things, all the things produced by our activity in the world. As God is Lord, so we too are called to be sovereigns of all the world's realities. We have not been called to be slaves—or to enslave others—but to gain dominion over creation and manage that creation responsibly in God's name. But we do not become nature's sovereigns by plundering the earth, destroying the ecological balance, and squandering the riches of nature. In so doing we show ourselves to be irresponsible governors and rebellious children. We are called to be responsible administrators of the inheritance we have received from God, and we shall have to give an account of our trust to the Supreme Sovereign.

We are not one another's sovereigns. We are one another's sisters and brothers. Siblings are equal. They should respect one another. They should be bound together by ties of service, not by structures of domination. Any discrimination, even in the Church—any relationship of enslaver and enslaved, oppressor and oppressed—represents an assault on the condition of sibling and thereby an assault on a brotherly and sisterly partnership and communion. For example, woman was not created primarily to be a wife and mother. In Genesis (2:18–23), woman is first and basically man's partner, the otherness of love, exchange, and dialogue, on an equal basis. She was not taken from the feet of man to be his slave, nor from his head to be his mistress, but from his side to be his companion. Obviously the story of the creation of Eve from Adam's rib is not to be taken literally. A metaphor is being used here to express the equality that ought to prevail between woman and man.

As for their relationship with God, women and men are God's daughters and sons. To be the daughter or son of someone is not the same as to be that person's creature. To be a daughter or son of someone implies a relationship. It acknowledges that this other, this cause of one's being, is one's progenitor. It implies obedience and a loving relationship. The more a son or daughter relates to, loves, respects, and listens to his or her parent, the more a son or daughter that one is. Being a child of God means that we can invoke God, that we can call on God with that name of infinite tenderness used by Jesus himself—*Abba*, "Daddy." It means that we can be exalted above the rest of creation and maintain a dialogue with the Absolute. Here is the human being's limitless grandeur. Our roots are of earth. We share with all the rest of creatures the weight of matter. We retain reminiscences of our brute origin. But we can burst these terrestrial bonds. We can rise infinitely high. We can gaze at God and cry lovingly, "Abba!" And our call is heard. Yahweh returns our gaze and cries, "My child!" When this occurs, the grace event bursts upon us. God abides in us and we in God. God is humanized, and we are divinized. The Reign of God begins. New heavens dawn and a new earth is born.

We human beings are not only children of God, sisters and brothers to one another and sovereigns over the earth. We appear in history, as the Scriptures attest, also as nonpersons. We are rebellious children, enslavers of others and the slaves of this world. We can open ourselves to God, but we can also close ourselves. We can be persons of magnificent response or magnificent refusal. We are vessels of the history not only of salvation but also of perdition. We have used our freedom as a means to sin: we have preferred a relative good to the absolute Good. We have absolutized a relative good; we have placed our ultimate hope in the world and not in God. The consequence of this treacherous, disloyal project is the distortion of all of life's relationships. The obedient child turns rebellious, the sibling becomes a dominator. Sovereigns become dependent on their own creation.

Sin not only introduces a distortion into the relationship between human beings and God, then. It also affects all other relationships, especially the key relationship with one's neighbor and with one's world and culture. The people we are today are not only human beings; we are inhuman beings, as well. A shadow person dwells within us, a counterweight we carry, and into our existence it injects trauma. With Paul we cry, "Who can free me from this body under the power of death?" (Rom. 7:24). We beg for deliverance from the polluting, contaminating atmosphere of our existence—sin, which produces divisions, hatred, war, exploitation, injustice, and wickedness of all kinds, lowering and demeaning human dignity. And a world unwilled by God is created. Prophets arise and denounce this human and social evil. They are persecuted and crucified by the powerful, who have organized themselves to protect their project of domination. But Yahweh takes pity on the little, the unprotected, the poor, the last of the earth. God takes their side and maintains a special presence in them. Any poor person is a sacrament of the living God (Matt. 25:31–46).

We seek God not only as Parent but as Liberator and Savior as well. How long, O Lord, how long shall we await your liberating intervention? How long before the gruesome, ghastly situation of this world comes to an end? Such questions pervade Holy Scripture from beginning to end. Two hearts beat as one—

the human being's and God's—as the Old Testament Scriptures implore the coming of the Reign. God's people call out for the advent of the Liberator Messiah.

4. JESUS CHRIST, LIBERATOR GOD IN THE FLESH

And God has heard the supplication of the centuries. The New Testament bears witness that, in a Jew called Jesus of Nazareth, God has become present as total Redeemer, total Liberator, incarnate, enfleshed in our fallen situation.

God Totally Incarnate in the World

The first and basic article of Christian faith is the Incarnation. God, Mystery ineffable, whose sacrosanct name must be on human lips with reverence or not at all, has been seen, touched, and handled by human beings. This God has entered the realm of human existence and become, in all things save sin, a weak, mortal creature. Here is an unheard-of assertion. Here is a claim verging on scandal for pious minds aware of the ontological implications. God has always been represented as the Utterly Other, the Holy, as unimaginable, absolute Mystery—in a word, as the Transcendent. But this is none other, we say on our knees, than the one who has bestowed himself utterly on this world! Yahweh has taken on physical existence, from the first moment of a wondrous conception, in a Jew of Galilee, Jesus of Nazareth. Truly human, Jesus is at the same time God himself. Behold the event we call the Incarnation, in which both human and divine nature genuinely, truly subsist in one and the same historical person. God has taken on human otherness without destroying it, diminishing it, or in any way modifying it essentially. And this concrete humanity belongs so entirely to God, is so perfectly appropriated to and assimilated by God, that we may call it, altogether correctly, God's humanity.

God's penetration of human life has a *historical* character. In taking on human life, God takes on the social and historical conditions that make that life possible. God does this in a process, since human life is a matter of process. Life is not suddenly "there," suddenly complete. Life acquires its reality in a succession of moments. It moves from process to process. Nor are these processes merely the unfolding of material already latent at life's beginning. They constitute the creation of a *novum*, something never before experienced. We do not come into being as finished products. We are created in seed; then we build ourselves, we construct ourselves historically. We interiorize, we assimilate institutions, habits, and social conflicts, working from a nucleus of capacities that is activated by interacting with what is around us. The Incarnation is a process, then. Throughout the course of history, God gradually assumes the various moments of this history, so that all history if brushed and penetrated by God. Human history becomes the history of God. In this first meaning, then, the incarnation of God is an *affirmation of the world and its history*. God abandons the divine distance and draws near—with sympathy, as the fathers of the Church said—with the love that finally identifies with the beloved.

Besides being an affirmation of the world, the incarnation of God is a *protest against the world*. The Incarnation is liberating. Jesus is shown to us in the Bible as the vessel and articulator of a project of liberation, principally for the poor. The Reign of God both announces and denounces. It proclaims and it condemns. It encounters projects in history and enters into conflict with them. It calls for total liberation, not just a liberation of certain regions of human existence or the world. It demands not just a particular kind of justice, as, for example, commutative justice alone. It asks not just a certain type of loving relationship among human beings. It does not accept just a particular kind of fidelity to God. It is an autonomous project, and it confronts totalitarian, controlling power as an autonomous project. Jesus provoked conflict with the social and religious status quo of his time, and he was defeated, physically eliminated by crucifixion. His death was a protest against his world, which discriminated against the poor, the little, and the marginalized. It had closed itself off to their need for justice by invoking its piety, its dogmatics, its established image of God. The murder of Jesus showed the world's refusal to consecrate values of justice and communion. Jesus' death was, and is, a denunciation: some things are unacceptable to God. For some values we must sacrifice our lives if we are to be faithful to God and neighbor.

The life and death of Jesus were the life and death of God. The human crime against the Just One is the crime of deicide.

Behold the final consummation of human iniquity. In Jesus' murder, original sin as the history of human refusal of salvation finds its extreme and perfect form.

The proclamation of the incarnation and rejection of God is part and parcel of the content of Christian faith. Christian faith professes God's most profound affirmation of the world: "To his own he came . . ." (John 1:11); "God so loved the world . . ." (John 3:16). It also professes God's most profound protest against this world, against the particular form in which the world has been organized. God affirms creation (the divine deed, the receptacle of the divine incarnation) even in its fallen state (as scarred and spoiled by sin). But God also refuses to legitimate its decadence—the defiling of creation in the interests of human selfishness. Hence the meaning of Jesus' life, of the conflicts he provoked, the demands he made, the death he suffered, and the manner in which he underwent that death. It is likewise part and parcel of the Christian proclamation to prophesy against the human rejection of God.

God Alive in the World Forever

Once he had become incarnate in the world, God never left it. The resurrection of Jesus is the sign of God's definitive presence in history. More than a miracle, more than the victory of life over death, the Resurrection represents creation's happy ending by anticipating that outcome in the present, old creation. The principal meaning of Jesus's resurrection is its interpretation of our hope. Either that hope is cheated forever or it becomes reality. Jesus' resurrection is God's token of the ultimate legitimacy of our imagination and our utopias.

Jesus' resurrection marks the definitive presence of a God incarnate in the world as its ultimate meaning. This meaning is manifested in both arenas of human life—the biological and the social. The biological order governs physical life; the social order pertains to human life structured as society.

On the biological side, we may ask: What is the term of human life? Are we born to die? Empirical verification says that indeed life is born to die. Death is life's period, the end of life's sentence. After death, nothing. But imagination, desire, and the utopian in us rise up in protest against this observation. We dream of immortality and desire it. Yet we find no such thing, either in the order of nature or in the order of history. Jesus' resurrection responds: Yes, we are born to die. But we die to rise. Jesus' resurrection marks the triumph of life—on a higher, fuller plane. But the higher includes the lower. Thus, the Resurrection is the triumph of human life, now fully realized in its identity as life, in its final framework in God.

Another question emerges from life in its social fabric. Here again the meaning of life is either realized or frustrated. In the social order the most profound conflicts of existence take place. This is the arena in which we experience just or unjust, tyrannical or relatively equitable human relationships. History is written by those who hold the monopoly of ownership, power, and knowledge. The defeated, the conquered, the great dominated portions of the human race write no history. In this context we may ask: What meaning can life have for those who die for a just cause? What future is there for those who have fallen in defense of the inalienable right to life and justice? What value can be ascribed to the sacrifice of those who lay down their very lives for others and in this sacrifice are rejected and forgotten by history itself? At stake, of course, is the meaning we ascribe to history. Does history have meaning only in terms of the designs of the high and mighty, the writers of history?

The Resurrection answers: the humiliated, the rejected, have a future. It was in one of their number that God wrought resurrection. Jesus' resurrection has its full meaning only against the background of insurrection. Jesus' resurrection is the reconciliation of a shattered societal life. Why? Because in Jesus' resurrection, God has taken the part of the humiliated and the wronged and shown that the existential absurdity of their crushing is not unto everlasting death. It is not absolute. On the contrary, the future of the world comes out of this absurdity. For it was in One rejected and crucified that God wrought the decisive deed of all history: the triumph of life and the triumph of a just cause defended by the sacrifice of one's life.

Suddenly utopia is real. The dream of our imagination comes true. Now we can dream of a reconciled world with all abandon, for that world is not only possible and imaginable, but also historical. The risen Jesus is the concrete prize of this quest. This is why the Resurrection is an article of Christian faith.

Jesus' resurrection perpetuates his presence in the world. Now Jesus adopts not only a particular world—that of the time and place of his becoming flesh in the Palestinian culture of long ago—but also that of the entire world. Now risen, he is present to and penetrates all existence, the whole reality of creation. Faith testifies to this presence and celebrates its actualization.

5. THE HOLY SPIRIT, GOD'S OTHER INCARNATION

The Holy Spirit too has a particular mission in salvation history. The Spirit also has been sent, by the Father and the Son, to reveal to us the Father's mysterious face. In a unique and real way, the Holy Spirit descended upon the Virgin Mary (Luke 1:35, Matt. 1:18). He raised this simple woman of the people to such a divine stature that the one born of her would be the Son of God (Luke 1:35). Mary, then, without metaphor or figure, is the true, physical temple of the Holy Spirit, in a way analogous to Jesus as the dwelling place of the eternal Son.

Beginning with Mary, this Spirit has penetrated Jesus' other sisters and brothers—all the converted—to become the yeast in the loaf of the world. Beginning with her, the Holy Spirit spreads out to every part of that world, purifying, elevating, and reconciling all history and causing it to converge in its happy ending, the Omega of its felicity, God. The mission of the Spirit consists in keeping the memory of Jesus alive throughout the course of history and across the whole gamut of humanity. The Spirit recalls to our minds all that we have been told by Jesus (John 14:26). The Spirit announces to us everything it has received from Jesus (John 16:15). The eschatological deed of the life, death, and resurrection of Jesus can never be exhausted. It has an eternal value, that of reconciling and joining humanity with God. To renew the perennial value of Jesus' liberation; to instill that value into the attitudes of all women and men, orienting the social order toward justice, communion, and love; to assemble groups who will live Jesus' project with intensity—this is the specific mission of the Holy Spirit.

6. THE CHURCH: COMMUNITY OF LIBERATION, SACRAMENT OF THE HOLY SPIRIT

The whole of humanity of caught up in Jesus' deed of liberation. All creation is penetrated by the Spirit of Jesus. The Church is the community of the faithful who come together in an awareness of this truth. The Church gathers to celebrate God's redemption in the world and to be a sign of that redemption. This is why we call the Church the sacrament of universal salvation. Salvation is not in the Church alone. Neither do the Risen One and the Holy Spirit act in it alone. Salvation, like the Risen One and the Holy Spirit, is in the world. But only in the Church does salvation become palpable, sensible, and identifiable by human beings. In Pauline language, the Church is the body of the risen Christ, an organism animated by the Holy Spirit. But this body, this organism, is alive only to the extent that its members live for the cause of Christ and realize his project in the strength of the Holy Spirit. Thus the community of the faithful is signed with the seal of love, that it may be the place of understanding, of forgiveness, of communion, of new being. Wherever discord and injustice prevail, there the sign is tarnished, Jesus is marginalized, and the Spirit is aggrieved. The Church does not enfold the totality of the Mystery of Christ, nor is it the only place where the Spirit is active. Christ and his Spirit act on all sides, secretly reaching the heart of every human being coming into this world. Christians are those who know this universal truth of strength and consolation. Christians are those who make themselves the sign of this activity of the Spirit, that all men and women may realize how close they are to God and may see how much their divine Parent loves them in the divine Child present in the world through the vitality of the Spirit, who helps us accept the gift of that Parent.

7. A WORLD DESTINED TO BE THE BODY OF GOD

The Scriptures speak, not only of human beings and God and the interplay of their relations, but also of the destiny of the human world. The Bible does not see the world simply as matter or even as life doomed to dissolution. The world too has a future, because it has always been the object of God's love. Nothing

God loves can disappear forever. The world is God's good creature, borne up at every moment and kept in existence by the divine love. The world is electric with God. It is also a grand, revelatory sacrament of the Holy Trinity. It will be this in all perfection when humankind beholds the new generation of all things, delivered at last from all imperfection.

Biblical texts like to represent the end of the world in apocalyptic imagery: "The sun will be darkened, the moon will not shed its light, stars will fall out of the skies . . ." (Mark 13:24–25; cf. Matt. 24:29, Isa. 13:10, Ezek. 32:7, Joel 2:10, Rev. 6:13, and elsewhere). These representations are to be understood not literally, of course, but as figures calculated to portray the astounding novelty of God's activity. When God installs the new sky and the new earth, everything that had seemed strong and secure (steady as the sky, regular as the stars, mighty as the sun, vast as the sea, and so on) will be as weakness and nothing. The message is not sinister but benign. And it is glorious: "What we await are new heavens and a new earth where, according to this promise, the justice of God will reside" (2 Pet. 3:13).

And that is the whole secret. In God's new world, justice, love, and everything good will flourish. The old will be over and gone. Then we shall be happy, with all of our fellow creatures, in the great house of our Father.

As we see, the central message of Holy Scripture is not one of sin and forgiveness but of God's overflowing love. God's presence in history is characterized by hope, the joy of living, joviality, and graciousness. The anguish of our times and the passion of our people, which we share, must not cloud our vision of the brightness that streams from God's revelation, the revelation and testimony of the Scriptures. The Bible not only offers us hope. It not only issues its calls and its challenges. It also invites us to imitate God and to follow Jesus Christ as ways of living in happiness now and of anticipating the Reign of God to come. Until that Reign comes among us, we believe in and hope for, we hope for and give thanks for, we give thanks for and love the resurrection of the flesh: life everlasting.

II. FAITH ON THE EDGE

5. The Two Eyes of Theology

All theology is built from a twin point of departure—a double locus. Theology is constructed from the locus of faith and from the locus of the social reality in which faith is lived. The locus of faith is common to all Catholic Christian theologians. The locus of social reality remains to be identified.

THEOLOGIA ANTE ET RETRO OCULATA

The fathers of our faith, in the early Christian centuries, spoke of theology as having two eyes, "one before and one behind" (*theologia ante et retro oculata*). With the "eye behind" theology looks to the past, where God's definitive salvific presence has burst in upon our universe. It beholds the Christian Scriptures. It beholds the conciliar texts—the documents of the ecumenical councils, which have defined the creed of the Church community. It beholds the testimonials of the saints and doctors of the Church. It beholds the tradition of the people of God.

With the "eye before," theology looks to the present. It detects the challenges of current social and historical reality. It sets about making connections between faith and life, between love of God and political love, between hopes and the divine promises.

Theological production is correct and good when it succeeds in expressing the truth of faith (glimpsed by its backward-looking eye) in such a manner as to produce an existential, social meaning in the present (viewed by the forward-looking eye). Only then are we certain that we are not seeing double; we are seeing both the reality of faith and the reality of our present day in a correctly balanced binocular perspective.

Each of theology's two loci or points of departure has its specific problems. Let us examine these problems.

LOCUS OF FAITH: THE KAIROLOGICAL "TODAY"

Theology does not invent its point of departure. It takes as its starting point the faith it receives from the apostles. What does

Christian faith tell us? Faith testifies to an ongoing "today," effected and created in our behalf by God. We shall call this "today" the "kairological today," inasmuch as it is a "today" so dense with salvation, so laden with the divine presence that it bursts out of the category of linear time and becomes an anticipation of eternity.[1] Because it has the structure of the definitive and the eschatological, this "today" abides as a constant present. It is neither swallowed up by the past nor overwhelmed by the future. Of what does this "now" consist?[2] It consists of the testimony and proclamation that through the divine Son God has intervened to liberate history from its distortions and lead it to realization and a fullness of life. The eternal Son took flesh in poverty and marginally in order that, beginning with the lowest of beings, beginning with "that which is not" (cf. 1 Cor. 1:28), he might save all that is. Now the Resurrection has confirmed the happy outcome of Jesus' life, a life surrounded by the perils of ongoing history. Thanks to the Incarnation of the Word and the Resurrection event, Jesus' life is called, not only to face the perils of history, but to absolute fulfillment as well. Jesus' life has been touched and sanctified by the divine reality. Thanks to Jesus Christ and his Spirit in the world, we have reached a point from which we can never fall back. The old Adam remains forever new, and the new Adam will always be *Novissimus Adam*, the "last Adam" (1 Cor. 15:45).

This is theology's starting point. It is received from Christian faith of the first century. It is the point of the witness and testimony of faith, to be pondered uninterruptedly and uttered constantly. The function of theology is to subject this testimony of faith to critical reflection—to transform the cry of faith (witness) into a rational, grammatical, regulated discourse (theology).

Lest theology distort faith—in order to be certain that it is maintaining a true understanding, arriving at the original meaning of faith and reuttering that meaning for the present—it has recourse to the hermeneutic sciences. Theology uses the historical method, seeking to reconstruct "that time" in which God's full communication was bestowed. It uses the most rigorous exegesis of the foundational texts of our faith (the Old and New Testaments) that it possibly can. It avails itself of linguistic and philological instruments. It uses the sociology of knowledge. It steeps itself in philosophy and hermeneutics, in order to disclose what kind of human being is concealed behind the sacred texts. Only in this fashion will the theologian appropriate, without illusions and without too many mistakes, the wealth of divine revelation.

For such a task, it is not enough merely to have faith, to be devout, and to have a heart full of love. Intelligence and intellectual versatility are also necessary. The function of theology is to generate light—to show that our hope has its reasons (cf. 1 Pet. 3:15). Further, theology must show that the *logos* or rationality of faith is not hostile to the universal *logos* (the sciences of the human being) but rather is in harmony with it, raising it to a plenitude unheard of in history.

Locus of Social Reality: The Chronological "Today"

It is not enough to unearth a spring of crystalline waters. If they are to benefit thirsting human beings, these waters must have a channel. The kairological "today" must be lived in the *chronological* "today."[3] Society is complex. The mechanisms of its functioning are not open to view. Between the analyst's eye and objective reality come ideologies (discourses that disguise and dissimulate), social preconceptions, and notions of common currency embodying the interpretation of reality provided by the dominant classes. In order to be able to see clearly the reality within which the discourse of faith is to be uttered, the analyst must use the sciences of the social and of the human being, such as anthropology, sociology, psychology, political science, economics, and social philosophy. These assist us in deciphering the complexity of the real—the workings of power, the mechanisms of the production of wealth and poverty, and the constitution of the social classes with their nearly always antagonistic interests.

Theology necessarily works within a particular type of analysis of historical reality, whether that analysis is a product of the empiricism, utopianism, idealism, and naiveté of a noncritical interpretation or whether it is developed critically through the social sciences. The former, noncritical analysis, can lead to theological mistakes. For example, it will typically yield a pastoral theology characterized by shortsighted solutions along paternalistic or, at best, reformist lines. The latter, critical analysis, is more likely to supply theologians with a less ambiguous socioanalytic text and hence a better chance of being accurate. For example, a socioanalytic reading of our own social reality reveals the extent of the economic exploitation and social marginalization of the working classes of our continent. The main cause of this exploitation and marginalization resides in the capitalism of our societies. A small minority of persons appropriates the bulk of the wealth constructed by the toil of all, controls the state, and holds the ideological monopoly.

Confronted with the reality of a chronological "today" that has been deciphered critically, how will Christian faith, seeking to grasp the truth of the kairological "today" by theological hermeneutics, comport itself? Unless it is to be untrue to itself, it cannot simply remain indifferent to the reality at hand. Using the arsenal of ideas, values, and visions that it has at its disposal, it can only pronounce a negative theological verdict on that reality. The social reality as we find it certainly does not suggest— let alone anticipate—the Reign of God. In order to become more like the Reign of God, prevailing social reality must be transformed. Christian faith is not an ideology. But it does help Christians define their sense of direction. It helps them adopt a fundamental option for the oppressed, for their struggles, for their rights. Christianity endorses an option for liberating the marginalized and all other persons—liberation to a more equal life in community, a life that is more a partnership of sisters and brothers.

To formulate such a judgment—to found it on and connect it with the more comprehensive vision of Christian faith, even in the transhistorical dimension of that faith—is the mission of theology. Theology is obliged not only to render a theological judgment on social reality—theology as theory—but to recommend the concrete steps that must be taken to live out a preferential option for the liberation of the poor—theology as practice. Theology's efforts here must be coordinated with those of other social forces. Furthermore, theology will have to take account of existing historical conditions—the interplay of class forces and the whole warp and woof of the global geopolitical system.

On the one hand, faith (and its critical discourse, theology) must strive for social transformation side by side with the victims of the prevailing system. On the other hand, faith must maintain its identify as faith, which it does only insofar as it retains its reference to Christ, the Gospels, and sacred tradition (the tradition of faith). In other words, it must toil in the "chronological today" in fidelity to the kairological "today." There will be a twofold danger, then. We shall be tempted to abide in a splendid isolationism, insensitive to the cries of the oppressed, cultivating "our" faith, celebrating "our" liturgies, and limiting the practice of faith to religious practices. Or we shall be tempted to commit ourselves to social liberation to the point of losing our identity, losing our Christian awareness, losing the integral meaning of liberation read in the light of faith. In either case faith is distorted. In the first case it becomes a religious ideology. In the second it becomes a secularized, profaned ideology. It is absolutely necessary to join faith and social liberation in such a way as to extract both the liberating dimension of genuine Christian faith (the only faith that saves), and the theological or faith dimension of social liberation.

Summarizing, we may say, the Christian message—that of the "kairological today"—places us at the side of the oppressed. At the same time, this commitment to liberation—in our "chronological today"—shows us that Christian message in a fuller light. These two moments are dialectically interconnected and mutually enriching.

THEOLOGY OF LIBERATION: CONJUNCTION OF THE LOCI

Liberation theology claims to be the most consistent approach today to a joining of Christian faith and a praxis of liberation. After long groping, after much ambiguity and even error, after beginnings marked by polarization, theoretical obscurity, and methodological inexactitude, liberation theology has at last succeeded in producing an adequate, rigorous elaboration of the various mediations required by the mission it proposes to itself.[4]

Before all else, the theology of liberation means to be genuine *theology*. In other words it should be and is an erudite discourse on the faith of the Church fathers. The theologian never abandons this horizon of Christian faith, not even when engaged in minute political or economic analyses. Ruled by this faith, and with the goal of producing works of faith, liberation theology is obliged to employ a socioanalytic mediation. Faith helps this theology take its position squarely within conflict—at the side of the poor, in the locus or situation of our marginalized people. Faith mightily sensitizes a person to the problems of the exploitation of the people, for it interprets these problems as manifestations of sin.

It is not enough, however, to maintain this enhanced sensitivity, this "raised consciousness" and its accompanying ethical indignation. We must also maintain a correct, critical view of the structures of reality. Otherwise we shall be unable to act effectively upon that reality and thus transform it. This is the first methodological step in the theology of liberation: to see sociohistorical reality clearly by using proper and adequate tools supplied by the social and human sciences.

This analysis will be governed by an antecedent option for the poor and for their liberation. Therefore it will be carried out "from the locus of the oppressed"—from their viewpoint, with their interests in view, and for the purpose of the social transformation that will do them the most justice. This analysis, this reading of reality, must also consider the analyses made by the dominant classes. Only thus shall we be able to maintain the objectivity we need to correctly appraise the social forces at play in our reality.

The theology of liberation then superimposes a philosophical reflection on this socioanalytic reading, with an eye to theological and pastoral practice. Here we seek to appropriate and reduce to rational categories the course of history, especially the experience of the individual and society within capitalism. Our goal is to reveal the background of subjugation against which this historical experience has unfolded while appraising the various forms of resistance this subjugation has encountered. We seek the alternatives, always defeated but never destroyed, that will prevail in history tomorrow.

Following that procedure, theology, in its quest for rationality, analyzes the text produced by a socioanalytic reading of reality.

This second step takes place within a different epistemological framework from that of the first step, "seeing." Now the task at hand is "judging." The second step, then, is to judge social reality, with the various practices that exist within that reality, in the light of Christian faith. This is a moment of special importance for the locus of faith, for here theology invokes the specifically Christian criteria for constructing a just society. Theology attests to the liberatory meaning of salvific faith (which is salvific only to the extent that it leads to practices of love), of the utopia of the Reign of God, of the person and message of Jesus, and so on. Faith is not indifferent to the ethical aspect of Christian and human practices, and the theologian must develop ethical judgments.

Finally, liberation theology studies the concrete approaches the pastoral practice of the Church might adopt. It maps out the possible pathways of Christian commitment. Prudential judgments enter into play here. We do, not what we would like to do, but what can be done—what the situation permits. We must examine the kind of bonds the Church establishes with other groups that work for social change. Theology must consider the precise manner in which the Church joins the specific practices of faith (sacraments, religious education, liturgy) to social and political practices, in order to avoid introducing a parallelism that would be deleterious to both realities.

As we see, the theological undertaking is a vast one. But we are not thereby exempted from the demands of a conscience ever alert to the following challenge: what is the Christian community doing, or not doing, for the liberation of a suffering people? In response to this challenge, and despite all of the theoretical and practical difficulties involved, liberation theology comes into being. As was once said:

Catholic scholars are all but impossible persons. They must know the entire deposit of faith, the Scriptures, the acts of the Holy See. At the same time, they must know what St. Paul calls the elements of this world. That is, they must know simply everything.[5]

A formidable task? By all means. But the theology of liberation is driven. It is unable to forget that we shall be called to account one day by history and by the supreme judge of history. "I was hungry . . . I was thirsty . . . I was away from home . . . naked . . . I was ill and in prison . . ." (Matt. 25:42–44).

6. Jesus Christ the Liberator, Center of Faith on the Edge of the World

To speak of Jesus Christ as Liberator is to choose liberation—release from subjugation. To reverence and proclaim Jesus Christ as our Liberator means thinking and living our christological faith from the social and historical context of domination and oppression. Faith then develops this contextuality in analytic fashion, producing a Christology that focuses on Jesus Christ as Liberator. This Christology thus implies a specific political commitment, a commitment to break with the oppressive situation.

SOCIAL LOCUS AND ALL LIBERATION: RELEVANCE FOR CHRISTOLOGY

An adequate Christology takes account of two data: (1) the christological relevance of social and political liberation, and (2) the social locus that functions as the starting point for developing christological reflection.

Christological relevance can mean two things. On the one hand it can refer to the demands of a given historical conjuncture for reflecting on a faith centered in Jesus Christ. In this case, the pressing question is, How are we to think, preach, and live Jesus Christ in the presence of the demands of a particular situation so that he may be seen in the light of faith, that is, as our Savior? *Christological relevance* might conversely mean theology's ability to explain or comprehend specific historical circumstances and then either maintain or transform those circumstances. Here the questions are, For whom is a particular image of Christ relevant? Who is aided or encouraged by this or that particular type of Christology or by this or that specific theme? What interests does it represent, and what concrete projects does it support and confirm?

Relevance thus carries an inherent ambiguity. To resolve it, we need to consider another basic question, that of the social locus (the practices, the commitments, the positions) constituting the point of departure for making faith in Jesus Christ explicit.[1] Theologians do not waft above concrete reality. They are social agents, situated within a particular place in society. They think with the instruments permitted them by their circumstances. They address their discourse to a specific group of hearers. Christological accents, indeed the choice of the subjects or topics to be treated by a given Christology, are defined by what is relevant to the theologian's social locus. Another way of putting this is that there can be no such thing as a neutral Christology. A Christology is necessarily partisan—committed, engaged. Its discourse has repercussions on a situation shot through with conflicting interests. In vain we style our Christology purely "theological"—historical, traditional, ecclesial, and apolitical. The first tendency of a Christology is to adopt the position of the powers that be. In this case, its social locus will be transparent, and its alleged apolitical character will vanish. It will emerge as a religious prop and stay of the status quo.

Every Christology is relevant to its particular social and historical circumstances. In other words, a Christology is always engaged and committed. Therefore we hold this basic proposition: Christology, as a body of regulated, erudite knowledge of our christological faith, is constituted in the matrix of a definite moment of history. That is, it is formulated under particular concrete conditions of material, ideological, cultural, and ecclesial production, and it is articulated according to certain concrete interests of which the theologizing subject may or may not be aware. The real question, then, is not *whether* a particular kind of Christology is partisan or engaged, but *to whom and to what* this particular kind of Christology is committed and engaged. What cause does it serve? The Christology that proclaims Jesus Christ as Liberator commits itself to the economic, social, and political liberation of the oppressed and dominated groups of society. It takes as theologically relevant the historical liberation of the vast masses of our continent, and it says, This is what

Christology ought to think, and in praxis this is the path it ought to encourage. In other words, liberation Christology seeks to compose and articulate its content and style in a manner calculated to bring out the liberating dimensions of the historical Jesus' life.

We might put it this way: a context of oppression and dependency in all aspects of life—to the detriment of the opposite pole and correlate, liberation—suggests to Christology in Latin America a way of thinking about and loving Jesus Christ as the Liberator of humankind. Latin American theologians do not generate this approach simply in order to afford interesting topics for discussion. They generate it in response to a demand of their concrete faith as Christians. By that faith they are bound by conscience to help their sisters and brothers overcome a humiliating, demeaning situation, and they have found in Jesus Christ the necessary impulse for a mighty attempt to liberate these persons.

Latin American Christology, then, like any other, supposes and depends on a particular social practice. That social practice takes into account the possibility and urgency of breaking with the prevailing context of subjugation.

The locus of this Christology is clear. Its social matrix consists of those social groups for whom a qualitative transformation of the prevailing social structure represents an opportunity to be liberated from domination. For many of our theologians, a clear definition of their social locus alongside the oppressed involves a veritable hermeneutic conversion. After all, in their new social locus new questions are being proposed for their reflection, and these questions, like other scientific questions, call for an appropriate epistemological vehicle.

However, this commitment to the locus of the oppressed—and let us keep this clearly in mind—does not guarantee the intrinsic quality of our Christology. A consideration of the social locus and relevance of a Christology merely demonstrates the inevitable connection between theory and practice, between Christology and politics. Now we see that the social locus of a Christology is a necessary and basic condition for that Christology's definition of its thematic object and the manner in which it will focus upon it.

In order to determine the content of a Christology, then, we shall have to consider something else. We shall have to distinguish between the *autonomy* and *dependency* of a Christology (or any other theology).[2] The former is guaranteed by epistemological considerations, since it arises from the epistemic locus. The latter concerns the sociology of knowledge, since it arises from the social locus. The autonomy of Christology resides in its discourse being developed through its own specific methodology. Christology has its own mode of theorizing. It need not justify itself to any other method in order to enjoy its own legitimacy, that is, in order to possess the adequate criteria of its internal truth.

In the epistemological sphere, then, it is meaningless to distinguish a Latin American Christology from a North Atlantic one, or a Christology of the oppressed from one of the oppressors. No such criteria are required or admissible among the theoretical tools by which a sound epistemology judges the value of a Christology. Internally, Christology is autonomous. It does not become better or worse *as Christology* in virtue of having been produced in the metropolitan center of an economic system rather than on the periphery of that system. The same is to be said of a liberating, progressive, or traditionalist Christology. The content represented by such adjectives is inadequate as a criterion for determining the truth or correctness of a Christology. They indicate an exterior and non-essential feature: that of the social reference or matrix of a Christology. (Of course, a particular Christology will have a particular social commitment and thus may strengthen a particular social group—conservative or progressive or liberating.)

Still, Christology (like any other theology) does have its external dimension. This is its dimension of dependency. In selecting the topics to be analyzed, Christology depends on the social locus of the theologian and on what this person perceives as relevant to a christological reflection on his or her social and historical circumstances. Establishing the various relationships between the social and epistemic loci constitutes an extremely complex problem, and we cannot address it here. But at least we have adverted to their intimate connections.

TWO LEVELS OF SOCIAL CONSCIOUSNESS: TWO CORRESPONDING CHRISTOLOGIES OF LIBERATION

Our next step is to identify the context in which a theology of Jesus Christ as Liberator has appeared.[3] We begin with a simple observation. The brutal fact is that the vast masses of our Christian continent live and die in inhumane living conditions. All around us we see malnutrition, infant mortality, endemic disease, subsistence wages, unemployment, and the absence of welfare programs, hygienic conditions and health services, hospitals, schools, or housing. In short, we observe a lack of the goods and services necessary to secure human beings their minimal subsistence and dignity as persons. This phenomenon commonly goes by the name of underdevelopment. Yet hand in hand with this demeaning reality goes another reality: our people's Christian faith, with its spectrum of values—its hospitality, its human warmth, its sense of solidarity, its immense longing for justice and a political voice, its taste for festival. But our cultural ethos is eroding and disintegrating. Why? Because of the myth of progress as defined in capitalistic terms and because of the elitist consumerism that myth entails.

Confronted with this scandal, Christian groups, at least those that have attained a certain degree of awareness, have reacted, hoping to rescue the practice of the faith on this continent from its traditional historical cynicism.[4] In theological terms, we see two broad reactions, each generating its own Christology in terms of Jesus Christ the Liberator.[5] One works in the empirical order—the order of experience. The other seeks a christological articulation of the order of analysis—the order of thought. The former arises out of an ethical indignation, the latter out of socioanalytic rationality. Both have this in common: they are a "second word" vis-à-vis the reality of misery, which is always "first word." Following is a brief sketch of each.

1. SACRAMENTAL CHRISTOLOGY OF LIBERATION

In the first of the two Christologies being developed on our continent, the basic contradiction of Latin American reality is perceived by an intuitive popular wisdom that we might call "sacramental." It brings to light and makes real the presence of oppression and the urgency of liberation. Many Christians, through the lens of their faith, have discerned that Latin American reality contradicts God's historical design. Poverty constitutes social sin, a condition contrary to the will of God. It is of the utmost urgency, therefore, to bring about a change. Our brothers and sisters must begin to obey God.

This perception is generally expressed in a language of prophetic denunciation, together with a motivating, encouraging demand for change, all translating ethical indignation.[6] It is embodied in a praxis of committed love. But it does not analyze the mechanisms and structures of the situation it decries and would transform or see transformed. Hence the effectiveness of the ensuing commitment is temporary and unpredictable. But its political position is clear. The situation must not be allowed to continue as it is. A change in social relations is in order, with more power going to the dominated groups for the purpose of creating new, less oppressive societal structures.

This practice, with its implicit, rudimentary theory, enables Christians to make a genuine christological faith reading of reality. All of the deeds, words, and attitudes of Jesus implying a call to conversion and a change in relationships—his position vis-à-vis the marginalized of the Palestinian society of his time, his preference for the poor, his conflicts with the religious and social status quo of his place and time, the political content of his proclamation of the Reign of God, the reasons for his execution—acquire a special relevance and make up the image of a Jesus who is a liberator. This is quite a different image from that of official dogmatic piety—Christ the celestial monarch—or from that of the defeated, suffering Christ of popular piety.

This liberation Christology is based on certain values, themes, appeals, and demands for change and liberation of some kind. No strategy or tactic is postulated. There are as yet no concrete goals. Viable routes of liberation from the concrete situation of captivity and repression have not been identified, as there has been no antecedent analysis of the general conjuncture. Praxis, at this level, is by and large pragmatic.

This Christology has a certain value. It reveals the inescapable connection between the salvation of Jesus Christ and historical liberations. It overcomes an intimistic, privatizing conception of the Christian message and respectfully rejects its inadequate identification with politics. This kind of Christology is at times even accompanied by a rigorous critical exegesis—a sound, wholesome reinterpretation of the fundamental christological dogmas and a development of the liberating dimensions of Christian faith. Sensitized by its perception of the demeaning condition in which so many persons must live, it reacts from the standpoint of faith itself and proceeds to think and live that faith in a way that endorses the task of economic and political liberation of society's humiliated and wronged.

From this viewpoint, a criticism can now be lodged against traditional images of Christ that are not conducive to liberation but that, on the contrary, prop up the colonial project of domination.[7] The agonizing, dying Christs of Latin American tradition are "Christs of the internalized helplessness of the oppressed."[8] The Sorrowful Mother, her heart transfixed by seven swords, personifies the submission and subjugation of women. Her tears express Latin American woman's grief over the massacre of her children by colonialism's lust for wealth and power. Besides criticizing this Christology of resignation, a sacramental liberation Christology likewise attacks a Christology of domination and its alienated Christs, either its imperial-monarch Christ, crusty with gold like Portuguese or Spanish kings, or its Christ the vanquished warrior.

But a sacramental liberation Christology suffers from palpable limitations. It presupposes no socioanalytic focus of reality. Hence its limited contribution to political strategy. Groups espousing this Christology can be theologically (that is, theoretically) revolutionary and yet be conservative or merely progressive in their practices.

2. Socioanalytic Christology of Liberation

A second type of liberation Christology—the socioanalytic articulation of that Christology—takes as its starting point this same spiritual experience of confrontation with the poor. Its ethical indignation is no less intense. But this indignation is channeled through an analysis of reality calculated to detect the actual mechanisms of this scandalous misery and to articulate an effective liberation praxis. It stresses a liberating praxis, against the practice of improving things here and there while maintaining the same framework of relations of force—the practice of reformism. What it calls for is the revolutionary will to alter the very framework of society. The basic commitment must of course be unambiguously to liberation. But to have any chance of reaching the goal of liberation, this praxis will require a social analysis of the mechanisms of the social inequity, understood in the light of faith as social and structural sin. Therefore the Christology arising from this focus can be called a liberation Christology in the strict sense.

This Christology of liberation is built with two basic theoretical tools. The *socioanalytic* tool bears on the reality to be modified. The *hermeneutic* tool pertains to theology, since theology uses it to read the "text" produced by socioanalysis in the light of Jesus Christ as Savior—that is, in the light of the word of revelation— thus guaranteeing that the resulting liberation theory and practice will be theological in character.[9]

We shall not be concerned here with hermeneutics, as it is already familiar to theologians and their audience. Instead let us concentrate on the socioanalytic tool. This is where the particular concerns of the various theological currents emerge to demonstrate the actual (and not merely claimed or imagined) social locus of these currents.

Any theological intervention on the part of theologians or the hierarchy in the area of society presupposes a basic sociological theory. But that theory may be either spontaneous or critical. Empiricism (a spontaneous, intuitive reading) in this area constitutes one of the "basic epistemological obstacles" noted by the French philosopher Gaston Bachelard. An empiricist reading of social and historical reality will tend to reinforce the status quo and prevent the adequate articulation of any theology. Such a socioanalytic reading, then, will not be appropriate as a tool for a Christology of liberation. And so the question arises: what social theory should we use if we intend to articulate a Christology of liberation?

The criteria for the choice of a theory intended to explain society do not emerge exclusively from objectivity and rationality. They are governed as well by the analyst's basic option and social locus. All reflection on human reality is oriented around a basic project—a utopia constructed by a group and constituting the reference point of that group's projection of its future. This reflection is not purely ideological, however. It is based on social and material conditions objectively at hand. Hence we can distinguish two series of projects or utopias: the project of the dominant classes of society, and the project of the dominated classes.

The utopia conceived by dominant groups advocates a linear progress, one without changes in society's structuring frameworks. It demonstrates immense faith in science and technology. It is based on an elitist conceptualization of society, whose benefits it expects will reach the masses only gradually. The utopia conceived by dominated groups seeks an egalitarian society. It regards the gulf between the elite and the masses as the greatest obstacle to development and denies that there will be any genuine progress, any genuine social justice, as long as that gulf persists. It expresses an unshakable faith in the power of the oppressed to transform society—to generate a new society, characterized by less social injustice and oppression.

One of these two basic, mutually exclusive concepts must enter into the selection of the type of analysis to be directed toward society. Dominant groups prefer the functionalist method in social studies. This method prioritizes the notions of order and balance, viewing society as an organic whole whose parts are mutually complementary. Dominated groups prefer the dialectical method, whose central notion is that of conflict and struggle. These groups see society as a contradictory whole. The former orientation (historically articulated in the liberal or laissez-faire tradition) sees society "from the top"—from the point where, precisely, a specious harmony prevails. The latter (historically articulated in the revolutionary, Marxist tradition) considers society "from the bottom," where it appears as struggle and confrontation.

Faith (and its erudite expression, theology) respects the autonomy of rationality. But it exercises discernment calculated to reveal which analytical approach is most compatible with the demands of a faith incarnate in a praxis. Faith urges the choice of the socioanalytic schema that will most decisively reveal the mechanisms of injustice, that will suggest the most appropriate means of overcoming those injustices, and that will most help to bring about a community of brothers and sisters and a society of universal participation.

Thus the Christology of liberation presupposes an option for the dialectical tendency in an analysis of society, preferring the revolutionary project of the subjugated. When it speaks of liberation it expresses a well-defined option. This option is neither reformist nor progressive but instead liberating, implying a break with the status quo. Of what liberation are we speaking? Here we must be very careful. We must use the same words in two different senses at once, without allowing either to be reduced to the other. We are dealing with a liberation from economic, social, political, and ideological structures. Structures, not only persons, are concerned. We seek to change the relations of power that prevail among social groups and thus permit the appearance of new structures calculated to further a greater political and social voice for the excluded. The Christology of liberation takes the side of the oppressed, believing itself constrained to do so by faith in the historical Jesus. On this continent, nonengagement will be tantamount to accepting the situation and thereby implicitly espousing the cause of the privileged.

An option for the oppressed does not automatically eliminate the inherent ambiguity of the liberation process. Not every liberation is an anticipation and concretization of the Reign of God. And no liberation may be absolutized in itself. The salvation proclaimed by Christianity is all-inclusive. It is not limited to economic, political, social, and ideological liberations. But neither is it actualized without them. Christian hope and a sound, correct eschatology stand warranty for our conviction that this world is more than the stage on which the salvation drama is played out. The world is part and parcel of the drama. Definitive, eschatological salvation is mediated, anticipated, and made concrete in partial, this-worldly liberations at all levels of reality in history, provided these liberations be open to a fullness, an all-comprehensiveness, attainable only in the Reign of God.

It is crucially important for a Christology of liberation to correctly interpret that common denominator of our continent, underdevelopment. Underdevelopment does not consist principally—as the functionalistic interpretation of the liberal system would have us believe—in a *technological* problem: how to accelerate the process leading from a traditional, pretechnological society to a modern, technical one. That is, the basic problem of underdevelopment does not consist in the technological gap between developed countries and develop*ing* countries. Nor is it mainly a *political* question of how to tighten interdependent but unequal relationships among countries within the same system with a view to achieving a homogeneous development. That is, it does not consist basically in the gap between developed countries and *under*developed countries. The problem of underdevelopment consists in a system of dependency of some countries on others, with the latter functioning as metropolitan or imperial centers around which satellite, peripheral, outskirt countries revolve and are kept in underdevelopment by an oppressive system.[10] Underdevelopment is the other face of development. Underdevelopment is a direct consequence of development. In order to maintain its acceleration and the level of benefits it achieves, development in capitalist molds must retain in its sphere of dependency countries that are required to contribute to the central countries whatever is needed for the wealth of the latter. The reason for our underdevelopment does not lie in biological and hygienic factors or a difference in cultural ethos. These are merely contributing factors. The determining cause of our underdevelopment is the system of dependency under which we live, a system of objective oppression and subjugation interiorized in the various peripheral countries by the representatives of the central imperium. This dependency marks all manifestations of life—the economic system, the division of labor, politics, culture, even religion.

The only escape from this situation lies through a process of breaking the bonds of our dependency and liberating ourselves for a self-sustaining national project. But we must be realistic with this sort of theoretical postulate. Such breaches cannot be effected voluntaristically. "People create only revolutions which actually occur."[11] We must attend to existing conditions of viability. The goal is not to be free at all costs; not all liberation brings liberty. A given liberation may mean independence but not necessarily development. Latin American countries have not been able to create a technology of their own, and none of them can develop on its own. Hence the bitter dilemma:

Liberation without development, or development and submission. The only other alternative is sheer compromise: limit our development to maintain a certain autonomy, limit our dependency by selecting the sectors to be developed. But this takes us beyond the simple theory of dependency.[12]

To further complicate the dilemma, in Latin America the forces of repression have won the day, and any organized liberation movement is paralyzed for the moment.

In these desperate conditions, are we to desist from our efforts for liberation? On the theoretical level, we must concede nothing. Our diagnosis of our ills continues to be correct and should be maintained. But on the level of praxis, we must search out practices that will render viable an authentic liberation process, however slow and lengthy that process may be. The existing situation obliges us to strive for changes *in* the system in order to arrive at changes *of* the system. This does not mean renouncing an option for liberation and an alternative society. It does mean allowing the concrete circumstances of a general situation of repression and captivity to enter into the picture as one of the factors in selecting a strategy to this end.

This analysis of reality must include concerns that may arise not only from the social sciences (sociology, economics, political science), but also from the historical, cultural, anthropological sciences, that is, considerations dictated by popular culture. The vast, downtrodden masses have created their culture of silence— their own ways of giving meaning to life, of liberating themselves, of resisting, of living in captivity. Many studies are available on the character of these phenomena present throughout practically the whole continent—on popular culture and piety as a seedbed of values not available to the imperialist ideology, and as a reservoir of the dynamism for an authentic theology of resistance and increasing liberation.

If we are to appreciate the gravity of a situation in which development means dependency and subjugation, we must move beyond mere sociological or other analyses of the human sciences and come down to structural, cultural considerations. Capitalism, consumerism, and the bonds of oppression and dependency are manifestations of a certain cultural ethos, a certain meaning of life and death, a peculiar tone in relationships with others, with material goods, with the Transcendent. Modernity has opted for a sense of being and living that receives its orientation from knowledge of and power over everything that confronts it, especially over the material world through domination, greed, and exploitation. Any revolution that fails to change this cultural ethos—as fundamental to Marxism as it is to the rest of Western history—will be only a variation on the theme. It will never be a genuine liberation, at least not in the sense in which more serious Latin American scholarship conceptualizes liberation.[13]

Reflection along these lines, together with a rapid communication of its conclusions, is regarded as a priority by the liberation Christology being developed on our continent. This reflection is all but nonexistent in writing, or at any rate it is rarely spelled out in theoretical detail. It is practiced mainly in small groups and is communicated in mimeographed documents passed hand to hand.

This brings us to the essential question. From a reflection practiced in these interests, what image of Jesus will emerge? How will Jesus' message and salvific praxis be read?

FRAMEWORK FOR UNDERSTANDING THE HISTORICAL JESUS IN A PERSPECTIVE OF LIBERATION

As we see, a whole Christology is implied here, and while we cannot present it in detail, at least we can propose some theses for discussion.

RELEVANCE OF THE HISTORICAL JESUS FOR LIBERATION

The Christology of liberation developed in its Latin American matrix prioritizes the historical Jesus over the Christ of faith. Why? First, because it sees a structural similarity between Jesus' time and our own—objective oppression and dependency in both instances, experienced subjectively as contrary to the historical plan of God.

Second, the historical Jesus is relevant because in considering him we come into immediate contact with his program for liberation and with his practices (his *deeds*).

Third, reflection on the historical Jesus shows that any liberation practice will stir conflict. It shows us an example of the likely fate in store for anyone mounting a genuine project of liberation.

Fourth, a consideration of the historical Jesus identifies, with perfect clarity, the key element of a christological faith: following Jesus in his life and cause. In this following, or discipleship, the truth of Jesus appears. This truth is proportional, first, to how well it can help persons transform this sinful world into the Reign of God. Second, it is proportional to its capacity to justify itself to human reason in terms of its openness to the infinite. Jesus is seen here, not as an explanation of reality, but as a demand for the transformation of that reality. It is in this sense that Jesus is the definitive explanation of reality.

Fifth, liberation Christology prioritizes the historical Jesus because he reveals the Father to us by showing us the path to that Father. There is no approach to the God of Jesus Christ other than that of conversion and change (a practice). There is no access to God in abstract reflection (theory).

Sixth, the historical Jesus criticizes the human being and society as they present themselves historically. Only through conversion can human beings anticipate and bring into being the Reign of God—God's ultimate intent with regard to the human being and the world. The historical Jesus stands for a crisis in the current world situation, not its justification. Far more than explanation, he demands transformation.

The *full* meaning of the historical Jesus cannot simply be deduced by way of a historical analysis. It is accessible only to a reading that begins with the fullest revelation of his life journey: his resurrection. Far from dispensing us from a historical consideration, however, the light of the Resurrection places us under the obligation of being even more attentive to history. The Gospels themselves demonstrate this.

REIGN OF GOD: UTOPIA OF ABSOLUTE LIBERATION AND THAT UTOPIA'S HISTORICAL ANTICIPATIONS

The historical Jesus preached, systematically, not himself or the Church or God, but the Reign of God. The backdrop of the notion of the Reign of God is the eschatological, apocalyptic understanding that this world as we find it is contrary to God's design, but that God, in this final hour, has determined to intervene and definitively inaugurate his Reign. The Reign of God, then, is the sign that translates this expectancy (Luke 3:15), and it presents itself as the actualization of a utopia of comprehensive, structural, eschatological liberation.

Jesus' singularity consists not in a proclamation that the Reign of God is to come, but in the message that, in his own presence and actions, it is already at hand (Mark 1:15) and in our midst (Luke 17:21). Jesus' fundamental project, then, is to proclaim and be the instrument of the actualization of the absolute meaning of the world: liberation *from* whatever stigmatizes that world—oppression, injustice, suffering, division, sin, death— and liberation *for* life—the open communication of love, freedom, grace, and fullness in God.

The Reign of God is total and universal. It blocks regional, immediate interests, whether religious, political, or social. To regionalize the Reign of God, whether as political power or in any of the frameworks of religious ("sacerdotal") power, or even in the framework of a charismatic ("prophetic") power, is to distort the Reign. This was precisely Jesus' temptation (Matt. 4:1–11), and it was with him all his life (cf. Luke 22:28). In other words, no purely historical liberation defines the final framework of the world and actualizes its utopia. Total liberation, generated by full freedom, constitutes the essence of the Reign of the eschatological goodness of God. History is en route to this goal. Our task is to hasten that process. The Reign of God has an essentially future dimension, one unattainable by human practices; it is the object of eschatological hope.

The Reign of God is not only future and not only a utopia. It is also present, embodied in historical actualities. It is therefore to be regarded as a process, beginning in the world and culminating in final eschatology. In Jesus we encounter the adequate expression of the dialectical tension of the Reign: on the one hand, a proposition of total liberation (the Reign of God); and on the other, mediations (deeds, words, attitudes) that translate this proposition in a historical process. On the one side, the Reign of God is future, to come; on the other, that Reign present and at hand.

Jesus' first public exercise of his ministry, in the synagogue at Nazareth, has a programmatic sense. It proclaims the utopia of the Lord's year of grace, made historical in altogether concrete liberations of persons oppressed or held captive (Luke 4:16–21). This proclamation, this program, emphasizes the material side of human life. The Messiah is the one who effects the liberation of real, actually suffering persons. Happy are the poor, the suffering, the starving, the persecuted, not because their condition embodies a positive value, but because their circumstance of injustice represents a challenge to the justice of the messianic king. Through Jesus, God has taken sides with these persons. The Reign of God as liberation from sin is part of the kernel of Jesus' preaching and of the testimony of the apostles (Luke 24:47; Acts 2:38, 5:31, 13:38). But that Reign must not be interpreted reductionistically by amputating the social and historical dimension of the figure of Jesus as portrayed in Luke. The historical Jesus has taken up the project of the oppressed—which is one of liberation—as well as the conflict it must entail.

Jesus' liberation assumes a twofold aspect. On the one hand, Jesus proclaims a total liberation of all history and not merely of one segment of that history; on the other, he anticipates this totality in a concrete process of partial liberations ever open to this totality. Had Jesus proclaimed a utopia of blessed outcome for the world deprived of any anticipation in history, he would have been fostering human phantasmagorias deprived of all credibility. Had he introduced partial liberations without the perspective of totality and the future, he would have been frustrating the hopes he himself had awakened, and he would have fallen into a self-contradictory immediatism of the Reign. But both dimensions of the Reign of God, the "already" and the "not yet," are found in Jesus' activity and are found there in dialectical tension.

JESUS' PRAXIS: A LIBERATION IN PROCESS

The *acta et facta Jesu*—Jesus' praxes—are to be understood as historical embodiments of the concrete meaning of the Reign of God: a liberating change of situation. In this sense Jesus has a project like that of oppressed groups struggling for liberation.

This is the key to understanding Jesus' miracles. Their meaning does not reside in their character as prodigies. Their meaning is that of signs (in Greek: *erga*, *sēmeia*) of the presence of the Reign of God (cf. Luke 1:20). The mightier one, vanquisher of the merely mighty one, has appeared in this world (cf. Mark 3:27), and the liberation process is under way.

Jesus' attitudes incarnate the Reign and embody his Father's love. He draws near those shunned by all others—the poor, public sinners, the shameless, drunkards, lepers, prostitutes, in short, the socially and religiously marginalized—not out of a mere humanitarian spirit, but because he is the historical embodiment of his Father's loving attitude toward these "least ones" and sinners. Their situation does not represent life's final structure. They are not forever lost. God can deliver them, liberate them.

Jesus' praxis is eminently social and political in nature and attains the very *structure* of the society and religion of his time. Jesus comes forward, neither as an ascetic reformer in the style of the Essenes, nor as a faithful observer of tradition like the Pharisees, but as a prophetic liberator.

Granted, Jesus performs his activity in the religious arena. But the religious element constituted one of the main pillars of political power. Thus all intervention in the religious area had political consequences.

Jesus' praxis with regard to religion, sacred laws, and tradition is one of liberation, not reform: "You have heard the commandment. . . . What I say to you is . . ." (Matt. 5:21, 27, etc.). He relativizes their imagined absolute value. More important than the sabbath, more important than tradition is the human being (Mark 2:23, 26). Our salvation is determined by our attitude toward others (Matt. 25:31–46). Jesus shifts the criteria of salvation. Not orthodoxy but orthopraxis now decides that salvation. Jesus measures the Torah and all the rest of the dogmatics of the Old Testament by the criterion of love, thus delivering human practice from its necrophilic structures.

The proclamation and practice of Jesus postulate a new image of and approach to God. God is no longer the old God of the Torah. Now God is infinitely good, "good to the ungrateful and the wicked" alike (Luke 6:35), approaching us with a grace bestowed apart from a practice of the Torah. God is not a monad, an *ipseitas* (existence unto itself) outside history, revealed only in epiphanies. God is revealed in history, in the act of accomplishing the Reign and thereby transforming the human situation. God is primarily to be regarded from the standpoint of the future, from the outlook of the coming Reign. But that Reign is one of the total liberation from the unjust, wicked mechanisms of the past and of fullness of life as never before experienced. God is not approached primarily in worship—in religious observance or prayer. These practices are genuine but in themselves ambiguous. God is best approached where the approach is unambiguous—in service to the poor, in whom God is truly present, albeit anonymously. The surest pathway to the God of Jesus Christ is the pathway of a liberation praxis.

The liberating character of Jesus' activity appears in his social relationships. Society in Jesus' time and place was extremely stratified. Neighbors were distinguished from strangers, the clean from the unclean, Jews from foreigners, men from women, and observers of the Law from the ignorant, those of ill repute, and the sick, who were regarded as having been struck down for their sins. Jesus enters into solidarity with all of these marginalized persons. For his pains he is slandered as "a glutton and drunkard, a lover of tax collectors and those outside the law" (Matt. 11:19). His irreverent attack on the theologians, Pharisees, and Sadducees has unmistakable social relevance.

Justice occupies a central place in Jesus' proclamation. Jesus declares the poor blessed, not because he regards poverty as a virtue, but because, as the fruit of unjust relationships among persons, it provokes the intervention of the messianic king, whose primary function is to do justice to the poor and defend the rights of the weak. He likewise rejects wealth, which he sees as a dialectical consequence of the exploitation of the poor. He therefore qualifies it directly as dishonorable (Luke 16:9). Jesus' ideal is a society, neither of opulence nor of poverty, but a society of justice and communion among sisters and brothers.

Again, the liberating character of Jesus' criticism of all dominating power (Luke 22:25–28) is demonstrated in his demystifying the idea of domination as coming from God. Jesus' relativization of power extends even to the sacred power of the Caesars, whose divine character (Matt. 22:2) and pretentions to the status of highest cosmic authority (John 19:11) he denies.

The *Pax Romana*, based on domination and subjection, is not an embodiment of the Reign of God.

The praxis of Jesus implies the establishment of a new kind of solidarity, one that transcends class and "natural" differences. Jesus seeks to defend the rights of all, especially of the lowly, the sick, the marginalized, and the poor. Jesus combats all that divides persons—envy, greed, calumny, oppression, hatred, and the like. He champions the spirit of the Beatitudes, which alone can transform this world into a world worthy of the divine regard.

Jesus' appeal for the complete renunciation of vengeance in favor of mercy and forgiveness springs from his keen perception of historical reality. There will always be structures of domination. But this should neither discourage us nor lead us to accept those structures. It only shows us the need for forgiveness, which will always be possible wherever love is strong enough to cope with contradictions and overcome them from within.

Despite his liberating practices, which made the reality of the eschatological Reign historically concrete, Jesus was not preparing to seize political power. He always regarded political power as a temptation of the evil one, inasmuch as it implied a regionalization or limitation of the universal Reign of God. The basic reason for his refusal was his understanding of the Reign of God according to which that Reign, being God's, is historicized only through freedom (conversion) and not by constraint. We must also take account of the cultural background of Jesus' time and place, with its apocalyptic mentality. And indeed the coming of the Reign is a deed of God's grace: we must prepare ourselves for it and anticipate it, but we must not force it. On this point Jesus takes his distance from the Zealots.

In a history with a future—in a world where the *parousia* or Second Coming of Christ is no longer regarded as temporally imminent—we must adapt this attitude of the historical Jesus and give the limits of cultural categories of expression their due. Jesus' attitude does not constitute a reason for theology to deny the value of political power as a legitimate and appropriate way of securing more justice for the marginalized. When subordinated to the rule of service instead of being absolutized, political power can be a tool for rendering the content of the notion of the Reign historically concrete. "Jesus does not advocate a love that is depoliticized, dehistoricized, and destructuralized. He advocates a political love, a love that is situated in history and that has visible repercussions for human beings."[14]

CONVERSION: GOD'S LIBERATION MAKES DEMANDS

The conversion demanded by Jesus is more than a mere change of conviction—a change in theory. It is also, and mainly, a change of attitude—a change bearing directly on practice. Nor is it a change only within a person—a change of heart. It is also a change in that person's living, functioning network of relationships. Considered positively, conversion is the radical modification of relationships in all aspects of personal and social reality, resulting in concrete liberations and thereby anticipating the Reign of God. The personal and social aspects of human life are locked in a reciprocal dialectic.

Conversion must not be understood as a mere condition for the coming of the Reign. It is its very inauguration, presence, and activity in history. Conversion renders the structure of the Reign, the liberation willed by God, visible. On the one hand, it constitutes a gift offered and received. On the other, it is an acceptance that becomes real to the extent that people cooperate in establishing the Reign through personal, political, social, and religious actions.

The Reign of God and the liberation it implies are typical of God's exercise of power. The divine power does not dominate human freedom. It is an offer and appeal to freedom and to freedom's deed, love. The Reign of God comes on the scene as proposition, not imposition. Under historical conditions, then, the Reign of God comes only if a person welcomes it and enters upon a process of conversion or liberation.

The proclamation of the presence of the Reign does not invalidate the historical struggle. The total liberation proposed by God advances by way of partial liberations. The latter are not the cause of the former, but they do anticipate and prepare for it. Hence a human being is never a mere spectator, any more than God is a magical gift giver.

Conversion reveals the dimension of conflict in the Reign. Jesus' good news is good only for the converted. It is not good news for the hypocrite who remains a hypocrite or for the champions of discrimination against persons. For all of these it is bad news. Thus Jesus and his proclamation effect a division among human beings, a division that is the essence of the Reign. We can enter into it only by breaking with this world and changing it, not by extending its structure. Jesus addresses all. He addresses the poor as one of their number and takes up their cause. He addresses the Pharisees by unmasking their self-sufficiency. He addresses the rich by denouncing the mechanisms of their injustice and their worship of mammon.

Finally, he died "so that it might be known that not everything is permissible in this world."[15]

The historical Jesus refused to countenance the imposition of God's will by force. This would have exempted human beings from their task of liberation. Women and men would no longer have been the agents of their own personal and social transformation but merely its beneficiaries. Jesus preferred death to the imposition of the Reign of God by violence. He could do no other; else it would not have been the Reign of God that appeared but a realm created by the will of human power, a reign based on subjugation and the privation of freedom.

JESUS' DEATH: COST OF GOD'S LIBERATION

Jesus' death was intimately connected with his life, his proclamation, and his practices. His calls for conversion, his new image of God, his freedom in observing or not observing tradition, his prophetic criticism of prevailing political, economic, and religious power provoked a conflict that ended in his violent death.

Jesus did not seek death. It was imposed on him from without. Nor did he accept it with resignation. He accepted it as an expression of his freedom and his loyalty to the cause of God and human beings. Isolated, rejected, and imperiled, he refused to strike a compromise with the privilege of power in order to survive. Instead, he kept faith with his mission of proclaiming the good news to all who would embrace conversion. He freely accepted the death imposed on him by the existing circumstances.

The cross is the symbol of the reign of power in its own service. Religious power is no exception. It was the devout who martyred Jesus. Whenever a present moment freezes and ossifies, it conceals the future and absolutizes itself. It checks the process of liberation and strengthens the mechanisms of oppression.

Freely embraced, death reveals a total freedom from oneself and one's projects. When endured for love, in solidarity with the vanquished of history, in forgiveness of those who have inflicted it, and in self-surrender to God despite the historical failure, our death is a demonstration that the Reign of God becomes real in history.

The motives for Jesus' murder were twofold, and structural. First, Jesus was sentenced as a *blasphemer*, for presenting a different God from that of the religious status quo.

Jesus exposed the subjugation of human beings in the name of religion. He exposed religious hypocrisy, which prostitutes the mystery of God as an excuse for closing one's ears to the demands of justice. In this sense the religious powers saw aright: Jesus preached a God who was the enemy of theirs.[16]

Second, Jesus' attitude was eminently liberating, and this is why he was rejected. At the hands of the political authorities he was sentenced to death as a *guerrilla*. His preaching and his attitudes were indeed akin to the words and deeds of Zealotism: his hope in the coming of the Reign of God, his radicalism, his statements about a "Kingdom that suffers violence, and the violent bear it away," his freedom vis-à-vis the established imperial power, his influence over a people who sought to make him their leader. And yet he remained distant from the whole spirit of Zealotism, renouncing a politically religious messianism based on power and hence incapable of making God's Reign concrete. The Reign of God is based on a more radical, all-embracing liberation, one that overcomes all breach of communion and that calls for a new human being.

The cross demonstrates the conflict inherent in any liberation process under structures of injustice. In these conditions liberation is possible only in the form of martyrdom and sacrifice on behalf of others and of God's cause in the world. Jesus consciously chose and adopted this path.

JESUS' RESURRECTION: ANTICIPATED IRRUPTION OF DEFINITIVE LIBERATION

Jesus' resurrection was of a piece with his life, death, and proclamation of the Reign of God. The Reign of God is the term for total liberation. But, as we see, Jesus' life was a liberated, liberating life and his death a completely free act of self-surrender. Thus his resurrection actualizes the complete liberation of the Reign of God and actualizes it in its eschatological form. The authentic Reign of God had been rejected by the people of Jesus' time and place. Hence it could not become concrete then and there in its universal, cosmic dimension. Instead it found its eschatological realization in token and in an individual: in the resurrection of one who had been crucified. As Origen put it, Jesus is *autobasileia tou Theou*—"God's Reign in person."

In other words, Jesus' resurrection is the triumph of life *simpliciter:* the concrete expression of all of life's latent potentialities, liberation from all of life's obstacles and historical conflicts. It is eschatological reality "already," and as such reveals God's ultimate intention for human beings and the world.

Jesus' resurrection reveals a life concealed in Jesus that could not be swallowed up in death: liberation in fullness, coming in the form of the grace of God. The Resurrection points toward the goal of every authentic process of liberation: total freedom.

The resurrection of the crucified one shows that to die as Jesus died, for others and for God, is not without meaning. The anonymous death of all the vanquished of history, for justice' sake—for the sake of openness and ultimate meaning in human life—finds its explanation in Jesus' resurrection. The Resurrection delivers us from history's most blatant absurdity: the sacrifice of one's life in anonymity. "The question of resurrection arises precisely from the fact of insurrection."[17] In Jesus' resurrection we have all the palpable evidence we could possibly require that "the hangman does not triumph over the victim."[18]

The meaning of the total liberation that constitutes Jesus' resurrection appears only when that resurrection is placed side by side with Jesus' struggle to establish the Reign of God in this world. Otherwise it degenerates into a devout cynicism toward the injustices of this world, allied with an idealism totally innocent of the facts of history. By his resurrection Jesus continues his life among us, inspiring our struggle for liberation. All genuinely human growth, all authentic justice in social relationships, all enhancement of life constitutes a mini-resurrection—a self-actualization, a self-anticipation, and a preparation for one's future completion.

Any Christology must be a systematic effort to decifer the reality of Jesus' life, death, resurrection, and ascension. Therefore it must take the resurrection event as its starting point and its explanatory background. It was the resurrection that enabled the first Christian communities to develop, to make explicit, the titles of grandeur of Jesus Christ, culminating in their profession of faith, "Jesus is the Christ, the Son of God, very God with us."

FOLLOWING JESUS AS A PATH TO PERSONAL LIBERATION

Human life during the postponement of the coming of the Reign as fullness of liberation has a paschal structure, manifested in the discipleship of Jesus Christ crucified and raised from the dead. This discipleship includes, first, proclaiming the utopia of the Reign as the full meaning of a world that is good and offered by God to all.

Second, discipleship means furnishing that utopia with anticipatory elements, through practices calculated to change the present world in its personal, social, and cosmic aspects. The utopia of the Reign is not ideology, but it does supply a foundation for functional ideologies by orienting and guiding liberation practices. The following of Jesus is never a slavish imitation. Discipleship presupposes a capacity to distinguish between divergent existential situations: that of Jesus, with his apocalyptic background of the imminent irruption of the Reign, and our own, in which history has a future, as the Reign has been postponed. The choice of organizational tactics of love and justice in society depends on these differences. Obviously, for Jesus as for us, God is future. The Reign of God is not only "already" but also "not yet." However, the manner in which history must be taken in hand changes constantly. Jesus has prescribed, not a concrete model of an *ideal* concrete history, but a *particular* mode of becoming present in a given historical circumstance. The common, ideal element in Jesus' formula consists in his option for the wronged, his renunciation of the will to power and domination, and his solidarity with any genuine token of a more participatory society of sisters and brothers, children of the same divine Parent. It is the task of his disciples to filter this common element through the sieve of the relativity of their respective historical circumstances and thus adapt it to those circumstances in a way that will be genuine and effective.

Third, God's liberation is expressed in a liberation process that implies struggle and conflict. This struggle, this conflict must be accepted and embraced in light of Jesus' own journey. That is, it must be accepted with a love that may be required to sacrifice itself, with an eschatological hope that must pass by way of political hopes, and with a faith that must move ahead gropingly because we do not have the key to political and economic problems just because we are Christians. Jesus' cross and resurrection are the eminent paradigms of Christian existence.

To follow Jesus is to pursue his work, further his cause, and thereby attain to his fullness.

This vision—with all the limits of a vision—seeks to place itself at the service of the political, social, economic, and religious liberation of our oppressed peoples. It is an attempt to contribute, at the level of theoretical expression, to the illumination and enrichment of an already existing praxis of liberating faith.

In a dependent third world, our Christian faith, formulated and lived historically, guides us to an ideological option for liberation. That is, it inclines us to use a specific kind of social analysis, by reason of a specific existential commitment of faith. In our context, surely, to read the gospel and follow Jesus in ways divorced from liberation is to plant our feet firmly in midair. Such a reading would constantly oblige us to submit to an ideological interpretation of our faith, in the pejorative sense of the word.

There are many ways of preaching the Reign of God. It can be proclaimed as the *other* world God is preparing for us, a world to come only when this life is over and done. Or it can be preached as the Church, which represents Jesus and prolongs his project, through worship, dogmatics, institutions, and sacraments. But both of these conceptualizations of the Reign of

God bracket the Christian task and obligation of building a world of more justice and broader social and political participation in view of the Reign. Both of these approaches to proclaiming the Reign of God withdraw us from the problem of the oppression of millions of our sisters and brothers.

Finally, then, we can proclaim the Reign of God as the utopia of a world of full reconciliation anticipated, prepared, and initiated in history itself through the commitment of men and women of goodwill. We hold this last interpretation to be the one that expresses the *ipsissima intentio Jesu*, Jesus' precise intention, on the historical level as well as the theological. The function of Christology is to develop and mold a Christian option in society.

IMPORTANCE OF A LIBERATION CHRISTOLOGY FOR THE UNIVERSAL CHRISTOLOGICAL TASK

We must not imagine that this new Christology is important for Latin America alone, where we experience in our very flesh the anomaly of underdevelopment as a phenomenon of subjugation.[19] As we have seen, our circumstances in Latin America are the product of a particular set of international relations between rich nations and poor ones. We in the poor countries constitute only one pole of the relationship. The theologians of the other pole have the problem as much as we do. They too must face this challenge to Christian conscience. They too will find that it imposes a particular orientation on christological meditation and living. It is not indifferent to us here how theologians of the economically central nations articulate their Christology. Christology has a political dimension. It can reinforce the attitude and behavior of the determining pole, the pole bearing the main responsibility for the unjust balance, or it can counter that attitude and behavior.

The problem facing christologists of the center is not how to lend assistance but how to do justice. Current international relations violate the basic rights of nations, violently maintaining underdeveloped countries in their modes of underdevelopment while concealing the entire unjust mechanism under the cloak of progress and friendly relations. This can easily deceive local and regional churches and disarm the theological intelligentsia.

Not infrequently progressive, secularizing, enlightenment theologies, critical in the extreme, mask conservative political positions and function to ideologically reinforce the status quo. Other theologies are liberating in intention but lack a sufficiently critical analysis of the prevailing system and thereby support the structural practice of paternalism through assistance.

In Latin America, the mechanisms of subjugation are more open and visible. They leap out at you. Thus it has been easier for theology to call itself into question here and to search out theoretical practices calculated to support a liberation project. In Europe and North America, these same mechanisms are present (since this is where the decision-making centers that control our economic, political, and cultural conditions are found), but they are present in more subtle and refined forms. This makes it more difficult for theologians of the North to arrive at a liberating social and theological position. They can do so, however, by adjusting their analytical instruments and by maintaining a more in-depth, more consistent critical distance.

We in Latin America dream—may we not dream?—of the day when the privileged intellectual community of European theology will grasp the importance for their churches and their societies of promoting a process of liberation from injustice. These are the theologians of the primary pole of our unequal relationship, and they could be of incalculable help to their brothers and sisters on our continent in opening the floodgates of the project of liberation. The theology of liberation and the concept of Jesus Christ the Liberator stand for a reality steeped in misery. They stand for the oppressed Christians of our continent, who cry out in pain and batter on the door of their wealthy brothers and sisters. And what do these oppressed ask? Everything and nothing. They ask only to be allowed to be people. They ask to be accepted as persons. They ask only that they be permitted to fight for the release of their captive freedom.

If the Christology of liberation makes a contribution to this messianic task, it will have fulfilled its prophetic mission. It will have been worthy of the sacred name of Jesus Christ, who wished for nothing in this world but to be able to liberate all persons in fullness.

7. Liberation in Fullness, the Christian Utopia

The theology of liberation is bound up with concrete practices undertaken by or in behalf of the poor. It therefore runs the risk of losing the broad perspective of Christian hope. Christian hope thrusts us not only toward liberations that are historical, hence never more than partial, but also toward a liberation in fullness, in the Christ event—in Jesus Christ who lived, died, and was raised again. Christians strive for a utopia: a state of absolute liberation, to be enjoyed by the individual, society, and the world. From this utopia, whose anticipation we celebrate in faith, springs our certitude that the cause of the oppressed is destined to triumph. Christians must continually reflect on their hope, lest they succumb to worldly sorrow (2 Cor. 7:10), lest they surrender to a sense of impotence in the face of the enormous obstacles thrown in the way of their utopia by the powers of oppression.

For Christian faith, there can never be a full social and historical anticipation of the liberation God wills for his sons and daughters. Only the event of Jesus Christ possesses the fullness of that liberation. The Church is Christ's sacrament, not Christ himself. The Church must itself be liberated, day after day. The Church is always a pilgrim Church, both holy and sinful.

Let us reflect briefly on full liberation in Jesus Christ as the mainstay of our pilgrimage. Our considerations will be anthropological, since the realization of the Christian utopian dream is anthropological.[1] The apostolic faith clearly professes that the new person—the human being fully free of internal flaws and external failure, the human being delivered from every kind of servitude—has at last emerged, has "imploded" and exploded, in the history of Jesus Christ. The longings of all the anthropologies—the ancient myths, the most ancestral dreams—have at length been realized. In one who was raised from the dead, Jesus of Nazareth, this new being, this person of reconciliation, this vehicle of the irruption of anthropological eschatology in the midst of history has appeared in the flesh. The whole of Christianity's contribution to comprehending the human drama is concentrated in its witness to and rational articulation of this event. From their immersion in the event of Jesus Christ, Christians understand what human beings are, what they are called to, and what future is in store for the reality around them. For suddenly the future has appeared in the midst of the present.

EMERGENCE OF THE NEW HUMAN BEING, JESUS CHRIST

The event that is Jesus Christ is important for defining the human, and it shows it in two ways. One approach concentrates on our decadent condition, focusing on the "nonhuman being." The other focuses on our utopian potential. It bears on the *homo eschatologicus*—the *homo revelatus*. Initially, Jesus of Nazareth is perceived simply as the human being who recovers our genuine identity as human. He takes nonhuman beings and makes them human. This in itself is liberation—the liberating aspect of the Christian event. But then we proclaim Jesus as the Christ, too. As the Christ, Jesus realizes the human utopia, introducing us into our eschatological state. Once more, this is the liberating dimension of the Christian mystery. Christ delivers us to our true and full realization as human beings. On the one side, Jesus is manifested and believed in as the human being of the *Ecce Homo*, the genuinely human person. On the other, he is the *homo novissimus*, the eschatological, new person. Let us examine these two lines of reflection.

JESUS OF NAZARETH: *ECCE HOMO*

For those who associated with and understood him, Jesus of Nazareth in his historical pilgrimage represented the realization of true humanity. That humanity resides in the complex knot of our relationships with all reality in which we function as sovereigns of nature, brothers and sisters of one another, and daughters and sons of God. Jesus of Nazareth rendered this human essence completely and absolutely concrete. In him was not a trace of the sundering within us whereby we are at once human and nonhuman. The Gospel accounts show us a human being whose whole existence consisted in being for others. They show us someone who passed through this world doing good—forgiving others, consoling them, and opening them to liberation, their neighbors, and God.

Jesus was a *child of God* in all radicality. The divine project in Jesus did not destroy the human project. Jesus experienced an extreme intimacy with his divine Parent, calling God *Abba*. He felt himself to be and lived as an obedient child of God, attentive to his Parent's voice and always ready to do God's will rather than his own. None of the rift between human and divine that characterizes decadent human experience could be found in Jesus' relation with God. He had no sin for which to beg forgiveness; he only strove to remain faithful (Mark 14:36 and par.). Nor did he experience any distance between himself and God, as would a sinner who has accepted a process of conversion. He lived an intimacy and spontaneity that constituted a unique religious phenomenon (cf. John 10:30). He appears as the *homo matinalis*, the human being in the state of original justice. He did not experience this dimension of God as the result of ascetic effort or as the goal of a journey of internalization or as the culmination of a closed life that gradually opens to mystery. No, in Jesus of Nazareth the divine irrupts in all its diaphany and epiphany, as in someone seized and possessed, someone who simply *is* this way by creation and birth.

Jesus appears before us neither as a theologian nor as a mystic. For both of these, God represents the goal of an entire life of striving. For Jesus, God is rather an immediate experience. Jesus is no *homo religiosus* then, someone living in a sacred order. Rather he is a secularized and secularizing person. For him there are no sacred and profane spaces. Jesus is always in the presence of the God who pervades all, who is as visible in the lilies of the field as in the sacred words of Scripture, in the temple, or in that ineffable Holy of Holies known only to the Utterly Other.

Jesus lives in another dimension from the rest of humankind. He lives as a child in his Father's house with his brothers and sisters. In Jesus has appeared the whole concrete reality of filiation—a child of God in all the fullness of that condition from one end of life's journey to the other. Jesus is dependent on his Father in all things. And yet in him the child is not an infant, as in the case of a neurotically dependent adult. Jesus is altogether grown up. He has his own route to take and his own project to carry out. He is a full and genuine individual, and he relates to God as an I to a Thou. He enjoys a strong, free identity.

In Jesus has likewise appeared the model of the human being as sister or brother of others. His relationship with his neighbor is not one of superiority, which would humiliate that neighbor. He is open to all without discrimination, to the point of causing scandal in the devout. Everyone is his neighbor, from the moment he approaches that person. Jesus draws near to all, especially to the socially and religiously marginalized and slandered, to the lowly, to the damned of the earth. And he makes of his neighbor a brother or a sister. As all men and women are children of his heavenly Father (Matt. 23:9), Jesus can regard them all as sisters and brothers of himself and of one another. He calls the lowliest persons on earth "my brothers," and he would have us recognize himself present within them (Matt. 25:40).

The relationship Jesus establishes with his fellow human beings is not legalistic, formal, or classist. It is a relationship of radical communion. Jesus receives everyone as his brother or sister—Jew, pagan, poor, sinful, oppressed, and oppressor. "No one who comes will I ever reject" (John 6:37). The supreme commandment is to love one's brothers and sisters, a love that ought to characterize his community (cf. Matt. 12:49 and par., 23:8, 28:10; John 20:17; Luke 22:32). Among sisters and brothers is no longer any servitude, only service. This is what Jesus preaches and demands—the kind of relationship that ought to obtain among human beings—and this is what he himself lives, in unquestioned radicality (Mark 10:45 and par.). Surely the Sermon on the Mount is the ideal model of any baptized Christian's discipleship. But prior to this it is a description of the new human being that was Jesus, the person who fulfilled the meaning of being human.

Jesus' behavior toward the world is that of responsible sovereignty. We find no selfish attachments in him, no preoccupation with business. On the contrary, his warnings concerning wealth are unfailing: wealth enslaves. People worship wealth, and this is idolatry (Luke 19:16–21, 16:13, 12:15, 22:31). He condemns the wealth that enslaves as well as the poverty that demeans (cf. Luke 6:20–26). Jesus urges upon us a solidarity with those who have less, a solidarity to be expressed by sharing (Luke 11:41, 6:30, 38). He summons people, not to flee from the world, but to be responsible for one another—responsible for justice, truth, respect, and honest work. Jesus is sovereign, and sovereignly free: "My father is at work until now, and I am at work as well" (John 5:17).

Jesus' praxis as God's Son, our Brother, and sovereign of the world, delivers us from our condition as God's rebellious children, the enslavers of our brothers and sisters, and despots over nature. In Jesus, for the first time in history, a human being has emerged who is genuinely free of the shackles of history that have oppressed human beings and prevented them from becoming what they feel to be their calling and fulfillment.

A study of the praxis of the historical Jesus is relevant for theology. We must know what human being we long for. Jesus makes genuine humanism utterly concrete. The reduction of Christology to a study of the Christ of faith, Jesus Christ as interpreted by the community, without any concern for the experience of the historical Jesus—Christology without Jesuology—impoverishes Christianity's comprehensive vision.

Jesus does not proclaim a myth. He does not fan the flickering flames of a utopia in the wild blue yonder. He preaches a historical event, an actual, concrete *topos*. In Jesus the new person bursts upon the scene of our everyday reality, the person of Jesus of Nazareth. Jesus is important for us because in him we see and know and can follow what a person can and ought to be: a child of God, a sister or brother to others, and sovereign in the fresh dawn of the new creation. Jesus of Nazareth delivers persons from their nonpersonhood. He delivers their captive liberty to enlist it in his own exploit, the deed he has been called to accomplish.

Jesus' free, brotherly, sovereign, and filial life provoked a crisis in his world, where abnormality had convinced the world that it was order, where persons considered it normal to walk with their feet in the air and their heads scraping the earth. Then Jesus came and practiced another practice. He made human beings human again.

He was taken for insane, subversive, possessed, a heretic, an atheist. He was rejected in the name of the God that religious culture had constructed and in the name of the humanism that nonhumanism had erected. The manner in which Jesus accepted this conflict, assimilated this crisis, bore his cross, and underwent death shows once more his profound humanity. He does not flee, he does not turn his back, he does not concede. He embraces his lot, he forgives, he suffers for the multitudes, and he dies in absolute surrender to the persons who killed him and the God who seemed to abandon him.

To die thus is a worthy thing. It liberates the human person from the dominion exercised by death over life. Death no longer has the last word. There are values for which it is worthy to give one's life. Death is embraced in a project that reaches beyond this life; thus it is overcome and integrated. Because Jesus submitted to everyone, he conquered everyone. He became Lord. But he became Lord not by imposing his power, divine or human, on anyone. He became Lord through service and through love without limit (see Phil. 2:5–11). Contemplating Jesus' historical journey—holding before his eyes the *Homo* of the *Ecce Homo*—Paul could demand of the community: "Your attitude"—your praxis—"must be that of Christ" (Phil. 2:5). The apostle proceeds to describe the stages of Jesus' act of service, a service to all men and women, to the very solitude of death. The discipleship of the historical Jesus is an attempt to implement Project Human Being in everyone alive—and in the ambiguity of a Project Human Being that must be realized in the presence of Project Nonhuman Being.

JESUS CHRIST: THE ESCHATOLOGICAL NEW HUMAN BEING

Jesus of Nazareth not only liberated human beings *from* something—from their inhumanity, thus restoring to them their genuine humanity. He did much more. He liberated human beings *for* something—for the complete revelation of the human person according to God's design. Through his resurrection, Jesus steps forward as the new and final Adam (1 Cor. 15:45), as the human being already come to his final term, the human being who shatters the frontiers of history and plunges into the sea of absolute fulfillment in God. *Homo absconditus*, who had groaned under the weight of history, is now fully *Homo revelatus*. The human being willed by God from everlasting is here.

Deprived of the Resurrection, we should find ourselves still moving along the horizons of the old human being, still on the way toward our radical humanity in sheer hope, looking to the future alone. But with Jesus' resurrection the fullness of time has already come (Gal. 4:4). The former age has passed away, and the eschatological age has dawned. In Jesus' resurrection we celebrate a definitive present. We are in some sense transported to anthropological consummation and fullness.

We must understand the Resurrection correctly if we hope to reap all of its fruit for humanity. Jesus' resurrection does not concern him alone; it concerns all human beings. In it is unveiled God's ultimate intention for human existence, a calling to life, not death. This is the will of its Creator and Liberator. Resurrection is not the resuscitation of a corpse. It does not mean a return to the kind of life a person had before—biological, mortal, and subject to limitations of every order. Resurrection is the enthronement of the earthly human being. Resurrection means having a spirit-body in the life of the Reign of God. Resurrection is human reality at last actualized in all of its latent possibilities, which now unfold and come to their complete flowering. Resurrection is the total extrapolation of the human being into God. Resurrection is the concretion of what is dearest to the utopian part of the human heart: a dream of the Reign of God.

In an attempt to formulate this new mode of existence—a risen existence—Paul coined the expression *spiritual body* (*sōma pneumatikon*, 1 Cor. 15:44). As for the precise meaning of these two words, let us notice that they have a Hebrew rather than a Greek meaning. *Body* here does not have the meaning it has in Greek—one part of a human being distinct from the other, the soul. In the Bible, *body* is the entire human being—and precisely as person, communicating in, communicating itself to, and forming the network of vital relationships with surrounding reality. *Body*, then, is synonymous with *person*.

The word *spirit* denotes the specifically divine mode of existence. *Spirit* (in Hebrew, *ruach;* in Greek, *pneuma*) constitutes the life of God—Life immutable, immortal, eternal, full, omnipresent, pervading and filling the cosmos. To say that the risen one is now a spiritual body is equivalent to saying Jesus of Nazareth, in his concrete, personal reality (his "I," his ego) now exists transfigured and transformed into the very life of God. Previously he existed in *sarx*, in the flesh. Now he exists in *pneuma*, in the spirit. To exist in the form of flesh means being "subject to decay" and "ignoble." Paul calls such an existence "weakness." To live in the form of spirit is to be "incorruptible" and "glorious"; this is "strength." Our previous, corporeal existence has been "natural"—"psychic," or belonging to a merely human soul. Now our corporeal existence is "pneumatic"—heavenly, or eschatological (1 Cor. 15:42–43).

A risen existence, then, is one's exhaustively realized existence in God. It is, in a sense, such a communion with the mystery of God that God becomes "all in all"—everything in all things (1 Cor. 15:28). It is complete communion, cosmic omnipresence, and mutual interpenetration with all spiritual, material, heavenly, and divine realities.

Jesus Christ raised from the dead is proclaimed to be the Messiah, the Son of God, God among us. Jesus is God himself in human incarnation, God forming with a human being an indissociable, immutable, and permanent oneness. Thus this human being becomes divinized, and God becomes humanized. Christ is the encounter of God and the human being. Christ is the realization, the actualization of the most radical and daring utopia of the human heart: the longing to be "like gods" (Gen. 3:5), to be as God. While remaining completely the person we are, at the same time we are totally extrapolated from ourselves to full communion and union with God.

Jesus who lived, died, and was raised from the dead is the realization and consummation of all human reality. Not only is the *homo* of the *Ecce Homo* delivered from nonpersonhood, then; but *Homo revelatus, Homo eschatologicus* has reached total culmination as well, to be completely reborn for good and all. Thus is realized the absolute utopia: oneness with the divinity. The process of humanization has reached its term in Jesus Christ raised, our Brother and God's Son, divine revelation and human gladness.

NOVISSIMUS ADAM AND THE PERSISTENCE OF THE OLD ADAM

Novissimus Adam, the "last Adam," the new and definitive Adam (1 Cor. 15:45), therefore constitutes the hermeneutic locus where Christian faith may read God's ultimate intention for humanity. From the starting point of this definitive event, the entire history of Jesus takes on a transcendent meaning. The history of the people among whom Jesus Christ was born and lived likewise becomes meaningful, since this is the people in whose midst occurs the event that will be most decisive for human history: the solution of the problem of the human being.

However, new being did not achieve its cosmic realization. Jesus was rejected. He was crucified. As a result, new being has been realized only in the reality of Jesus Christ. Nature and history live under the sign of the old Adam. New eschatological being is present only in Jesus raised. And yet history and nature are charged with something utterly new: they *contain* new, eschatological being, the being that is eschatologically realized by anticipation. Jesus is realized eschatology, and as such he represents the end of history in a twofold sense. First, history has reached its end in the sense of a goal. There is nothing more to be hoped for, salvifically, that has not already happened in Jesus who lived, died, and was raised again. Second, history has reached its end in the sense of fullness, since Jesus' resurrection is the fulfillment of the human being in God.

New being, now present, is realized only alongside a humanity in disrepair. At the heart of the former age is a new core, a new center, a new axis—a yeast capable of revolutionizing all things and moving in the direction of eschatological fullness. Human beings under the sign of the old Adam can now share in the *novissimus Adam*. Between the Ascension and the Second Coming is an interim, an intermediate time of sharing, discipleship, and celebration of the new eschatological being, Jesus Christ, under the conditions of our stifled existence in process of liberation. This is the time of the Church.

Two basic tasks are set before us as human beings. One, the more basic task, is to follow the new human being Jesus. But following Jesus does not mean blindly imitating his words, deeds, praxis, life, and death. It means having the same attitude as Jesus (Phil. 2:5). It means seeking to have the same experience as Jesus and thus to be, by participation, "new creation" (2 Cor. 5:17). At the root of this new being we discover a new praxis—an imitation of Jesus that is not the hypocrisy of external deeds but the expression of an internal, new, filled and fulfilled truth.

Our second task is to celebrate the presence of the new Human Being in our midst. We worship him, we revere him, we proclaim him to our fellow humans as their hope and future as the denouement of the human drama in the form of a liberation. Praxis and worship, conversion and celebration, task and festival have always constituted the great moments of the Christian mystery. We struggle to put off the old human being and put on the new. It is a painful, burdensome, dramatic struggle, and it is without respite. At the same time it instills in us a serene joy, for we are assisting in the victory of life over death, of love over hatred. We are witnesses to the happy ending of the human drama. We are not doomed to live the anguish of a Sisyphus or the ridiculous *hybris* of a Prometheus. Myth is not the last word. Sisyphus has pushed his rock to the mountain top. Prometheus has returned to the house of the gods. Jesus Christ raised is the reality and symbol of existence. To declare Jesus of Nazareth to be the Christ is to profess utopia to have become *topos*. To declare Jesus of Nazareth to be the Christ is to use the eschatological symbol of the Christ, the Messiah, to testify that, amidst this old world and these sinful human beings, a new world is in ferment. A leaven is at work in the dough. Jesus Christ is already free. One of our number is totally liberated—free at last.

8. For What May We Hope Beyond the Skies?

We now address the loftiest question of human existence. What is the ultimate meaning of freedom? For what are human beings free? Must we not be delivered utterly from ourselves and only then be genuinely free? Broadening our horizon still further: the most disquieting question that can be posed in anthropological terms is not "What is the human being?" but "For what can the human being hope?" We might reformulate the latter question as follows: To what are we ultimately called? What is the human being's definitive framework?

LEVELS OF APPROACH, LEVELS OF RESPONSE

It is difficult to enunciate our question in such radical, ultimate terms. In our culture we generally pose certain intermediate questions instead, contenting ourselves with intermediate answers.

We understand life as the fulfillment of historical tasks, as the fulfillment of a calling completely inscribed within the limits of this life, between birth and death. Surely we already have an abundance of challenges and responsibilities right here! For example, to what are we called, in this life, in psychological terms? We are called to a process of personalization capable of creating an ego vigorous enough to relate to and integrate the sea of realities that surge and plunge around it: the dynamisms of the unconscious; the intimidations of the conscious; the provocations of the sensory world; the encounter of otherness in other persons; the successes and failures of human existence.

For what can we hope in this life in social terms? At best we hope that we can discharge our social role in the network of social relationships in such a way as neither to be swallowed by the role we represent nor live in permanent conflict with it; and that our position in the overall process may contribute to a growth in partnership, equality, and social participation for the greatest possible number of human beings.

On and on, the various segments of human knowledge project an image of the human being and society, each slice of knowledge having its own theories, practices, values, and expectations. All of the sciences project utopias. They present the ideal (Max Weber's *Idealtypus*) toward which the human being should hope to move in order to approach perfection.

Each of these complex visions affords us a wealth of material for faith reflections. Faith, in the light of the word of God and sacred tradition, reads the presence of grace or sin in such views. It discerns in each of these various ideals its respective degree of compatibility with or departure from God's design as manifested in the life of Jesus Christ. It judges human projects in their ethical quality: do they open out to our ultimate destiny in God, or are they closed in upon themselves in a personal or collective selfishness? Faith ascribes supreme importance to such a reading. After all, faith knows that salvation and perdition are at stake in everything. For faith there is no merely natural, neutral order outside the scope of grace and sin. Everything we do, even our smallest act, whether or not it consciously refers to God, is related to salvation or perdition, to absolute realization or absolute frustration.

The community of the faithful renders this objective, implicit reality explicit, in doctrine, worship, and praxis. But the realities of salvation and perdition overflow the limits of religious consciousness. They exist even where they are not explicitly recognized. Therefore the personal and social utopias projected by psychology, sociology, political science, economics, cultural anthropology, the sciences of communication, and the various philosophies are of interest to faith. Faith knows that these channels are vehicles of grace or sin, justice or injustice, humanity or inhumanity, and anonymous acceptance or rejection of God.

As we see, it is the task of faith to formulate responses to various human projects. And it is the task of theology, as the learned, regulated discourse of faith, coherently and intelligibly to articulate faith's stance toward social and historical realities in terms of their approach to or withdrawal from God.

But faith does more. Faith is not concerned only with a religious and theological reading and elucidation of reality. It not only creates a reflection *pro paganis*, as the church fathers expressed it, a reflection for nonbelievers. It also composes a reading *pro Christianis*, for Christians themselves. In other words, faith not only passes judgment on the utopia of others; it develops its own utopia for persons and society. With its own versatile brush and rich palette, faith paints a picture of the future. Here the incarnation of God in Jesus Christ—his life, his historical project of liberation, his violent death, his resurrection, and the consequent presence of the Holy Spirit in our history— are the cardinal elements of the positive side, the utopian side. In terms of the vision of faith: to what, when all is said and done, are we called?

THE CHRISTIAN PERSONAL AND SOCIAL UTOPIA

Faith must hand down a verdict on persons and society. It must seek the meaning of meanings, the transcendent meaning of all historical meanings, a framework calculated to establish humanity's definitive situation. Obviously, then, it must move outside the limits of history. The ultimate meaning of life can only be transhistorical.

For what can we hope, then, in terms of absolute human realization?

1. By way of a preliminary, as yet external, response, faith says: We are called to heaven. Heaven, or the sky, is a religious symbol borrowed from the uranic religions, which employed this spatial representation to indicate that the transcendent, the infinite, that which appears as empirically inaccessible to us (like the sky over our heads) is actually our (and the world's) absolute realization in the future. Christianity says the same. Disastrous as history may seem, it is destined for a happy ending. Everything—human beings, living nature, and the cosmos—lives to die, yes. But it also dies to live. Resurrection implies a great deal more than the perpetuation of life beyond death. Resurrection

represents a form of life so full, so flawless, that death will be unable to wedge its way in. The process of nature and history does not end in cosmic catastrophe. Rather, it is consummated in perfection. On the human level, this denouement is not predetermined. Human beings are free to do as they will. Consummation in God is ordained only for those who have lived a life so that objectively, in their practices, and not only subjectively, in their convictions and consciences, they have shifted the center of their existence to something greater than their own lives.

Here is an outlook charged with optimism. It proclaims the favorable outcome of the processes of our present history—processes whose drama and conflict of themselves scarcely tend toward consummation in convergence! But faith shows us a God who is sovereign of all history, who can write straight with crooked lines, who knows the secret of the reintegration of dissonance into harmony, and who recalls all things to the font from which all have proceeded. It is profoundly heartening and animating to know that, ultimately, meaning will triumph over all historical absurdities.

2. To profess that we are called to heaven is to profess a great deal. But it is not everything. What is this heaven like? What does it mean concretely—for existence, for the world? It is not enough to know that we have dropped anchor in a safe haven. What is the landscape, what is the climate here? To what land have we come?

Theologically, the first thing to be said is that heaven is profoundly human. That is, all of the dynamisms of goodness, truth, beauty, and identity in the human being and the cosmos will converge utterly, to burst into full bloom. We think of heaven, then, as hearth and home, identity, felicity, goodness, reality's self-encounter in utter transparency. All destructuring, dismantling conflicts will be resolved, and utopian growth, development, and fulfillment—free of charge, to beings accustomed to paying for happiness in the coin of suffering—will become real.

The second part of the answer is more profound and more commensurate with the reality under consideration. Heaven is radically divine. We shall see, we shall relish, we shall be united with God as God actually is. We shall discover ourselves to be sprung from the divine, eternal source. We shall feel that source penetrating us and constituting us in the most intimate recesses of our being. We shall contemplate all things in God. We shall be privileged to assist with and share in the "self-generation" of the triune God—Father, Son, and Holy Spirit. Heaven is a new world—a new sky and a new land (Rev. 21:1)—where God will be all in all (1 Cor. 15:29).

Had its content not been revealed by God, faith could not accept its own utterances. And indeed, at the summit, at the vertex of mystery, a reverent silence communicates more than the chatter of our words. The apostle cites the prophet Isaiah: "Eye has not seen, ear has not heard, nor has it so much as dawned on man what God has prepared for those who love him" (1 Cor. 2:9; cf. Isa. 64:3).

Thus the human being and creation are called to an absolute transcendence of whatever is capable of being made real in history. In history, something always remains merely implicit— something unspoken in the spoken, something unknown in the known. In heaven, all is unveiled, open, evident, and explicit.

Heaven, then, is both divine and human.

HUMAN CONSUMMATION: TO ALLOW GOD TO "ACHIEVE REALITY" IN THE HUMAN BEING

Can we take one more step, a step beyond all human limits? Until now our reflections have begun with the human being. The dynamics of the human being yearn toward a blessed outcome. Faith guarantees us a happy ending. It goes further and presents heaven as the absolute realization of all that is latent within us. It shows what God ultimately means for the human being. But everything in this equation, even God, has been stated only in terms of human beings and their vocation.

What if we turn our thinking around? Instead of asking what God means for the human being, let us ask what the human being means for God. Not only is the human being in God; God is in the human being as well. Indeed, the latter relation has prior value. Looking at the equation in reverse reveals our ultimate, definitive, concrete calling.

We are called, we exist, we achieve our radical realization, in allowing God to become real by means of ourselves.

This is a conclusion, not of faith, but of theology, in a theological reflection on the mysteries of the Incarnation of the eternal Son in human nature and the personalization of the Holy Spirit in human persons. Unlike our twofold reflection on heaven, this is not a datum of faith but a theological elaboration created by joining two of the key data of our faith. Thus the degree of certitude attaching to it is not the same as for our considerations on heaven, and it does not compel assent. Still, it belongs to the task of the "intelligence of the faith"—the educated understanding of our faith, which is the definition of theology—to try to plumb the remotest depths of the mysteries of God and the human being. Theology must be indefatigable here. God is not reason's repose but its eternal challenge. Nor need we be reminded that God is exempt from all human necessity— that God has no need of human beings in order to become real. But God has deigned to take flesh. And in order to do so God created the human being and the whole cosmos. Thus God has tried to involve us in the project of divine self-realization. In performing this service that God has asked of us lies our radical plenitude, the realization of our ultimate calling. Ultimate perfection resides in a self-actualization not of oneself but of another. True greatness consists not in being served but in serving. The culmination of freedom is to be free from oneself and thus to be free for others and for God. The fullness of love is not to be loved but to love. This is true for the human being, and this is true for God.

Let us begin with this basic certainty of faith: the incarnation of God. What is meant by the incarnation of God? It means God's total self-bestowal on someone entirely different, the human being. In order to make a gift of self, God creates someone whose ultimate meaning, whose definitive fulfillment and *raison d'être*, consists in an act of complete self-surrender, making it possible for God to enter into that one utterly. And so God thinks, wills, and creates the human being, a being with the capacity to absorb God fully, to receive God utterly. Well did the ancients say, the human being has a capacity for the Infinite, and a natural desire for God's love. The human being is constructed by God (through the mediations of history, nature, and society) in such a way as to possess an infinite openness. This infinite openness is the door by which God can enter into and assimilate human nature, appropriating it so completely that it can be called the *humanity of God*. And God does this without the least injury to the integrity of this human nature. On the contrary, God does this in all respect for that nature, actually rendering it even more profoundly human.

Thus human nature contains the possibility of receiving God. This possibility is real and objective (ontological), and not merely "of reason" or imaginary. Our whole grandeur, our ultimate end, consists in being at the service of a God who has this design: to emerge from the divine Self and take on human nature. Thus what the mouth is for food, the eye for light, intelligence for thought, the womb for offspring, this human being is for God's will to become flesh. And as a concrete human nature is always both masculine and feminine, so the incarnation of God takes on these particulars, thereby conferring upon the masculine and the feminine a divine meaning.

Once in human history this design of God's was completely realized. In a Jew called Jesus of Nazareth, God caused this potency to be actualized, this possibility to become reality. In Jesus, from the first moment of his conception, God was totally present and incarnate. Faith tells us that this was accomplished in history once and for all. And so Jesus is presented, accepted, and loved as the human being of the *Ecce Homo*, as *novissimus Adam*, as *Homo eschatologicus*, as *Homo revelatus*—as the first human being utterly to accomplish that to which he was called: total self-bestowal for God's incarnational design. In him we read our own calling and final end.

The possibility, become reality in Jesus, exists in us as well. Historically it has been realized only in Jesus. In all the rest of humankind, in the siblings of Jesus, his consubstantial blood relatives, it has remained and remains for now pure possibility. But like any other real possibility, it too cries out for actualization. On earth it is realized, imperfectly, in the discipleship and following of the "firstborn of many brothers" (Rom. 8:29), imperfectly because of our personal and collective sins.

But are we to remain ever thus? Do we not groan, as in the pangs of childbirth, burning with the hope that God will fully realize all the potential that he has placed within us? Paul reminds us, "We know that God makes all things work together for the good of those who love him, who have been called according to his decree. Those whom he foreknew he predestined to share the image of his Son, that the Son might be the first-born of many brothers" (Rom. 8:28-29).

If our reflections are correct, we may conclude, heaven is not only absolute human realization nor merely the vision, enjoyment, and possession of God by human beings but also, and principally, the possession of human beings by God. God will become flesh in each of us. God will assume, in the degree proper to each of us, the human nature of every human being. God will render himself concrete—eschatologically, in heaven—in the fulfillment of that possibility to whose realization we have all been called. This is our supreme vocation: that we should be called and be able to renounce ourselves altogether in order to be entirely God's. Thus it is our absolute realization, as well, a complete self-bestowal on another in order to abide in the very being of that other. Nor is God's perfect realization anything else; it is an eternal self-giving to another, an emerging from the divine Self and a going forth to meet another self, in order to abide in communion with that someone else for everlasting, joining him or her to God's life and glory. This is what occurs in the trinitarian process, and this is what has occurred in the Incarnation.

The divine person who became incarnate is God the Son. That divine person took on human nature. Thus God is humanized, and the human being is divinized. But human beings are more than their individual natures. We are also a communion of persons, expressed by a network of the social bonds that unite us and thereby constitute human society—"us." But human society enjoys a relative autonomy vis-à-vis the individuals that make it up. To society too a specific calling is addressed. For what may human society hope?

As the Son has become incarnate in human nature, theology tells us, the Holy Spirit has been "incarnate," or personalized, in human persons. The community of persons, even as community, is open to the reception of God. The One who comes and assumes them substantially is the Holy Spirit, who thereby makes of many persons "one mystical person" with himself. Thus the human "we" as well finds its fullness; it places itself at the service of God the Holy Spirit who has deigned to emerge from the divine Self and adopt the substance of human society. The personalization and socialization of the Holy Spirit is as real and concrete as that of the Son who became flesh in Jesus and dwelt among us, as in heaven that Son will dwell in each of us.

This final calling, which renders human beings supremely happy because we exist totally for that for which we have been created, is only realized in the righteous. Those who, by the evil quality of their life on earth, are condemned to perdition will live in eternal frustration; their potency to receive God will remain forever empty. That potential will cry out for God, but its cry will burn like fire, as it can have no response or fulfillment. It will live in blight, like a bud condemned never to burst into bloom. Here the human being fails to attain what human nature most longs for—to be God, to be God's.

For the righteous, however, this potency will be filled to the brim. By their lives, by their love, by their justice, by their humanity they will have become, now that they are in heaven, the "matter" in which God will achieve a new self-realization, a self-communication to them as they receive and welcome God in an ineffable, definitive, everlasting espousal.

9. The Church's Contribution to the Liberation of the Oppressed

Let us not fall into facile oversimplifications or futile idealism. We must see the liberation process in proper perspective and balance, with each element in place. We must likewise see the whole liberation process in relation to the Church, which is intimately connected with that overall process. We strongly believe not only that the Church has an effective contribution to make to the process of liberation, but also that this contribution is irreplaceable if liberation is to be integral.

We must therefore define (1) the meaning of liberation, (2) the specific relevance of faith to liberation, and (3) the Church's presence in and the contribution of the religious life to the liberation process.

SOCIAL AND HISTORICAL CONTENT OF LIBERATION

Liberation here means principally, though not exclusively, the economic, political, and social liberation of oppressed peoples.[1] Liberation here is not, in the first instance, liberation from sin, selfishness, and the other vices that injure human community and compromise human beings' relationship with God. Spiritual liberation is indeed the ultimate meaning of liberation; without it no other liberation would have definitive significance. To reach this goal, however, we must await the intervention of certain social and historical processes. In other words, ultimate liberation (liberation from sin and liberation for grace) implies penultimate liberations (economic, political, social, pedagogical, and so on). It is in these latter areas that social sin—any wicked and unjust human relationship—becomes historically concrete. These are likewise the areas where grace is mediated and which anticipate the coming of the Reign of God. To speak of sin and grace while ignoring the practices in which they become concrete would be to rob liberation of its authentic content. We would deprive liberation theology's social analysis of its historical reality. We must take care not to allow the language of liberation to be translated into purely spiritualistic and idealistic meanings.

The content of liberation is not exhausted in its social and historical process. In order to be authentically human, a given process of liberation must open out to other dimensions and, at least in its intentionality, be integral. It is precisely because liberation intends to be integral that it postulates an economic and political liberation. A spiritual liberation or liberation from sin that fails to include the material realities of human life is a mutilated liberation. To be real, liberation, even spiritual liberation, must reach the "lesser" liberations, which not only are part and parcel of integral liberation, but also are the vehicles of spiritual liberation itself. Material liberations have a spiritual, theological dimension, which it is the task of faith to recognize. The economic is more than economic; it is the locus of grace and sin and thus can become a mediation of the Reign of God. Accordingly, a liberation confined and reduced to the economic and the social, a liberation that opens out upon no transcendent horizon, has to be denounced as myopic—unsatisfactory vis-à-vis the basic human exigencies. The human being is more than economic and political.

And yet our liberation will have comprehensive and genuine meaning only if we do not conjure away the economic and political liberation of the great poor majorities of our world. It is here that today's great social conflicts crop up. It is here that the great decisions are made that can mean life or death for such vast numbers of people, even an entire class of human beings. In theological terms, it is in the area of the economic and the political that God is most grievously offended today, if not outright rejected and denied. Only this consideration can justify the commitment of the Church and its communities to the economic and political liberation of our oppressed peoples.

LIBERATION: LANGUAGE OF THE OPPRESSED

Liberation is the cry of the oppressed. It is the goal of their strategy for action. We scarcely need recall the extent of the marginalization and poverty of the immense majorities of the people on the periphery, people who are ideologically labeled "underdeveloped." What is important is to be able to identify the cause that produces both impoverishment and its perpetuation. Here we must go beyond moralism, utopia, and idealism, of which Christians are so fond. We must give up circumlocutions like "Human selfishness is the root of all evil; it must be abolished by a society of fellowship and justice, a Christian society, built up through mutual assistance, coresponsibility, and love." Such generalizations contribute nothing to diagnosing or treating realities of conflict. We must get down to the concrete, historical realities and practices that create and sustain generalized poverty. Any ethical or religious discourse must follow upon this analysis.[2]

What, then, is the dominant cause of the poverty of the great peripheral majorities of our system? We say dominant cause, not sole cause, because there are other, secondary causes or cocauses. To abbreviate a detailed analysis in terms of the social sciences: the poverty of the underdeveloped countries of our Western system is a consequence of the development of the other countries of that system.[3] The system in question is capitalism in its current phase of transnational imperialism. The dynamics of development in capitalistic molds create a center and a periphery. Relations between the center and the periphery are not interdependent; rather, the periphery is dependent in economics, in the division of labor, in the social and cultural arenas, and in the political arena. The consequence of this dependency is subjugation and impoverishment. The encyclical *Populorum Progressio* defined capitalism as "a system . . . which considers profit as the key motive for economic progress, competition as the supreme law of economics, and private ownership of the means of production as an absolute right that has no limits and carries no corresponding social obligation."[4] This definition is a clear statement of the rules of the capitalist game, even when in the face of new historical conditions it has had to change tactics (to that of capitalism plus state intervention) in order to give the impression that the system has been humanized. "Profit as the key motive for economic progress" is socioanalytic parlance for the plunder and expropriation—today formally internationalized—not only of the working class, but also of whole nations. The dominant cause of the scandalous poverty of millions of persons in our system is the accumulation of wealth in the capitalist mode and on an international scale.[5]

In order to reproduce itself, our system has a certain limited need for internal consent. This consent is generated by the ideology of the dominant classes, who profit from maintaining and reinforcing the status quo. Using a jargon bubbling with expressions like "interdependence," "one world," "human rights," and so on, these classes manage to dissemble the inequities of their system. Their goal is to lull to sleep consciences that might otherwise mount a protest.

In these historical circumstances, the oppressed raise their cry. The oppressed people have now become aware of their oppression and are organizing for a struggle. They demand more than reform, development, and the general improvement of living conditions. Their goal is liberation, in the framework of a different kind of society. And their cry grows louder. The objective dynamism of history is calling for another type of social ordering. Capitalism has run its course. In this context, the question of socialism arises, not merely as an ethical political alternative, at least not on first examination, but simply as the historical phase dialectically subsequent to capitalism, the next concretion of history's own dynamism. Only when the time is ripe will history propose socialism to human freedom as a historical project and political option.[6] Socialism's basic demand is the ordering of the productive process to the real needs of society rather than to profit realized by a minority. But in order to become historical, this economic demand supposes another, political demand: the building of mechanisms by which all may have a voice in decisions. "For the economy to function for the benefit of all, it becomes necessary that it function through the intermediary of all."[7]

Aspirations to liberation are growing and spreading. The status quo is driven more and more frequently to use repression and violence in order to contain these aspirations. This itself is an index of the instability of the system. Further, the failure of popular consent betrays the system itself as repressive.

As a result of the unequal relations of dependence created by global capitalism, each country is linked to the fate of all. The affluent countries of the North Atlantic constitute the main pole in the relationship and are the culprits. The marginalized peoples of Latin America are the other pole and constitute the victims. Thus the appalling drama unfolding on the outer edges of the empire reaches sensitive spirits in the center itself. To what extent have Christians been made aware of the causal relationship between rich countries and poor countries? To what extent have they been shown their own responsibility to defeat the capitalist system and build a more egalitarian society, a communion of genuine partnership in production and decision making?

SPECIFIC RELEVANCE OF THEOLOGY TO THE LIBERATION PROCESS

We have reached the point in our discussion when we must address the theological problem proper. How will Christian faith judge this objective situation of oppression and this longing for liberty? How will the Christian community interpret, in the light of the gospel, this particular, concrete social process? What is the relationship between liberation, salvation, and the inchoate Reign of God in this world?

The answer, we think, presents itself under two aspects, one theoretical (theological) and the other practical (pastoral). Under the first aspect, the correct procedure is to reread the analytical text of reality from the starting point of the resources of faith and the gospel in an effort to determine whether the reality we have described is in harmony or discord with God's historical project. Under the second aspect, we must address the specific contribution of faith and of the Church in the concrete process of liberation.

Let us state at the outset that the basic task of the Christian community cannot be reduced to a moral condemnation of the capitalist system with its ideals and practices of social injustice and demeaning poverty. The principal Christian concern must be with the historical defeat of these ideals and practices. In other words, the basic problem is more political than moral. Certainly we must mount a prophetic denunciation of structural injustice. This is abstract. But more basically, we should strive to overcome the unjust structures. This is concrete. Further, we must form a critical judgment of the various liberations postulated by interested groups. What is the role of the Church here as Christian community? What is the role of the vows of religion within that Church? Not everything claiming to be liberation is liberation according to the mind of Christian faith.

Let us briefly consider the first, theoretical (theological) question. How does Christian faith interpret a desire for liberation from the structural mechanisms of economic and political oppression?

First, let us observe that Christian faith always demands and encourages social change. No historically given situation offers human beings and the world an ultimate framework. No social formation embodies the whole Reign of God. Accordingly, Christian faith approves in principle the actions of groups seeking social formulas that will give the people a greater share in the processes of society, give them more political voice. Surely such formulas represent a more adequate embodiment of the Reign of God.

The Reign of God is the core of the proclamation of the historical Jesus. It is the classic concept for translating the total, structural liberation of creation *from* its decadence and *for* its complete fullness in God. As such the Reign of God embraces all dimensions of reality—spiritual and material, religious and political. Therefore it implies the economic, social, and political arenas of reality. The liberation of the Reign cannot be reduced to liberation at this level. But it would not be the liberation of the Reign if it did not include this level. The Reign of God is built by way of a liberation process that runs directly counter to the reign of this world, which is structured in terms of selfishness. A conflict, to be undertaken in the spirit of the Beatitudes, must be waged if the Reign of God is to be built. The two reigns will inevitably collide.

The salvation that Jesus has gained and offered to us all is certainly not limited to the "end time." It overflows that time, surging back to the present. Its eschatological character requires its anticipation here and now, and it becomes history in manifold personal and structural processes. To the extent that they are just, furthering the realization of a community of brothers and sisters, these processes are the concrete (though still relative) presence of God's definitive salvation. That salvation is offered in the form of a series of historical liberations, each open to a greater one, until they all issue in full, transhistorical salvation in God. Speaking of the theological bonds between evangelization and liberation, Pope Paul VI asserts in his apostolic exhortation *Evangelii Nuntiandi*: "One cannot dissociate the plan of Redemption. The latter plan touches the very concrete situations of injustice to be combatted and of justice to be restored." In its document, *Justice in the World*, the 1974 Synod of Bishops emphasized that "the mission of proclaiming the Gospel in our times requires that we commit ourselves to man's integral liberation, here and now, in our earthly existence."[8]

For Christian faith, there is only one real order, and its destiny is supernatural. There are not two historical orders, one profane and one sacred. History is ever the history of salvation or perdition, of humble acceptance of God's self-communication or of refusal of the same. This outlook permits us to read historical economic phenomena in terms of salvation history, the history of our salvation or perdition. The Church's interest in these realities resides precisely in this theological aspect inherent in them. The economic and political arenas are the scene of justice and injustice, communion or its derangement, or, in the theological language, grace or sin, the realization or negation of God's project for history.

Christian faith therefore asks a theological question about the capitalistic system. To what extent does that system set the stage for the concrete anticipation of eschatological grace and holiness in persons' relationships with one another and with God? If *Populorum Progressio*'s definition of capitalism is correct, then capitalism is an element of the history of sin rather than grace. Granted, God's gracious presence is never wanting. But when we consider social structures, that presence is far more palpable in capitalism's victims (the majority of persons) than in its champions. The ultimate, transcendent meaning of this social and economic order, which has penetrated all aspects of our culture, is a mystery for theological reflection. Faith asserts, without fully understanding the content of its assertion, that God and Jesus Christ are the Sovereigns of history, including history in this disastrous dimension.[9]

The Gospels ascribe to the poor an altogether special privilege. Their poverty and marginality, being the fruit of injustice, constitutes a challenge to the messianic king. The Reign of God, as the actualization of right order and the reestablishment of the rights of the humiliated and the wronged, begins with them. The poor have a sacramental function. They provide the rest of us with an opportunity to encounter the Lord, who is concealed in them anonymously. Their longings for liberation and their thirst for justice have been taken up by the "Son of Man." Whenever the Church takes sides with the impoverished, then, the Church is infallible, since it thereby establishes and proclaims its presence in Jesus' own social locus, where he uttered his proclamation of liberation and then fitted his actions to his declared intent.

Our theological reading of social and economic reality shows us why the Christian feels impelled to assume a particular place within society. Not everything is valid for a Christian. Faith encourages us to take the part of the poor, to make their hunger for liberation our own. Faith includes an inherent political dimension, independent of particular social and historical circumstances. However, faith is more than a relationship to politics. Directly, it defines the total position of the human being before God as the ultimate meaning of reality, including politics. Indirectly, precisely because it orders all human life, faith bears on political practices. These practices always have the theological content of grace or sin, independently of any awareness on the part of their agents. For the Christian understanding, only that faith is salvific that is informed by charity—only that faith that generates solidarity, especially with our "least brothers" (Matt. 25:40). This is why Christian faith must necessarily have a liberating dimension. The bishops at the 1974 Synod stated, "According to the Christian message, human beings' attitude toward other human beings is part and parcel of their attitude toward God. Their response to God's salvific love for us through Christ demonstrates its effectiveness in their love and service of their neighbor."[10]

What service does the Church render to the oppressed? What is the place of the Church in the overall process of liberation presently under way at the hands of the poor and those who have taken their stand at the side of the poor? An answer to this question demands something over and above the theoretical, theological reflection we have just entertained. A practical, pastoral contribution, in terms of the objective conditions of history and society, is likewise required.

SPECIFIC CONTRIBUTION OF THE CHURCH TO THE LIBERATION PROCESS

The concrete contribution of the Church, as an institution and historical reality, has been ambiguous where the process of liberation is concerned. Especially in Latin America, the only continent on the face of the globe to have been entirely the property of colonial Christendom, the Church (considered sociologically, not theologically) has been the structural ally (not to judge its intentions, then, but only its social functions) of colonial Christendom and the accomplice of its mechanisms of oppression and subjugation. Iberian colonization meant oppression for the Indians and blacks, both as individuals and in their cultures. The presence of the Church in movements for liberation and the abolition of slavery was negligible. The formation of the Christian conscience was excessively centered on individualistic moralism and religious practices. There was a scandalous absence of practices determined by a sound social ethics. In millions of suffering persons, Lazarus languished at the rich man's door. But this was not perceived by faith as a serious matter. The Church functioned as a contributor to the prevailing moral disorder, and the prophets of the colonial era, like Las Casas or Vieira, shouted this from the housetops.

Today, however, the Church has heard the cry of the oppressed—both the Church universal and the regional church of Latin America.[11] The Church has entered into solidarity with the liberation of the poor. How is this solidarity presented and interpreted on the level of praxis? On precisely what front does the Church do battle? The liberation process maintains many fronts: the economic, the political, that of the union movement, the ideological, and, in some cases, the military. The Church cannot autonomously decide what position it will take in the ranks. It takes the position assigned it in the framework of social forces. It plays a particular role in a particular kind of society. It is not an autonomous reality from every point of view. It is not a reality apart. Rather, as *Gaudium et Spes: The Church in the Modern World* asserted decades ago, the Church is *in the world of today.* Its autonomy is relative. It must accept being part of a society and then decide in which direction to move.

Let us begin with the premise (which we cannot pause to establish here) that society is constructed, developed, and modified through the dialectical interplay of three instances or arenas: the economic, which is responsible for the material realities of life; the political, which is responsible for the social order; and the symbolic or ideological, which is responsible for human values, ideals, and aspirations. We shall likewise assume that ultimately it is the economic instance that organizes the complexity of the real, inasmuch as it is the economic arena that supplies the most basic needs of life and human subsistence. Not that economics is automatically dominant. It is merely the ultimate with respect to the others. The political instance, for example, or the symbolic can confer unity on a particular social phase. The arena that actually confers this unity thereby becomes the dominant one.

In the social division of labor the Church is part of the symbolic arena. After all, the Church is a social organization functioning as the vehicle of religious values—a message, and religious and ethical practices flowing from that message. Because it is organized as an institutional system, the Church qualifies analytically as a symbolic (or ideological) apparatus.

At the root of all dialectical interaction among the several arenas is the symbolic one, which includes the Church. This symbolic arena itself carries a certain political and economic weight, although not specifically and directly.[12]

In all of society, the Church constitutes one symbolic apparatus among many. It must share the symbolic arena with prevailing ideologies, schools, the media, and so on, and it is in competition with them. As a specifically religious symbolic apparatus it must also compete with other religions, which also produce religious symbols (the various Christian confessions, the sects, the non-Christian religions). Symbolic values act directly on individual and collective awareness and indirectly on the other political and economic instances.

Now the basic question arises. In the process of the liberation of the oppressed in our capitalistic society (and more specifically, under the particular conditions prevailing in each country), what is the influence of the symbolic Catholic Christian arena? The answer cannot be given a priori. It presupposes a concrete analysis of the historical situation, of the identification of the dominant instance (economic, political, or symbolic), and of the de facto social influence of the Church on society.

Generally speaking, we may say that in our transnational, pluralistic, pragmatic, and secularized capitalistic system the influence of the symbolic Catholic Christian instance is in decline.[13] That specific arena no longer enjoys either the monopoly or the hegemony of the production and distribution of religious goods. But through its historical tradition, to which nearly all of our Western countries are tied owing to the direct influence of the Church over their birth and early history, the Church, in its proper element (the symbolic), still maintains great influence. Then we must add the fact that, in the ideological confrontation with communism, the Church continues to be regarded as a powerful ally of the liberal or bourgeois forces by virtue of its so well defined official anticommunist doctrine. Today, however, the influence of the Church is weakened by conflict and division, which are shaking the ecclesial body from its grass roots to its hierarchical vertex. The conflict is not over the creed but over divergent political options, various judgments regarding the form of society we live in and the one we wish to live in, the type of activity performed or to be performed by the Church where politics is concerned, the social classes, the question of human advancement, and so on.

Despite these many limitations, the church institution, in its specific arena (symbolic, religious, and Christian), still has great importance in our societies (in varying degrees from country to country). The important thing for the Church is to be able to dovetail its specific practice—pastoral, catechetical, liturgical—with other social practices, especially political ones. Here the decisive consideration is the basic option of the Church with respect to the meaning of social change. Either the Church will opt for the established order, organized by the dominating class, with its capitalistic interests, or it will opt for the marginalized groups—more explicitly, for the exploited class—making their yearning for freedom and their aspiration for a different society its own.

The signifying practices of the Church acquire a political relevance—a relevance in the social arena. These practices relay the Church's basic option to every nook and cranny of society and its mentality through church work among the people—pastoral work, religious education, and the base church communities, to cite a few examples. We need only consider the recent contribution of Christian theology. The content of Christian faith has obviously driven the Church to choose a particular theological method. The Church's pastoral activity, merely in and of itself, acquires a political meaning. It raises the consciousness of those served poorly by the system, rendering them explicitly aware of their implicitly felt need for liberation. It then functions as the voice of these voiceless, their support and their organizing element.

As we see, symbolic practice is never politically neutral. Its political weight does not depend on any particular religious agents—neither their will and intent nor their thematic message. This weight is structural, and it reverberates against the social sounding board in the relationships of force prevailing in a given society.

For example, the pastoral (symbolic) option of Vatican II to live the faith within the world obviously includes a political dimension. In Vatican II the Church pledged to live in solidarity with "the joys and the hopes, the griefs and the anxieties of the men of this age, *especially* those who are in any way afflicted."[14] Likewise, the Latin American bishops gathered in Medellín, 1968, decided to adopt their continent's aspirations to emancipation and liberation from all servitude. This is taking sides. An option is being made here with an evangelical basis in the eminently meaningful practices of Jesus, who incontestably practiced a preference for the poor and suffering. Medellín states explicitly, "The Latin American church has a message for all women and men who, on this Continent, 'hunger and thirst for justice.' "[15] There is no vagueness here, no churchly dangling modifier. There can be no doubt about the identity of the addressees: those who hunger and thirst for justice. These, or the vast majority of these, are the poor.

Now let us return to the question. In what way does the Church as an institution cooperate in the liberation of the oppressed? The answer: from the starting point of its specific arena, the symbolic (ideological). This is not the most important arena. In our society, the political and economic arenas dominate, while the symbolic is secondary. The latter is important, however, in terms of the Church's social weight. The official option of the Church for the people and their liberation is significant from the standpoint of political ideology. First, it represents the removal of an obstruction, as it demonstrates that the symbolic religious arena does not necessarily legitimate the established order. Indeed, the religious contribution becomes social criticism by virtue of the prophetic nature of faith. Furthermore, the Church's adoption of the aspirations for liberty on the part of the poor bestows a certain legitimacy on these yearnings and in large part removes the subversive label imposed on them by a dominant class that would like to have these longings regarded as hostile to society itself.

Next, the Church performs the function of encouraging and inspiring liberation. What is the Church doing for the liberation of the poor? Paul VI asks the question in *Evangelii Nuntiandi*, and answers:

She is trying more and more to encourage large numbers of Christians to devote themselves to the liberation of men. She is providing these Christian "liberators" with the inspiration of faith, the motivation of fraternal love. . . . The Church strives always to insert the Christian struggle for liberation into the universal plan of salvation which she herself proclaims.[16]

The function of the Church, then, is to call attention to the dimension of liberation inherent in the Christian message and the practices of Jesus. This dimension must become explicit in all areas of the pastoral ministry—for example, in religious education and homiletics—as well as in all interventions of the Church in society.

Up to this point we have been considering the liberating function of the Church as a system organized in the symbolic (ideological) arena. We have seen the scope and the limits of its contribution. The function of Christians and groups of Christians is another matter. The church institution does not span the whole of Christian reality. Sensitized by the Church and by the liberating dimensions of their faith, Christians can extend their activity over a far vaster area than that of the Church as an institution. They can and should be active in political parties, unions, and other organizations, inspired by their liberating faith. This struggle is waged outside institutional boundaries of the Church. But it embraces an essential Christian and ecclesiological task, working in the midst of the world, alongside other women and men, to construct a society with more just human relationships.

The significance of the Church is not restricted to its liberating dimension. The Church's meaning is broader than politics and historical processes. The Church is the sacrament of definitive salvation, already achieved by Jesus Christ and being realized not only in the Church but in the vast field of the world. The Church is the locus in which this total salvation becomes awareness, proclamation, and celebration. Transcending the division of society into oppressed and oppressor, transcending historical struggles, the Church offers to all the opportunity for God's reconciliation and presents an *eschaton* already realized in the earthly journey of Jesus who lived, died, and was raised from the dead. In Jesus all historical processes converge. Liturgical, spiritual, and sacramental practices therefore render the *eschaton* visible, and they cannot be exhausted by political practices. The Church is the vessel of a store of symbols that transcends politics. Faith must always see things in terms of the Meaning of meanings. As Saint Thomas said, "With regard to the totality of his beings and his possessions, man does not exist for the sake of the political community. On the contrary, whatever man is, can, and has, must be for the sake of God."[17]

From the starting point of this absolute instance—God—faith and the Church relativize politics and liberation processes. Politics, which is a form of organizing and exercising power, faces a permanent temptation: to add power to power without acknowledging any limits and thus to fall into an implacable totalitarianism. Faith tells political power, to reiterate Emmanuel Mounier's observation: everything is political, but the political is not everything. Power is legitimate in proportion to its function as instrument of right and justice. Only God can be absolute. Only God can claim the totality of the human being. And so faith and the Church as its organized locus make possible practices that transcend politics, such as prayer and celebration, practices that contact the Absolute immediately as that Absolute is anticipated and worshiped in history. Historical liberations have a theological content. They are not, however, the eschatological. They are not the liberation achieved in the Reign of God.

Accordingly, faith is the large space. The greater includes the lesser, so that we may formulate the relationship between faith and politics as follows: Faith (the greater) always contains a political dimension (the lesser).

SPECIFIC CONTRIBUTION OF THE RELIGIOUS LIFE TO THE LIBERATION PROCESS

The whole series of considerations just discussed is required for identifying the liberating sense of the religious life. The life of the vows is not a kind of knight errancy, freelance and autonomous. It presupposes an elucidation of the Church's own thematic concerns. The religious life is a part, a specific manifestation, of the Church. If the Church is a sacrament of God's eschatological liberation, then religious life is the sacrament of the sacrament. Whatever is true of the Church is true even more so of the religious life, which, while it does not pertain to the divine structure of the Church, springs from the same source. The religious life is eminently charismatic, then. It enjoys more freedom of activity and can therefore perform that activity where the institutional Church, as official institution, cannot or ought not to act.

What should the religious life contribute to the process of integral liberation?[18] In answering this question we shall follow the same sequence as when asking the question with regard to the

Church: first we shall entertain a mainly theological reflection, then a mainly practical one.

The identity of the religious life resides in its particular expression of the experience of God in the following of Christ. That experience is expressed in a total consecration to God through the three vows of religion, lived in a communion of sisters or brothers where this life is a prophetic sign—a token and embodiment in the world itself—of God's future promise to everyone.

It is possible to live the religious life in a nonliberating fashion. There are interioristic forms of the religious life that uphold the interests of the powerful. If the religious life is to serve the evangelical cause of liberation, sensitization to the contradictions of reality will be necessary, along with a consciousness-raising that is not partial but radical—going to the root of the causes of oppression.[19]

With this conscientization or consciousness-raising presupposed, the religious life now must ask, Do the requirements of liberation call for reinterpreting the theology of the religious life and its practices? How can the religious life, on the strength of its own identity, and without compromising that identity, cooperate in the integral liberation of the oppressed? We are convinced that the religious life is characterized by evangelical values so explicit that, reread in terms of liberation, they can only impel religious women and men to embrace a process of authentic liberation. Let us examine some of these basic values.

Experiencing the God of the Reign. The religious experience of God as Sovereign of the Reign comes to see that this God is the same God encountered in a process of liberation from oppression. God seeks to inaugurate the Reign even in this world, beginning with those who thirst for justice—the poor and their allies. The Reign is built by opposing the structures and behavior of this world. And in this conflict God, who hears the cry of the poor, takes sides with the oppressed. God is therefore perceived as Liberation, Hope, Future, Justice, and Communion, and as a God who sends religious men and women forth to serve the poor and thereby help those poor build the Reign in this very world.

Following Jesus Christ. Following Christ is a fundamental category of the life of the vows. Against a background of liberation, discipleship of Jesus implies communion in his life and lot. Communion in his life implies partnership in his liberating project. It implies sharing the twofold fidelity that characterizes the entire life of Christ: loyalty to God, who wills the liberation of the children of God together with that of all creation, and loyalty to human beings, especially to those most loved by God, the marginalized and the sinful, the humiliated and the oppressed. To follow Jesus means, among other things, accepting the conflicts provoked by his message, enduring them as a way of redeeming his very enemies, and being willing to live and suffer his own lot. If we are to follow Jesus and commit ourselves to building the Reign, then we shall have to regard persecution and defamation as radically normal even when, as for some, these lead to physical elimination or martyrdom.

Consecration as mission. Religious publicly consecrate themselves to God so that, with God as their portion and strength, they may live all of the tasks implied in the charisms of each congregation. For centuries, this consecration or setting apart for God was interpreted inadequately. It was restricted to renouncing the world. Renunciation had, and still has, its permanent value. However, renunciation must be complemented by the biblical meaning of consecration as mission, as a sending forth. The religious is sent by God with the mission of bearing witness to the reality of the eschatological Reign and of living that Reign, by anticipation, here and now. This sense of consecration as mission is at the root of our religious commitment to building a world of greater liberty and communion.

Public nature of the vows. The demands of liberation vigorously underscore the public or prophetic and critical dimension of the three vows. Poverty does not mean merely stripping ourselves of our goods in order to be free for God and free for human beings. It means striking a solidarity with the poor in order to join forces with them in overcoming the poverty that displeases God by reason of the obstacles it places in the way (not of wealth but) of universal justice. Chastity is the expression of an entire love for God. In the context of liberation, it "represents a prophetic response to the problem of the relation between the world of money and the eroticization of such a large portion of the human race."[20] Obedience is not exhausted in a quest for God's will for our interior life or our religious services to society. In includes a search for the will of God for the society in which we live and offer those services.

Rereading the theological content of the religious life with a view to liberation is not enough, however. We must also join the religious life to concrete practices of liberation springing from the specific identity of the life of the vows and producing fruit in the form of actual liberation. Here we may recall the scope and limits of the Church's activity as a symbolic arena. The religious life constitutes a smaller piece of the larger symbolical apparatus of the Church. By virtue of its charismatic rather than institutional nature, however, the religious life enjoys more freedom of action than does the Church. It can therefore express itself across a wider spectrum of meaningful deeds of liberation than can the institution Church, especially in practices more directly bound up with the area of the political.[21]

First, religious ought to strive to be liberated persons themselves. They will be able to engage in liberation practices only if they are free themselves. Liberation here is to be understood not in its *petit bourgeois*, psychological meaning but in its socioanalytic meaning. What is required is a determined option for the oppressed, an option to embrace their aspirations and to see and interpret reality from the starting point of their demands for structural transformations. This will define the hermeneutic and social loci of our theoretical and practical practices. Naturally it will also imply rejecting the bourgeois schemas of our intellectual training. It will require a fresh awareness of the mechanisms of our national society in its interconnections with international capitalistic society, and it will call for ideological vigilance over our discourse lest it be manipulated by the status quo. Here and now, in our communities, we ought to live a more responsible freedom.

Second, we must critically review of our presence in society through the works of our various institutions. To what extent does our institutional presence promote the interests of the status quo? Here our whole effort should be to confer on our works a liberating, conscientizing function, one of real service to the underprivileged in the prevailing system. But to this end, we must have a realistic political sense. We cannot always do as we please. We must do what is permitted and tolerated by the dominant forces in society. We must be able to bear up under these difficulties and make concessions—not in our strategy of liberation, but in our tactics—in order to maintain our presence in society with a view to eventual liberation from the system.

Third, we must stay at the people's side, without trying to usurp their autonomy. This means we must appreciate popular culture, popular piety, and the popular ways of being people and being free, which are frequently far removed from the categories of our academic training. We must intensify our commitment to the people, supporting them when they take up their struggle and, when need be, pronouncing the prophetic word of denunciation, revealing and decrying the injustice and oppression of their lives, and proclaiming the will of the Lord, which is the creation of a brotherly and sisterly partnership of justice for all. In this context we must consider it important for the religious to insert themselves into the popular milieus of the oppressed and poor—of shouldering the people's burdens, of sharing their deprivations and communicating in their yearnings. This solidarity with the poor will show us why it is they to whom the gospel is first addressed and, if the Greek fathers are to be believed, our very instructors, our "lowly doctors." Evangelized by us religious, the poor turn the tables and evangelize us.

The option for the poor offers a variety of concretions. For some of us it means living *for* the poor. A religious may live elsewhere than among the poor, taking up their liberating project, their outlook, and their cause. In the central countries of the capitalist economic empire, religious of the Americas will familiarize themselves with what is transpiring in underdeveloped countries and acquire the ability to understand both the international mechanisms of neocolonial exploitation and their own country's participation in this neocolonial enterprise. Or again a religious may actually live *with* the poor, switching social positions and moving into the popular milieus in order to share—as a religious—in the process of conscientization and liberation. Third, some carry this solidarity so far that they are granted the grace to live *as* the poor, sharing their anguish in all of its dimensions. Here participation in the self-liberation of the poor consists of walking at their side and sharing with them the burden of their oppressed existence.

Finally, any religious presence in the liberation process should be inspired and animated by the religious charism. That charism consists in contemplating and experiencing history and the world from the standpoint of God. Viewed from this absolute perspective, politics and liberation processes are relative. They are mere mediations. Their importance is not diminished; but the mode of our presence in the midst of these realities takes on a particular character. We perceive the element of transcendence, contemplation, and eschatology in politics. The ultimate sense and meaning of all human searching for liberation and justice is revealed. This theological dimension will be perceived as real, however, only to the extent that religious men and women become incarnate in the world by accepting the challenges of liberation in the way demonstrated by the eternal Son in his Incarnation.

Religious who make an option for their own integral liberation and that of their sisters and brothers must be armed with the living experience of a great hope, a hope that goes beyond all visible limits of our history. They must work for a world that will probably not be realized. But the small amount that can be accomplished is the little stone that God asks today's religious to contribute to the construction of the Reign. We must have the patience for great enterprises. This will require the ability to love the invisible and to make sacrifices for those who will come after us. Christian hope is our warranty that history is not an endless circle but a growth toward the eschatological Reign of God. Until that Reign comes, let us love and believe and hope in the one who promised us: "Stand erect and hold your heads high, for your deliverance is near at hand" (Luke 21:28).

10. The Universal Mission of the Church and Concrete Liberation

It is sometimes argued, in circles hostile to liberation theology, that the Church must not descend to involving itself with the oppressed. The Church recognizes the equality of all classes of persons, we are told. Historical struggle on behalf of the poor requires preferring one class of people over another, which would force the Church to compromise its universality—its mission of providing pastoral care to all men and women regardless of social status.

By now it should be clear that such criticism is irrelevant. The universal mission of the Church is bound up with concrete liberation. The concrete realization of the mission and universality of the Church must pass by way of the particular—in the case at hand, by way of the liberation of the despoiled. Otherwise that universality will remain abstract and that mission vacuous. Let us illustrate this process by citing practices of our own Latin American Church.

WHAT IS MEANT BY THE UNIVERSALITY OF THE CHURCH?

Investigating the meaning of the term *catholicity* or *universality* of the Church throughout history produces five basic meanings.[1]

First is a descriptive meaning. The term *catholic* can refer to the *universitas Christianorum* or the body of the churches made up of the aggregate of the local churches. This universal, total aggregate is greater than the sum of its parts, since the unity of this body emerges from the communion maintained by all of the local churches among themselves. *Catholic* is used here in the historical, sociological sense of this phenomenon as an analytical quantity.[2]

Second, *catholic* can have a meaning in the sense of anything destined for all and valid for everyone without exception. The Church, particular or universal (or, for that matter, any individual member of either), is catholic in its quality as a community open to all human beings without distinction. It is also open to the whole human being without neglecting any of the integral parts that make up human nature. This catholicity is rooted in the christological focus of salvation history: salvation, of which the Church is the conscious, organized bearer, is offered to all. Mission, as proclamation of present salvation and call to conversion, is likewise universal: the Church is conscious of being sent to all peoples.[3] To be catholic is intrinsic to Christian reality at each level of its realization—personal, communal, and global.

Third, the word *catholic* can mean worldwide in the geographical sense, referring to the Church as found *toto orbe diffusa* ("throughout the world," from the Roman Canon), the *per totum orbem terrarum Sancta Ecclesia* ("the Holy Church throughout the world," from the *Te Deum*). This meaning is derived; it follows upon the Church's universal mission.

Fourth, the word *catholic* can have a polemical meaning of true or orthodox. The Church is called catholic because it accepts the totality of the gospel truth in communion with all of the local churches.[4] *Catholic* is opposed to *heretical* or sectarian as the whole is opposed to a mere part. The sectarian is characterized by the absence of a reference to the whole truth of the gospel. It universalizes a mere part, as we may speak of the *Pars Donati*, the Donatist party, as opposed to the *Ecclesia Catholica*. This meaning first appeared in the third century, gaining broad currency in the sixteenth.

Finally, *catholic* can have an anthropological and cosmic meaning that signifies plenitude or totality. On the basis of the eschatological events of Christ's resurrection and sending of the Holy Spirit, Christian faith becomes a response to the totality of human aspirations and to the fullness of all of the cosmic forces in their tendency toward a final convergence. Human nature itself manifests an intrinsic catholicity in its openness to an unlimited, universal capacity for communion. Christianity, with its essential catholicity, claims to attend to and realize, on the level of ultimate questions and absolute meaning, this anthropological and cosmic catholicity.[5]

All of these meanings of *catholic* except the last gravitate around the very nature of Christian faith. Christian faith is intrinsically catholic. Granted, full, unconditional catholicity is an eschatological gift. As long as history lasts, no concretion of catholicity or universality will exhaust the universal calling and mission of the Church. That mission is to be carried out continuously, and not merely on the occasion of socioanalytic observation. From the fact that this obligation is continuous, we can only conclude that, while the Church is catholic, it is not fully so. History presents it with constant opportunities for intensifying its catholicity. Accordingly, catholicity must be conceived and experienced not only from above (from the standpoint of God's universal salvific will, the universal mission of the Church, and the catholicity or universality of human nature), but from below, as well (starting with social and historical demands that can claim universality).

The Church is not universal by sole virtue of its intrinsic catholicity and its own universal mission. It becomes universal to the extent that it takes up universal human and social causes. It becomes universal in proportion to its adoption of the universality articulated by others. From this point of view universality is defined from the starting point of mission, and mission is understood as the process of a liberating incarnation within a historically defined setting. In other words, through embodiment in universal causes the Church itself becomes universal.

BOND BETWEEN THE CHURCH'S MISSION AND ITS CONCRETE UNIVERSALITY

Whenever the Church redefines its mission in history it also redefines its conception of universality. The current historical setting is a new case in point. We think the Church is undergoing a spiritual and political experience that is endowing it with a new universality, one that it has never had to the same degree. This new universality manifests itself principally in the new churches on the periphery of the first world—in Latin America, Asia, and

Africa. The catholicity emerging in these churches is their contribution to the old mother churches, and it is a rich acquisition for the Church universal.

What is this new universality? Let us briefly sketch the Church's pilgrimage over the last few decades in terms of a correlation between mission and universality.

A CHURCH OUTSIDE THE WORLD: UNIVERSALITY EMERGING FROM FAITH

For centuries, and in official circles until the Second Vatican Council, the typical Christian practices of the Church were limited to religious practices, which were regarded as antithetical to secular or profane activity. As indicated in chapter 1, this generated the concept of a Church *outside the world* and in confrontation with it. The Church was the sole vehicle of a universal mission to the world. Its purpose was to bring salvation to that world. The Church held a self-image of an indispensable sacramental instrument of salvation. The Christian mission monopolized salvation; hence that mission must expand the ecclesiastical system and make the world a part of the Church. One of the results of this practice and this theory was medieval Christendom. The universality or catholicity of the faith was realized through uniformity in theology, liturgy, canon law, language, and so on. Identity and homogeneity were the watchwords, and the particular characteristics of the local church of Rome were imposed on all the other churches of the world. These churches were romanized, then. But authentically, as we have seen, universality or catholicity consists in an openness to all peoples and cultures, coupled with a readiness and a capacity to assume their values. Unfortunately, the universalization of the particular can masquerade as universality. The cost to the medieval Church was high in terms of poverty of expression, rigidity, and a reductive standard of unification. The universality and catholicity of the faith were not, however, simply throttled for good.

This Church outside the world and in confrontation with it practiced a religious colonialism in Latin America and Africa, imposing the frameworks of European Christianity in the Tridentine mold and destroying or neglecting the precious cultural witness of the civilizations flourishing on those two continents.

The reason is clear: an institution that regards itself as the sole possessor of the truth of salvation, the solitary vehicle of the instruments of redemption, will necessarily become intolerant and repressive of its potential competitors. This principle became traumatic reality in the evangelization of the native peoples of South America. Now universal mission might only achieve historical incarnation through the forced subjugation of all local churches and all the faithful to a single doctrinal, liturgical, canonical, moral, and linguistic formula.

A CHURCH IN THE WORLD: UNIVERSALITY BEGINS WITH MODERN WOMEN AND MEN

At Vatican Council II, the bishops of the Catholic world redefined the mission of the Church. Not a few Christians were no longer performing their practices exclusively within the framework of the ecclesiastical system. They had long been operating in the profane, secular world built by the spirit of modernity. Now the Council delved deep into the theoretical conception of Church and rediscovered an essential note, long forgotten at the explicit level but always implicitly present: that of a *Church in the world*. The title of the most important document to issue from Vatican II indicates the value the bishops ascribed to this rediscovery: "Pastoral Constitution *Gaudium et Spes:* On the Church in the Modern World." *Gaudium et Spes* understands salvation historically. Salvation comes to us through variety of historical mediators, which the fathers of the Church called *sacramenta*. The most important of these—though not the only one—is the institution of the Church. The Church is a sacramental instrument of redemption. But this does not specify its function in salvation history. The salvific function of the Church consists in being precisely the sacramental *sign of universal salvation*. The Church is the "grammar" of the definitive salvation of the world wrought in the life pilgrimage of Jesus Christ. Salvation is in the world because Jesus Christ is in the world. But Jesus Christ is in the world in three ways: as the Word for whom, with whom, and in whom the world was made; as incarnate in the world; and as raised from the dead and established as the world's *Plērōma*. The Church is the historically organized sign—the sacrament—of something greater than itself. Salvation and grace cannot be fully contained by the Church because the world too is their vehicle.

The mission of the Church "is truly and intimately linked with mankind and its history," according to *Gaudium et Spes*. The document catalogues the objects of "the deeper and more widespread longing" of the human race and seeks to understand the universality of the Church in its capacity to respond to these aspirations universally. The Church does not act *from without* but *from within*, embracing all human beings.[6] "The proposals of this sacred Synod look to the assistance of every man of our time, whether he believes in God, or does not explicitly recognize him. Their purpose is to help men gain a sharper insight into their full destiny, so that they can fashion the world more to man's surpassing dignity, search for a brotherhood which is universal and more deeply rooted, and meet the urgencies of our age with a gallant and unified effort born of love."[7]

This redefinition of the mission of the Church implies a new universality. Rather than being founded on the specific nature of Christian faith, the universality of the Church now rests on the universality of the historical aspirations of our current world, taken up and assumed by the Church. Thus faith incorporates the deep longings of a civilized humanity steeped in the spirit of a scientific and technological culture. It assimilates their aspirations for a new person, a new community, and a new activity in the world, yearnings that spring from specific problems of family, promotion of culture, the social and economic life, and the building of the international community. (These are actual subtitles of *Gaudium et Spes*.) How could it be otherwise, in light of the Church's Christian identity? The Council is clearly aware of the disparities between wealthy countries and dependent countries, between highly developed cultures and backward cultures.[8] But its language betrays its preference for modernity, for the human being born in Europe and now to be found in the four corners of the earth. Those to whom the document is addressed, in principle all human beings without distinction, are de facto modern human beings with their formal education and scientific, technological bent. That is, the document is not addressed to all human beings but to the dominant people of the world today, those who monopolize the world's being, power, and knowledge. In short, the person addressed by *Gaudium et Spes* is the person formed by the world of the Enlightenment. This is the type of person whom the Church of Vatican II went out to meet in its theology and its pastoral ministry. Henceforth the Church would live among such persons. They would constitute the starting point of the Church's self-understanding. The universality of the Church would no longer be evinced in the strength of its uniformity, but in its capacity for adopting the plural values of the modern world without losing its Christian identity. What we have here, in eminent form, is the qualitative, anthropological, and cosmic sense of catholicity, in the framework of the bourgeois class of the enlightenment.

A CHURCH IN THE SUBWORLD: UNIVERSALITY BASED ON THE NONPERSON

Medellín, in Colombia, was the site of the 1968 Second General Conference of the Latin American Episcopate. The purpose of this gathering was to interpret the intuitions of Vatican Council II for the specific conditions of our own underdeveloped continent. At Medellín, the Church came to grips with the problem of the colonial domination that has prevailed in Latin America in recent centuries. Against this background it redefined the mission of the Church. "This destitution, as a collective fact, is an injustice that cries to heaven," the Church proclaimed. It adopted the desire of the great, impoverished majorities "for total emancipation—liberation from all servitude whatever."[9] Now the Latin American Church defined its mission in altogether concrete terms: "The Latin American Church has a message for all on this continent who hunger and thirst for justice." Accordingly, it addressed in a particular way all nonpersons— those denied the minimal rights and dignity without which human life can no longer be rightly regarded as human.[10]

Now the Church wishes to take its stand not vaguely and simply "in the world" but in a particular world, a hidden, lower world, the subworld of the poor and the nonperson. There it "seeks a more intense, a renewed kind of presence in the current transformation of Latin America."[11] The addressees are not the same as for *Gaudium et Spes*. They are not enlightened persons but totally uneducated, illiterate persons. They are not those who have been integrated into the prevailing social, economic, and political system but those who have been marginalized by that system. The universality of these persons' demands for justice and longings for liberation has now placed its stamp on the universality of the Church, and the Church is determined to commit itself to their causes.

If we review our three models of Church in light of this new option on the part of the Latin American Church, we observe the following pattern. In the first model, the Church as an institution relied on its own faith, on itself, on its faithful in order to become Church and to carry out its universal mission of evangelization and redemption. In the second model—that of the Church in the world—it relied on the person of enlightenment, the beneficiary of modern culture's advantages, and on that person's progressive ideals. In the third model—that of the Church in the subworld—the Church seeks its support among, and understands itself in terms of service to, society's abandoned, the poor and marginalized.

In the first model the Church faced the problems of orthodoxy and heresy. Here was the true Church versus the Christian sects, faith versus atheism, agnosticism, and secularism. In the second model, the burning problems were those of faith and science, the Christian spirit and the modern spirit, Christian tradition and scientific and technological progress. In the third model, the problem of faith and the transformation of society, of Christian love and a liberating solidarity with the poor—the Church and social justice—bursts upon the scene. The first series of questions are by and large those of Vatican I; the second, of Vatican II; and the third, of Medellín.

Let us examine this third model of Church, so dear to the faith of Latin American Christians. The problem is how the Church in the subworld, the Church that espouses the cause of the nonperson, can be the Church *universal* in that subworld. Here we must insist on a concrete universality (the only universality deserving of the name). The universal must be defined as that which is valid for all without distinction. The "for all" in this definition, in turn, must not be understood as transcending the individual in the sense of being without incarnation in any individual. On the contrary, the universal in the sense of "for all" constitutes a veritable "trans-descendence," to use a contrived expression. It can and must take flesh in all and in each without exhausting its potential in this or that particular incarnation. The universal is universal because it possesses, intrinsically, an intentionality directed to the concrete and thus directed upon every concrete member of the whole. A disincarnate universal—one without limitation, without the courage for the transitory and concrete—is lost as a universal. It represents abstractionism and, at bottom, the particular imposing itself on the whole by masquerading as a universal. It is merely a false front for an oppressive, cowardly particularism in the face of history. Hegel called this attitude *une bell'âme* (*die schöne Seele*), as opposed to the mind ever in quest of concrete universality.[12] A Church of this kind of "universality," to use an image of Péguy, tries to maintain the purism of its formulas and doctrines without getting its hands dirty in the politics of the world. But the reason this Church has no dirty hands is that it has no hands.

The Church does not compromise its universality when it takes up the concrete causes of the world and human beings. On the contrary, this is the condition of its realization. It is not the concrete that falsifies universality. It is the falsity of certain causes that places at risk the universality of the Church. An authentic cause enjoys an intrinsic universality. It is a true cause for all, and all the more so for the Church. In making such a cause its own, the Church becomes truly universal.

Thus in the third world the regional and local churches have joined hands with the damned of the earth. Their causes have a "blindingly evident" claim to universality (*d'une aveuglante evidence*): minimal justice, the freedom simply to be human, the dignity and the rights without which a human being is degraded to a level lower than that of the beasts (which are legally protected in almost every country). But justice, by definition, is justice for all. Likewise freedom, rights, and dignity must be the perquisites of all human beings; otherwise they belong to none. Justice, freedom, rights, and dignity for only one part of humanity means the legitimation of injustice and the canonization of discrimination for another part. But this would contradict the very essence of justice, freedom, rights, and dignity, since these values are by their essence universal. Either such values exist for all, then, or they simply do not exist. The meaning of life does not tolerate their private appropriation. That meaning is always a meaning for all. It is clear, then, that to the extent that the churches espouse the claims and demands of the poor, they assume a universality inherent in these claims and demands. Let us detail the manner in which our churches carry out this truly messianic task.

THE SAME CHURCH: NETWORK OF SERVICES, NETWORK OF COMMUNITIES

Ever since its colonial beginnings, the Church in Latin America has been a strong institutional presence in history and in society. Of course, it began and continued as a power that strengthened, and in some cases legitimated, the colonial and neocolonial powers. With Vatican II, and especially with Medellín, a conversion process began. The institutional Church began to turn toward the people.[13] First a large number of committed priests, religious, and laity began to move out of their social and ecclesial locus and strike roots among the poor and marginalized. There was an actual geographical shift. Church people moved physically, and this changed their hermeneutic locus. From the heart of the cities they went out to the outskirts to work, and they began to conceive and live their Christian faith and their being-Church from a locus of deep identification with the urgent needs of the poor.[14] Little by little this conversion became the choice of an entire continental church, a choice canonized by the Medellín documents and constantly being updated by significant documents published by the national or regional episcopates. On the margins of the Church and society, a vast network of base church communities of a popular, lay character began to spring up. This network was generated, and continues to be encouraged and supported, by the old Church, the larger institution. Initially there seemed to be two churches. On one side was the institutional Church of the population centers, traditionally rooted in the affluent milieus of society; on the other, a seedling church of base communities, constituted of the poor, the "little people of God," those who live out on society's margin. However, each of these two expressions of the one Church has come to understand its specific mission. The larger institutional Church has adopted the network of base communities and today offers the newer entity services that only an organized institution can offer, conferring its universality upon these communities and inserting them into the mainstream of the apostolic tradition. For its part, the network of base communities has restored the larger Church to its status as a community, enabling it to root its faith in history and integrating into the mystery of the salvation of Jesus Christ the burning desires of the people for more humane living conditions. This phenomenon occasions a genuine "ecclesiogenesis"[15] or birth of a Church, in the sense of a Church reinventing itself in new ministries, a new liturgical expression, and new accents to be placed on Christian truths as the new Church develops an original synthesis of life and faith.

Two incarnations of one and the same Church are gradually converging; two faces of the same entity, each requiring the other, are becoming one. Together they are constructing in the world the sacrament of complete liberation in Jesus Christ.[16] And each of these realizations of Church renders the universality of the Church a historical reality.

CONCRETE UNIVERSALITY OF THE CHURCH AS NETWORK OF SERVICES

The commitment of the wider institutional Church to transforming society, with a view toward liberating the marginalized, has occasioned unavoidable conflict that the Church is willing to endure in the spirit of the Beatitudes. The state and its secret owners, the dominant classes, feel betrayed by the Church. The Church had been their principal historical ally. They had protected it and showered it with privileges. But the Church had paid a price: it had lost the people. Now the Church is leaning toward the people, and the more it does so, the more it is castigated and harassed by the state. Suddenly the state uses its "political vigilance" and police tactics to repress the pastoral practices of the Church. The Church opts for the people, and it pays a different, and costly, price. In nearly every Latin American country, martyrs have sealed with their blood the covenant of the Church with the passion of its people.

Now the greater institutional Church is confronting the state and the dominant classes. It has taken sides with the popular cause. And a paradigmatic concrete universality springs into being. Let us examine the principal traits of this new universality.

Political Diakonia of the Church

The flagrant social and economic injustices of the neocolonial system, with its massive multinational capital at the disposal of a Latin American bourgeois society, have brought forth an authoritarian, even totalitarian, state. The owners of this capital must protect their interests by force. Thus nearly every Latin American country has fallen into the hands of the so-called national security state. The historical ties of the national security ideology to the totalitarian ideologies of Nazism, European Catholic traditionalism, and the Pentagon are not particularly relevant here. Our concern is to understand the strategic function of the national security state in the current setting. That setting is dominated by multinational capitalism.

The motto of the national security state is "Development and Security." But the development in question is obviously not the development of the nation as a people. Rather what is meant is development in capitalist categories, a development whose sole subjects and beneficiaries are the elite minorities. Nor is the security in question the security of all of the people and of their rights. What is meant is the security of the elite and of the mechanisms of their private benefit and enjoyment.

The national security state has commandeered the nation. The absolutist state prevails. It has broken the autonomy and power of all intermediate entities between the citizen and the apparatus of state: unions, political parties, class associations, the universities, and so on. As a result, persons find themselves subject to the direct control of the power of state. The national security ideology presupposes and promotes the image of a human being, a society, and a religious function reduced to the dimensions of the political power of state.[17] The state is now universal; all else is but a dimension of it. Suddenly all formerly autonomous entities, including the Church, are faced with a terrible dilemma: either integrate or be repressed.

In general, the institutional Church has been slow even to recognize the absolutist and totalitarian character of the new state.

The hesitancy of its reaction has been consonant with the rudimentary level of its political awareness. Yet in some countries, as in Brazil, Paraguay, and Chile, the Church has adopted a most courageous, prophetic posture, with an unprecedented effect on the public perception of the new political situation.[18] Here the national bishops' conferences have refused to be integrated into the national security system, recognizing fully the risks involved in such a refusal. While never formally severing relations with the state, which would entail disastrous consequences for Church and state alike (not to mention the people), the Church has managed to develop a political theology and pastoral practice marked by an authentic, concrete universality. Principally, it has forthrightly reasserted the limits of the authority of the state vis-à-vis the absolute value of the person, human liberty, and religion. It has proscribed the Manichaeism of the national security doctrine, denouncing its totalitarianism and reductionism. It has condemned the prostitution of Christian themes and symbols by the civil authority.[19] The episcopate in various countries has grasped the demands of the historical setting and has now lent its voice, whose freedom it has managed to preserve, to those who have lost their voice or who have never had the suffrage. In some situations none but the Church had the freedom plus the courage to condemn the almighty state to its face. In these cases the Church has cited the violation of public liberties, the torture of political prisoners, and the massive means of repression invoked against any who hold opposing views. Today the Church is still performing its ongoing prophetic and political *diakonia*, which has won it universal gratitude.

At stake here are not incidental issues, which might be overlooked for the moment, but the universal foundation of human community and the legitimacy or illegitimacy of forms of social and political power. By refusing to be manipulated as the legitimating totem of established political power, a function it has so often exercised in Latin American history, the Church has asserted and demonstrated, in teaching and in practice, the transcendence of gospel and Church alike. The primordial function of the Church is not to sacralize the powers of this world but to point to another dimension, another definition of the final meaning of human life and history. The Church goes beyond the political contradictions of capitalism and socialism, of West and East.

The Church's Diakonia of Prophetic Criticism

Another practice of the concrete universal mission of the Church is to denounce the capitalist system as the principal producer of destitution and social injustice. Here too the Church has molded and nuanced its critique only gradually.[20] At first we heard only a rather naive criticism of "abuses in the system," or "flaws of capitalism," as if capitalism could be a good system once it had amended its faults. Subsequently, however, the Church explicitly characterized generalized poverty as a "by-product of the capitalistic development of Western society, a derivation of its own internal essence."[21] From there it moved to disclosing the illusions of the capitalist ideals, the unchecked accumulation of goods in the hands of a few, and the antipopular nature of the activity of the state, which is committed to fortifying the capitalistic system in order to protect it from any transformations that might damage the fortunes of the elite. The national security state is deliberately antipopular. It refuses to credit the ability of the people to make decisions concerning national objectives. It relegates the people to the status of a mass, cutting off the avenues to any real participation of the people in the goods and services their labor helps to produce.

Broad regional episcopates have formulated postures of open confrontation. Peru's episcopate has said, "The construction of a just society in Latin America means liberation from the current situation of dependence, oppression, and spoliation in which the vast majority of our peoples subsist. On the one hand, liberation will be a breach with everything that maintains human beings in their inability to be fulfilled as such, individually and in community; on the other hand, it will be the construction of a new, more human society of genuine fellowship."[22]

The people must be permitted to participate in civil and economic affairs really and directly. Liberation is not *for* the people unless it is *of* the people: "We believe that this world will be built especially by the toil of those who today are held in scorn—our people."[23]

In not a few instances the Church has gone beyond the phase

of criticism and called for an alternative socialistic economic model: "Christians have a duty to show that the true socialism is Christianity, lived integrally, with a just sharing of goods and in basic equality. Far from rejecting socialism, we gladly accept it as a form of social life more adapted to our times and more in conformity with the spirit of the Gospel."[24]

But not just any kind of socialism is called for, nor just any route to it. The Church "goes its own way to a socialistic society." It does not seek a Christian socialism, "for then we should be absolutizing socialism and relativizing Christianity, as in the past we have absolutized Western society or democracy, or humanism, or religion itself, by insisting that they be specifically Christian in order to be genuine and authentic. By relativizing Christianity, which is the vital presence of God in history, we have diminished it. We have relegated it to ancillary status."[25]

In today's world, especially among the peoples of the periphery, the human being has a burning thirst for an ever greater sharing by all in everything—an authentic socialization of the human experience. The Church is adopting this universal aspiration. Thereby, against the background of its own Catholic identity, it is becoming universal itself.

A Universal Diakonia: The Defense of the Rights of the Poor

The Church most transparently actualizes its universality in the defense of human rights. Underdevelopment involves an ongoing, structural violation of the fundamental rights of the human person. The Church has come to understand that the gospel is intrinsically tied to the proclamation and defense of human dignity; human rights are essential to the gospel and not merely historically contingent. Accordingly, in its articulation of faith, in catechetics, in homiletics, and in its official interventions, the Church perceives the proclamation of the gospel and the promotion of human rights to be of a piece.[26] In dangerous situations like ours, when all other voices have been violently silenced, that of the Church rings loud and clear: "You shall not oppress your brother!" "I have heard the cries of my people!" These are the actual titles of two documents published by the Brazilian church. Another document is called "Marginalization of a People, Cry of the Churches."[27] Nor has the Church been content with simple public proclamation and denunciation. Almost all of the bishops have visited jails and prisons to speak with prisoners and torture victims. Cardinal Paulo Evaristo Arns, Archbishop of São Paulo, has been one of these visitors. The bishops have done everything they can to locate and defend political prisoners, and they have created associations for the defense of human rights.

The Church has also been intelligent enough to identify the ambiguity so often lurking beneath the cloak of a defense of human rights. It is not enough to call for individual rights. Capitalist governments do that loudly. The crucial thing is social rights. The capitalist system, today globalized, plays by its own rules. It imposes its structures without any concern for personal and social rights. By the way they function, these structures create a situation that all but forces governments to violate human rights. The cause resides, not so much in the malice of the governments or the sadism of their repressive apparatus, but in the structures of the system itself. These structures are controlled by the central countries, whose governments fly the banner of personal human rights without referring to the fact that it is they who are the principal culprits. It is their own game rules that lead to these manifest violations of human dignity and to the structure of national society.[28] Not a few local churches have now awakened to the hypocrisy that lurks beneath the official cloak of a defense of human rights by the central countries of our economic and political system. These governments denounce the effects but refuse to treat the cause.

CONCRETE UNIVERSALITY OF THE CHURCH AS NETWORK OF COMMUNITIES

A Church begotten of the people by the Spirit of God is emerging everywhere. It is structured in a network of base church communities, which owes its origin to the great traditional, institutional Church, but whose organization is different. The Church born of the people is based first and foremost on the principle of lay evangelization.[29] The sociological center of these communities is in the world of the poor, where the bonds of a sisterly and brotherly communion becomes reality. Here this "people of the poor" forges the links of an evangelism of promoting and furthering the liberation of the oppressed, carried out in solidarity. The development and proliferation of the base church communities is pregnant with theological as well as social and political consequences in what these communities represent for the process of liberation. Theologically, these communities demonstrate that the Church can reinvent itself *institutionally*, creating new structures more adequate to the social milieu and more likely to generate an up-to-date interpretation of the content of the faith of the apostles. We are witnessing a veritable "ecclesiogenesis," as our theologians term it. Politically, these communities provide a counterweight to the centralizing new state, by virtue of their efforts to safeguard precisely that societal and social minimum without which the people are reduced to a mass.

At this altogether concrete level, the grassroots Church achieves another kind of universality, different from but abundantly and profoundly articulated with the universality of the larger institutional Church.

The Small Church Community as Church Universal

Is the small base church community identical with the universal Church or distinct from it? The answer is that it is identical with it, in terms of a real but incomplete or inadequate identity. It contains, offers, and bears witness to the universal salvation of God the Father in the mediation of Jesus Christ and his Spirit. While it does not represent every possible manifestation of universality, it does realize the note of universality common to all communities of orthodox faith that are in communion with all of the others. We live the same faith, love, and hope as all the other members of the Church; we read the same Christian Scriptures; we follow the same Christ, in communion with his life and his lot; and we embody the same community gathered together for love of the word of liberation and deliverance. On the outskirts of the cities, in little villages, in the immense hinterland where a priest is almost never seen, the lowly people gather with their coordinator to hear and celebrate the message of liberation. They organize community tasks. They set up means of mutual assistance. The Church universal, sacrament of the Reign, is taking shape and form before our very eyes.

Unity of Life and Faith

Under regimes of surveillance and repression, prohibited from holding civil gatherings, the people gather as Church. The Church is the only place where the people of the grass roots, the poor, are legally permitted to build or rebuild their community spirit. In the light of the gospel, they learn to interpret life and to develop a critical awareness of the mechanisms of misery and decay. The base communities are eminently religious. Everything they do is done in terms of Christian thought and Christian symbols. But they live a profound oneness of life and faith. The people know no euphemisms. They translate the gospel message into practices consistent with that message. Hence it is in this context that they experience the social and political dimension of Christian faith as a commitment to the conversion of their attitudes and the rehabilitation of their community structures. Before it can be a theory practiced by Latin American theologians, liberation is the spiritual and political (in the broadest sense of the word) experience of countless little communities of laity. The people pray, they meditate on the words of the gospel, but they also practice a liberating solidarity with the needy. Here their concerns are food and health, mutual assistance, small associations to defend the price of their products, and study groups to reflect on the defense of their human and civil rights, guaranteed by legislation but relentlessly violated by the powerful.[30]

Thus a genuine pedagogy of liberation has sprung up among us. By means of their own resources, the oppressed learn to unite, organize, and act in community solidarity. Thereby they become the agents of their own liberation. Faith is ever the creative vehicle of a community spirit and community practices. The universal values of human advancement and liberation appear, to be implemented fully in a long, determined process. The Church knows its place as spiritual patron of material enterprises. But in our situation in Latin America, where secular roads to community encounter are all blocked off, the only way the Church can exercise its spiritual patronage is by taking up a mission of popular organization and education. There will be more freedom tomorrow. Then the people themselves will take up their own tools and their own cause. The Church is educating them in coresponsibility and in the sacred art of letting the light of faith and the liberating message of Jesus Christ shine on their commitment to history.

Defense of Human Rights at the Grass Roots

Unlike the great institutional Church, the base church communities exercise no direct influence on social mechanisms. They can exert no pressure in this area. Their relationships are exclusively horizontal. They simply live in brotherly and sisterly communion. They have no access to the media. Thus they are completely exposed to the tyranny of the mighty. But despite all, the great majority of their members are deeply committed to the defense of human rights. First, they practice a systematic consciousness-raising with regard to their rights and dignity. Then they try to live, right in their own communities, a new alternative ethos, different from that of the dominators with its constant violence, an ethos of more solidarity and participation in the spirit of the Beatitudes. As a group they practice a discreet prophetic denunciation, accepting the risks entailed and preparing to offer solidarity when one of their members suffers the consequences of courage. The Church has come to realize that the more it becomes the people, the more the people become Church. The Church is no longer a Church simply *for* the poor and the unprotected. Now it is a Church made up *of* the poor and unprotected. The cry of the victims of poverty, injustice, and marginalization have a universal appeal. It touches every human conscience that has not lost the last vestige of its sense of solidarity with the other members of its species.

Faith lived in a community has bolstered and made concrete this appeal springing from the heart of the earth and determined to be heard by all women and men of goodwill. The gospel guarantees us that the power of the weak is invincible.

CONCLUSION: CONVERGENCE OF THE PATHWAYS OF THE CHURCH

Naturally the Latin American ecclesial experience has repercussions on ecclesiology. In particular, it demonstrates two facts of special importance. First, it is now clear that the Church as broader institution and the Church as a network of communities need not stand in mutual opposition or contradiction.[31] The current historical situation requires that the Church be institutionally strong and united if it is to confront the authoritarian state and the totalitarian tendencies at work in that state. It must be strong to lift its voice in the name of the gospel and the universal conscience of humankind; it must be united to express its claims on behalf of human rights and the preservation of that minimal quality of social life without which society is shattered and the people are reduced to an amorphous mass. The larger institutional Church, then, is an indispensable form of being Church in Latin America today.

At the same time, the base church community constitutes a new way of being Church. This new form of Church is the vehicle of the incarnation of the gospel among the people and in the popular culture. Welding theory and practice, the community performs a political function in the best sense of the word, inasmuch as the community is evidently the only viable historical avenue by which the people can join together, forge bonds of solidarity, and keep on being a people.

The Church that embraces a *diakonia* on behalf of the highest human values as part and parcel of the christological project itself becomes universal. For these values are universal, and the Church that genuinely succeeds in living them as Church becomes universal in its own right.

Notes

Chapter 1. Pilgrimage of the Church with the Oppressed

1. Paul VI, *Evangelii Nuntiandi*, no. 34.
2. Puebla Final Document, no. 515.
3. Paul VI, *Evangelii Nuntiandi*, no. 32; cf. Puebla Final Document, no. 483.
4. *Evangelii Nuntiandi*, no. 38; cf. Puebla Final Document, no. 483.
5. Paul VI, *Populorum Progressio*, no. 26.
6. Puebla Final Document, no. 542; no. 494, no. 55, no. 546.
7. Ibid., no. 30; cf. 64, 70, 437, 778, 1136, 1258.
8. Ibid., no. 1307; emphasis added.
9. Ibid., no. 85.
10. On Latin America's institutionalized injustice, see Puebla Final Document, nos. 437, 46, 536, 562, 1259.
11. Puebla Final Document, no. 312; no. 26; nos. 1264–65; cf. nos. 427, 501, 1065.
12. Ibid., no. 92; cf. the Bogotá document, "system clearly marked by sin."
13. Puebla Final Document, nos. 55, 1065; nos. 542, 494; no. 546.
14. On abuse of power, see Puebla Final Document, no. 508; cf. nos. 46, 793; on its violation of human dignity, see no. 41; cf. no. 1259.
15. On the national security doctrine, see Puebla Final Document, no. 547; no. 314; no. 549; no. 49.
16. On condemnation of Marxism, see Puebla Final Document, no. 543; nos. 543–46.
17. Ibid., no. 41; no. 1209; no. 28; no. 476.
18. Ibid., no. 515; cf. no. 824.
19. Ibid., no. 516; no. 521, cf. no. 291; no. 558.
20. On structural changes, see Puebla Final Document, nos. 134, 388, 438, 1055, 1155, 1250. On a new society, see nos. 12, 642, 848, 1128, 1119, 1192, 1305.
21. Puebla Final Document, no. 1140.
22. On not excluding other persons, see Puebla Final Document, nos. 1134, 1165. On solidarity with the masses, see nos. 1134, 974; cf. 27.
23. Puebla Final Document, no. 79. On misunderstanding and hostility encountered by the Church, see no. 83.
24. On the causes of poverty, see Puebla Final Document, nos. 30, 1160. On the struggle for a more just society, see nos. 1136, 1154.
25. Puebla Final Document, no. 1149.
26. On the ability of the poor to evangelize, see Puebla Final Document, no. 1147. On the Church joining the poor, see nos. 1154, 1156; cf. no. 40.
27. Puebla Final Document, no. 320; no. 316; nos. 1254, 1283; no. 1254.
28. Ibid., no. 327.
29. On the rights of the poorest, see Puebla Final Document, nos. 1217, 320, 324, 711, 119. On social rights, see nos. 1270–73.
30. Puebla Final Document, no. 368.

31. Ibid., no. 26, citing *Evangelii Nuntiandi*, no. 30.
32. Puebla Final Document, no. 480.
33. Ibid., nos. 355, 476, 480, 562, 1254, 1283.
34. Ibid., no. 479, citing *Evangelii Nuntiandi*, nos. 29, 38.
35. Puebla Final Document, no. 482; emphasis added. On liberation spanning all reality, see no. 483.
36. Puebla Final Document, no. 485. On liberation beginning in history, see no. 483; on its culminating in eternity, see nos. 475, 141.
37. Puebla Final Document, no. 1145. On liberation: and evangelization, see nos. 485, 487, 488, 491; and liturgy, no. 972; and education, no. 1031; and youth, no. 1183; and charismatic groups, no. 958.
38. Puebla Final Document, no. 320; cf. no. 552.
39. Ibid., no. 864.
40. Ibid., no. 783; cf. nos. 864, 320. On responsible reflection, see no. 470.
41. Puebla Final Document, nos. 96, 262, 1309; no. 96. On bishops' endorsement of base church communities, see no. 156.
42. Puebla Final Document, no. 173. On the base church communities: as wealth of the Church, see no. 368; calling for a voice in society, no. 125; experience of Church as family, no. 239, cf. no. 261; giving rise to new ministries, no. 97.
43. On the base churches as communities of solidarity, see Puebla Final Document, nos. 273, 622, 629, 640, 643; on their bringing out the evangelizing potential of the poor, see no. 1147.
44. For the effect of the base church communities: on bishops and priests, see Puebla Final Document, no. 626; on deacons, nos. 119, 672; on vocations to the religious life, nos. 850, 867; on evangelization, no. 1309; on religious education, no. 983; on ecumenism, no. 1122; on popular piety, no. 462; on prayer, no. 952. For the expression "Church of the people," cf. 263.
45. Puebla Final Document, no. 648; no. 1309.
46. Ibid., no. 445. On the legitimacy of popular Catholicism, see no. 447.
47. Ibid., no. 450; no. 452.
48. Ibid., no. 466. On the negative side of popular religion, see no. 45. On adopting various aspects of popular piety in the liturgy, see nos. 506, 465. On necessity of popular piety for the Church to be universal, see no. 462.
49. Puebla Final Document, no. 1186. On youth: as hope for renewal in society and Church, nos. 1170, 1178; as workers, no. 1176; as repressed by government, no. 1179.
50. Puebla Final Document, no. 1188.
51. Ibid. On steering youth toward social action, see no. 1196; on their becoming factors in transforming society and Church, see nos. 1187, 1196, 1197.
52. On women: as most oppressed group of the poor, see Puebla Final Document, no. 834; as marginalized by the Church, no. 839; as supported by the Church in their aspirations for advancement, no. 847; as sharing in the transformation of society, no. 848; as having a voice in pastoral planning and religious education, no. 845. For Mary as model of Latin American Christian women, see nos. 293, 297, 302.
53. John Paul II, Balice Airport, June 10, 1979.

Chapter 2. Christianity and the Liberation of the Oppressed

1. A translation of Boff's Portuguese version of this quotation from Karl Marx & Frederick Engels, *The German Ideology* (New York: International Pubs. Co., 1970).

2. Puebla Final Document, no. 521.
3. Ibid., no. 79.
4. Ibid., no. 327.
5. Dom José Maria Pires, *Do Centro para a Margem* (João Pessoa, Brazil: Editora Acauã).
6. Puebla Final Document, nos. 51, 403.
7. José Maria Pires, *Do Centro para a Margem*, p. 10.

Chapter 3. Theology and Political Commitment

1. Thomas Aquinas, *Contra Gentiles*, lect. 1, chap. 4.
2. Ibid.
3. The word *nonperson* is used in a historical sense, not an ontological one, which would be absurd. Ontologically the oppressed are persons as much as anyone else. Historically and analytically, however, the oppressed have been deprived of their dignity and rights. That is, they are dealt with by the oppressor *as if* they were nonpersons ontologically. The word *nonperson* seeks to convey a prophetic denunciation of anthropologies that restrict their considerations to the area of the ontological, thus overlooking the effects of historical realities.
4. Thomas Aquinas, *Summa Theologica* I, q. 1, aa. 3, 7.

Chapter 4. Spirituality and Politics

1. Paul VI, *Evangelii Nuntiandi*, no. 30, quoted in Puebla Final Document, no. 26.
2. Puebla Final Document, no. 29.
3. Clodovis Boff, *Teologia e prática: teologia do político e suas mediações* (Petrópolis, Brazil: Vozes, 1978), in English as *Theology and Praxis: Epistemological Foundations*, trans. Robert R. Barr (Maryknoll, NY: Orbis Books, 1987).
4. Puebla Final Document, no. 539.
5. *Gaudium et Spes*, no. 44.
6. John XXIII, *Pacem in Terris*, no. 159.
7. Paul VI, *Octogesima Adveniens*, no. 33.
8. Ibid., no. 34.
9. See Puebla Final Document, no. 1147.

Chapter 5. The Two Eyes of Theology

1. *Kairos* is the term used in biblical Greek to denote a special time, a moment of particular density of meaning, of which we say, "*Haec est dies, haec est nox, in illo tempore*," and so on: "This is the day the Lord has made, this is the night you led your people out of Egypt, at that time [Jesus did or said such and so]." The Incarnation, the Resurrection, the institution of the Eucharist, Jesus' washing the apostles' feet, and the apostles' decision to carry their mission to the gentiles are examples of such "kairological moments."
2. The Pauline writers have this "now" (in Greek, *nun*) very much in mind: "Now is the acceptable time! Now is the day of salvation!" (2 Cor. 6:2; cf. Rom. 13:11).
3. *Chronological* here refers to linear, historical time, with its particular content and its challenges to Christian awareness.
4. The most important contribution in this area: Clodovis Boff, *Theology and*

Praxis: Epistemological Foundations, trans. from the Portuguese by Robert R. Barr (Maryknoll, NY: Orbis Books, 1987).

5. Locardaire, cited by Yves Congar, *La foi et la théologie* (Tournai: 1962), p. 195.

Chapter 6. Jesus Christ the Liberator, Center of Faith on the Edge of the World

1. A. Vieira Pinto, *Ciência e consciência: Problemas filosóficos da pesquisa científica* (Rio de Janeiro, 1969), chaps. 12–14; Clodovis Boff, *Theology and Praxis: Epistemological Foundations,* trans. from the Portuguese by Robert R. Barr (Maryknoll, NY: Orbis Books, 1987), pp. 159–74, "The Theologian's Social Commitment"; Michel de Certeau, *L'Ecriture de l'histoire* (Paris: 1975), pp. 65–79; P. Blanquart, "L'acte de croire et l'action politique," *Lumière et vie* 19 (1970):12–30.

2. A detailed treatment of this question is found in Clodovis Boff, *Theology and Praxis,* pp. 14–17, 159–74, 186–94.

3. Leonardo Boff, *Teología desde el cautiverio* (Bogotá, 1975), pp. 13–56.

4. If the state of domination and dependence in which two-thirds of humanity live, with an annual toll of thirty million dead from starvation and malnutrition, does not become the starting-point for *any* Christian theology today, even in the affluent and powerful countries, then theology cannot begin to relate meaningfully to the real situation. Its questions will lack reality and not relate to real men and women. As one speaker at the Buenos Aires Seminar observed, "We have to save theology from its cynicism."

Hugo Assmann, *Theology for a Nomad Church,* trans. from the Spanish by Paul Burns (Maryknoll, NY: Orbis Books, 1975), p. 54.

5. Following are some of the more significant titles in Latin American Christology. H. Borrat, "Para una Cristología de vanguardia," *Víspera* 17 (1970):26–31; A. Zanteno, "Liberación social y Cristo," *Cuadernos liberación* (Secretariado Social de México, 1971); Gustavo Gutiérrez, *A Theology of Liberation: History, Politics and Salvation,* trans. from the Spanish by Caridad Inda and John Eagleson (Maryknoll, NY: Orbis Books, 1973), pp. 168–87, "Christ and Complete Liberation"; F. Bravo, B. Catão, and José Comblin, *Cristología y pastoral en América Latina* (Santiago, Chile, and Barcelona, 1965); Hugo Assmann, *Theology for a Nomad Church,* pp. 69–70; idem, "La situatión histórica del poder de Cristo," *Cristianismo y sociedad* 13 (1975):43–54; Jon Sobrino, *Christology at the Crossroads: A Latin American Approach,* trans. from the Spanish by John Drury (Maryknoll, NY: Orbis Books, 1978); Ignacio Ellacuría, *Caracter político de la misión de Jesús,* MIEC-JECI Document 13–14 (Lima, 1974); Rubem Alves, *Cristianismo: opio o liberación?* (Salamanca, 1973), pp. 187–91; Segundo Galilea and Raúl Vidales, *Cristología y pastoral popular* (Bogotá, 1974); José Porfirio Miranda, *Being and the Messiah: The Message of St. John,* trans. from the Spanish by John Eagleson (Maryknoll, NY: Orbis Books, 1977); Vidales, "Como hablar de Cristo hoy?" *Spes* (January 1974), pp. 7–8; idem, "La práctica histórica de Jesús," *Christus* (Mexico City) 40 (1975):43–55; *Cristianismo y sociedad,* no. 43–44 (1975), the entire issue; J. Severino Croatto, "La dimensión política del Cristo liberador," *Cristianismo y sociedad,* no. 45; Leonardo Boff, *Jesus Christ Liberator: A Critical Christology for Our Time,* trans. from the Spanish by Patrick Hughes (Maryknoll, NY: Orbis Books, 1978); idem, "Salvação em Jesus Cristo e processo de libertação,"

Concilium (Brazilian edition), no. 6 (1974):753–64; idem, in *Theology in the Americas*, ed. Sérgio Torres and John Eagleson (Maryknoll, NY: Orbis Books, 1976), pp. 294–98; idem, *Teología desde el cautiverio* (Bogotá, 1975), pp. 145–71, "Liberación de Jesucristo por el camino de la opresión"; idem, *Passion of Christ, Passion of the World*, trans. from the Spanish by Robert R. Barr (Maryknoll, NY: Orbis Books, 1987); Segundo Galilea, "Jesús y la liberación de su pueblo," in *Panorama de la teología latinoamericana* (Salamanca, 1975), 2:33–44.

6. "One becomes a revolutionary not through science, but through indignation. Science comes later, to fill and fine-tune this empty protest." M. Merleau-Ponty, *Humanisme et terreur* (Paris, 1956), p. 13. Durkheim's thesis is familiar: Socialism arises from passion—a passion for justice and the rescue of the exploited. Emile Durkheim, *Le socialisme: Sa définition, ses débuts, la doctrine Saint-Simonienne* (Paris, 1928).

7. See also S. Trinidad, "Cristología—Conquista—Colonización," *Cristianismo y sociedad* 13 (1975):12–28; P. N. Rigol, "Cristología popular: alienación o ironia?" *Cristianismo y sociedad* 13 (1975):29–34; H. Lepargneur, "Imagens de Cristo no catolicismo popular brasileiro," in *Quem é Jesus Cristo no Brasil?* (São Paulo, 1974), pp. 55–94.

8. See Hugo Assmann, "The Actuation of the Power of Christ in History: Notes on the Discernment of Christological Contradictions," in *Faces of Jesus: Latin American Christologies*, ed. José Míguez Bonino, trans. from the Spanish by Robert R. Barr (Maryknoll, NY: Orbis Books, 1984), pp. 125–36.

9. Clodovis Boff, *Theology and Praxis*, pp. 221, 225.

10. The bibliography here is immense. We might single out: F. H. Cardoso, *Sociología del desarrollo* (Buenos Aires, 1970), pp. 19–20, "Desarrollo y dependencia: perspectiva en el análisis sociológico"; O. Fals Borda, *Ciencia propia y colonialismo intelectual* (Mexico City, 1970); T. Santos, *Dependencia y cambio social* (Santiago, 1970); G. Arroyo, "Pensamiento latinoamericano sobre subdesarrollo y dependencia externa," *Mensaje* (October 1968), pp. 516–20; P. Negre, *Sociologia do Terceiro Mundo* (Petrópolis, Brazil: Vozes, 1977).

11. José Comblin, *Théologie de la pratique révolutionnaire* (Paris, 1974), p. 65.

12. Ibid., p. 127.

13. See also J. C. Scannone, *Hacia una pastoral de la cultura*, MIEC-JECI, no. 16 (Lima, 1976).

14. Jon Sobrino, *Christology at the Crossroads*, pp. 369–70.

15. José Porfirio Miranda, *Being and the Messiah*, p. 1.

16. Jon Sobrino, *Christology at the Crossroads*.

17. Fernando Belo, *Uma leitura política do Evangelho*, (Lisbon, 1975), p. 133.

18. M. Horkheimer, *Die Sehnsucht nach dem ganz Anderen* (Hamburg, 1972), p. 62.

19. Jon Sobrino, "El conocimiento teológico en teología europea y latinoamericana," *ECA*, (1975), pp. 322–23; Ignacio Ellacuría, "Tesis sobre la posibilidad y sentido de una teología latinoamericana," in *Teología y mundo contemporaneo*, by various authors (Madrid, 1975), pp. 325–50.

Chapter 7. Liberation in Fullness, the Christian Utopia

1. The present subject is dealt with in greater breadth in other writings of mine: *A ressurreição de Cristo e nossa ressurreição na morte* (Petrópolis, Brazil: Vozes, 1973); *Jesus Christ Liberator: A Critical Christology for Our Time*, trans. from the Spanish by Patrick Hughes (Maryknoll, NY: Orbis Books, 1978); *Teologia do*

cativeiro e da libertação (Lisbon, 1976), pp. 155–86, "Libertação de Jesus Cristo pelo caminho da opressão." See also Paul Tillich, *Systematische Theologie* (Stuttgart, 1958) 2:129–50; Inácio R. Strieder, *Die Bewertung der Leiblichkeit in den Hauptbriefen des Apostels Paulus und in seiner Kulturwelt* (Münster, 1975). Along more spiritual lines, see Thomas Merton, *The New Man* (New York: Farrar, Straus, & Giroux, 1963).

Chapter 9. The Church's Contribution to the Liberation of the Oppressed

1. Leonardo Boff, *Teología de la liberación y del cautiverio* (Madrid: Editorial Paulinas, 1977), pp. 13–33.
2. Clodovis Boff, *Theology and Praxis: Epistemological Foundations*, trans. from the Portuguese by Robert R. Barr (Maryknoll, NY: Orbis Books, 1987).
3. For a detailed analysis, see P. Negre, *Sociologia do Terceiro Mundo* (Petrópolis, Brazil: Vozes, 1977), with its extensive bibliography.
4. *Populorum Progressio*, no. 26.
5. See also the collection of studies edited by Hugo Assmann, *Carter y la lógica del Capitalismo*, 2 vols. (San José, Costa Rica: Centro Universitário de Centro América, 1978).
6. Clodovis Boff, "A justiça na história: capitalismo-socialismo e a doutrina social da Igreja," *Vozes* 71 (1977):765–78; idem, "A justiça na história: capitalismo-socialismo, discernimento cristão," *Vozes* 72 (1978):85–96.
7. "We cannot fail to interpret this gigantic effort at a rapid transformation and development as evident signs of the presence of the Spirit who guides the history of human beings and peoples to their calling." Medellín, *Presença da Igreja na atual transformação da América Latina*, introduction to "Conclusões," no. 4.
8. Pope Paul VI, *Evangelii Nuntiandi*, 1975, no. 31; 1974 Synod of Bishops, *Justice in the World*, no. 35.
9. For a more detailed reflection see Leonardo Boff, *Teología de la liberación*, pp. 157–78.
10. *Justice in the World*, no. 34.
11. For the Church universal, see *Gaudium et Spes*, no. 1. On the regional Latin American church, see the Medellín document, *Presence of the Church in the Current Transformation of Latin America*.
12. Throughout this third part of the present chapter, see also the more detailed treatment by Clodovis Boff, *Comunidade eclesial, comunidade política: Ensaios de eclesiologia política* (Petrópolis, Brazil: Vozes, 1978).
13. L. Laeyendecker, "Le catholicisme devant l'ébranlement de son système d'emprise," *Archives de sociologie des religions*, vol. 28 (1969).
14. *Gaudium et Spes*, no. 1, emphasis added.
15. *Justice in the World*, no. 3.
16. *Evangelii Nuntiandi*, no. 38.
17. Thomas Aquinas, *Summa Theologica*, I–II, q. 21, a. 4, ad 3.
18. CLAR, "Vida religiosa e compromisso sócio-político," *SEDOC* 8 (1976):851–79; Equipo-Teólogos-CLAR, *Pueblo de Dios y Comunidad liberadora*, CLAR, no. 33 (Bogotá, 1977); idem, *Tendencias Proféticas de la Vida Religiosa en América Latina*, CLAR, no. 24 (Bogotá, 1976); Leonardo Boff, *Testigos de Dios en el corazón del mundo* (Madrid: Instituto de Vida Religiosa, 1977), pp. 265–331.
19. On the various levels of awareness of reality and their corresponding prac-

tices, see CLAR, *Vida religiosa e compromisso sócio-político*, pp. 859–65, esp. p. 863.
20. Ibid., p. 870.
21. Regarding the various meanings of the word *political*, see chapter 2 above, pp. 33–43.

Chapter 10. The Universal Mission of the Church and Concrete Liberation

1. For Christendom, see Henri de Lubac, *Catholicisme: Les aspects sociaux du dogme*, Unam sanctam, no. 3, 5th edition (Paris, 1952), pp. 25ff., 241–60; M. Briek, "De vocis 'catholica' origine et natura," *Antonianum* 38 (1963):263–87; Yves M.-J. Congar, "A catolicidade da Igreja," in *Mysterium salutis* 4, no. 1: 478–502; Hans Küng, *Die Kirche* (Freiburg in B.: Herder 1967), pp. 353–78.
2. The term *universitas Christianorum* comes from Hugh of St. Victor. Gregory the Great used *catholic* to mean the body of the churches, as does *Lumen Gentium*, nos. 23, 2.
3. See Matt. 28:18, Acts 1:8, also *Lumen Gentium*, no. 13.
4. Vincent of Lérins's celebrated definition runs, "Catholic is what has been believed in all places, always, and by all persons," *Commonitorium*, I, 2 (*PL* 50:640).
5. See also Congar, "Catolicidade da Igreja," pp. 491–94.
6. *Gaudium et Spes*, nos. 1, 9 and 10, 11.
7. Ibid., no. 91.
8. Ibid., nos. 9, 66, 56.
9. Medellín, Document on Justice, no. 1; Introduction to Conclusions, no. 4.
10. Medellín, Document on Justice, no. 3.
11. Medellín, Introduction to Conclusions, no. 8.
12. G. W. Hegel, *Phänomenologie des Geistes*, ed. J. Hoffmeister (Hamburg, 1952), p. 463.
13. See also some fundamental texts: R. Muñoz, *Nueva Conciencia de la Iglesia en América Latina* (Salamanca: Sígueme, 1974); Raúl Vidales, *La Iglesia latinoamericana y la política después de Medellín*, IPLA, nos. 15–16 (Quito, 1972); P. Bigo, *L'Eglise et la révolution du tiers monde* (Paris: Presses Universitaires de France, 1974); L. Proaño, *Pour une Eglise libératrice* (Paris, 1973); Leonardo Boff, *Teologia do cativeiro* (Lisbon: Multinova, 1976), pp. 201–9 (bibliography): "A Igreja no processo de libertação: uma nova consciência e etapas de uma práxis"; G Arroyo, F. van der Schueren, J. Rojas, and P. J. Krischke, *The Church and Politics in Latin America* (Toronto: 1977).
14. Julio de Santa Ana, *El desafío de los pobres e la Iglesia* (EDUCA, Centroamérica, 1977).
15. A. R. Guimarães, *As comunidades eclesiais de base no Brasil* (Petrópolis, Brazil: Vozes, 1978).
16. See also the CLAR document, *Pueblo de Dios y Comunidad liberadora: Perspectivas eclesiológicas desde las comunidades religiosas que caminan con el pueblo* (Bogotá: CLAR, 1977).
17. See also José Comblin, *La Iglesia y la ideología de la Seguridad Nacional*, MIEC-JECI, no. 19 (Lima: MIEC-JECI, 1977); *Bibliographie sur la Sécurité nationale* (Paris: Centre Lebret, 1976).
18. See also *Iglesia y Estado: Documentos de Obispos brasileños*, América Latina Boletín, MIEC-JECI, nos. 13–14 (Lima: MIEC-JECI, 1977).

19. See also the important document from the National Conference of Bishops of Brazil (CNBB), "Exigências cristãs de uma ordem política," *Revista eclesiástica brasileira* 37 (1977):188–96.
20. See also M. M. Alves, *L'Eglise et la politique au Brésil* (Paris, 1974), pp. 187–206.
21. National Conference of Bishops of Peru, "Documento sobre a justiça no mundo," *SEDOC* 39 (1971):426.
22. Ibid., 427, 432.
23. See also the document from the bishops of the East Central region of Brazil, "Marginalização de um povo: grito das Igrejas," *SEDOC* 69 (1974):1021.
24. See also "Manifesto de Obispos del Tercer Mundo (1967)," *Cristianismo y Revolución* 6–7, no. 14 (1968):44.
25. Bishops of Peru, "Justiça no mundo," p. 428.
26. Dom Sérgio Mendes Arceo, "Discurso," *SEDOC* 54 (1972):620; see also Ivo Lesbaupin, "O episcopado da América Latina e o socialismo," *Concilium* (Brazilian edition) 125 (1977): 630–41.
27. For "Não oprimas teu irmão" ("You Shall Not Oppress Your Brother") see R. Azzi, "A Igreja do Brasil na defesa dos Direitos Humanos," *Revista eclesiástica brasileira* 37 (1977):106–42. *Eu ouvi os clamores do meu povo (I Have Heard the Cries of My People)* is the title of the 1974 declaration of the bishops of São Paulo, issued in Brodósqui in 1974. "Marginalização de um povo: grito das Igrejas" is the document from the bishops, clerics, and religious of the Northeast of Brazil, 1973, published in *SEDOC* 22 (1973):607–27.
28. See also no. 22.
29. See also Juan Luís Segundo, "Direitos humanos, evangelização e ideología," *Revista eclesiástica brasileira* 37 (1977):76–90.
30. Leonardo Boff, *Ecclesiogenesis: The Base Communities Reinvent the Church*, trans. from the Spanish by Robert R. Barr (Maryknoll, NY: Orbis Books, 1986).
31. R. Muñoz, *Solidaridad liberadora: misión de la Iglesia* (Santiago, 1977), 49–72.